East German Civil-Military Relations
The Impact of Technology, 1949-72

PRAEGER SPECIAL STUDIES IN INTERNATIONAL POLITICS AND GOVERNMENT

Praeger Publishers   New York   Washington   London

Library of Congress Cataloging in Publication Data

Herspring, Dale Roy.
   East German civil-military relations.

   (Praeger special studies in international politics and government)
   Bibliography: p.
   1. Germany (Democratic Republic, 1949-   ) Nationale Volksarmee—Political activity. 2. Civil supremacy over the military—Germany (Democratic Republic, 1949-   ) 3. Technology and state—Germany (Democratic Republic, 1949-   )
   I. Title.
   UA719.3.H46   321'.5'09431   73-11035

PRAEGER PUBLISHERS
111 Fourth Avenue, New York, N.Y. 10003, U.S.A.
5, Cromwell Place, London SW7 2JL, England

Published in the United States of America in 1973
by Praeger Publishers, Inc.

All rights reserved

© 1973 by Praeger Publishers, Inc.

Printed in the United States of America

East German Civil-Military Relations

Dale Roy Herspring
foreword by
Peter C. Ludz

The Praeger Special Studies program—utilizing the most modern and efficient book production techniques and a selective worldwide distribution network—makes available to the academic, government, and business communities significant, timely research in U.S. and international economic, social, and political development.

To Joseph Nyomarkay

ACKNOWLEDGMENTS

In preparing this book I was helped by many persons, to whom I owe a major debt of gratitude. None of them, however, is in any way responsible for the analyses or conclusions of this study.

Among those who supplied expert comments on various parts of this study are Professors Robert Goodman and Peter Berton of the University of Southern California, Professor Roger Harrel of San Fernando Valley State College, Professor Max Azicri of Edinboro State College, Drs. Thomas Simons and Raymond Garthoff of the Department of State, Dr. Dietrich Herzog of the Institute for Political Science at the Free University of Berlin, and Professor Richard Lowenthal of the Otto Suhr Institute of the Free University of Berlin. In addition, I should like to express my appreciation to Professor Dr. Peter Christian Ludz of Bielefeld University, who consented to write the foreword to this study. Most of all, however, I should like to thank Professor Joseph Nyomarkay of the University of Southern California; although somewhat less than enthralled by the subject matter with which this work deals, he gave unselfishly of his time and energies in its behalf. Whatever value this study may have is in large part a result of his efforts.

This book was made possible by a Fulbright Research Fellowship in the Federal Republic of Germany from 1969 to 1971. I am profoundly grateful to the Fulbright Commission for this assistance.

A number of persons played an important part in making this study possible by helping to locate primary and secondary source material. Among them are Dr. Leimbach of the Institut für Gesamtdeutsche Fragen, the staff at the Bundeswehr Bibliothek in Dusseldorf, Hartmut Zimmermann of the Institute for Political Science of the Free University of Berlin, and Dr. G. Wagenlehrer of the Studiengesellschaft für Zeitprobleme. In addition, a number of persons in the German Democratic Republic, both officials and private citizens (who must remain unnamed for obvious reasons) assisted in locating important primary source material. Since most of the research for this study was carried out in the German Democratic Republic, their help was invaluable.

I should like to thank my wife, who demonstrated an amazing degree of patience and understanding during the two years we spent in Berlin. She also devoted innumerable hours to typing and reading the manuscript and to the never ending task of attempting to teach her husband the fundamentals of writing style.

FOREWORD
Peter C. Ludz

Communist political systems find themselves under growing pressures from the so-called technological revolution. Some of the problems involved are particularly evident in the military section of their body politic and they can be studied to special advantage in the case of the most advanced, "most modernized" of the Soviet-controlled countries, the GDR. Dr. Herspring's book then, by concentrating on the "dual executive" perspective, devotes itself to changes in the GDR military-party relations.

The book attracts our attention because its author proceeds with great care. As his point of departure he offers the following proposition: ". . . the greater the use of technology required by the group in fulfilling the goal desired by the political leadership, the less the party leadership will be able to interfere in the group's internal affairs, and thereby affect the type of individuals who are members of that group." Although referring to the GDR situation from 1949 to 1972, this proposition is also meant to include the historical background of strained relationships between the party and the army in communist systems. Lenin's "single leadership principle" is interpreted as an early answer to the fundamental dilemma of gaining political control over the military skill group.

Explicitly the military skill group is distinguished from other, especially the economic, expert groups. On the grounds that in communist systems the military may be among the most important skill groups, Herspring argues and proves that here, in contrast to the economic and partially, the political fields, the dual executive problem is handled in such a way that in reality a type of dual (i. e., politico-technical) military executive is emerging. Indeed, these results contradict earlier findings in GDR research on the rise of economic experts. In my book The Changing Party Elite in East Germany (Cambridge: M. I. T. Press, 1972), which investigates changes within the SED that took place between 1958 and 1967, I tried to prove that the rising technocrats within the party and the economy were replacing the pure party functionaries; that party loyalty became less a criterion of social ascent than economic expertness. It is in discussing these theses that Herspring develops his views on the military skill group.

The methodological approach that Dr. Herspring has applied provides an original and valuable contribution to GDR research. Using his wide knowledge of the politico-historical development of the East German military, the author sets up a number of "indicators" for "technology" and for "political control." For example, the technology set of 17 indicators includes: "educational level required for entry into officer's training schools"; "percentage of total officers classified as engineers or technicians," and "existence of technical awards." Among the 15 political control indicators Herspring lists: "length of training period for political officers"; "activity of the military party organization," and "handling of disciplinary questions." Furthermore, the time period 1949-72 is divided into five subperiods. Each indicator, after a competent discussion within the politico-historical context of each period, is classified and scored in order to gain a basis for comparisons. What makes this approach so valuable to me is its intertwining of the methodological principles of quantification and qualification. Qualitative changes in the subsystem under investigation, i.e., the GDR military, are classified and quantified. But once they are scored, they are not treated as mathematical devices, but rather qualitative viewpoints are brought in again in order to insure a valid interpretation. In other words, Herspring embeds his quantifications in a broad historico-political description, thus avoiding the danger of abstract modeling, which is of little use in area research anyhow. On the other hand, it is extremely impressive how Dr. Herspring succeeds in systematizing the broad materials he consulted in such a way that they become quantifiable.

With research work like this the author is breaking new ground. Nothing has been published on the GDR military that can be compared to Dr. Herspring's study. Furthermore, this work is of great use to all those who are engaged in comparative research based on the analysis of indicators.

The results of the study justify its author's immense expenditures of time and energy. At the end of his investigations Dr. Herspring can state with authority that between 1949 and 1972 the levels of both technology and political control in the East German army have risen; that with regard to the military skill group the dual executive seems to exist not only in ideology but in reality also. Or more precisely and in Herspring's own words: "Despite the increased use of technology by a group fulfilling a need desired by the party, the political leadership will be able to interfere in the internal affairs of the group to produce a dual executive. Emphasis on one aspect of the dual executive will not necessarily result in a decrease in the other. Strong emphasis on one half, however, will decrease the degree to which the other increases."

The political consequences that can be drawn from such an outcome seem to be as weighty as the scientific ones. By supplying some substantial information to both an assessment of the NVA and an evaluation of its specific problems, Dr. Herspring provides for a better political understanding as well as a more subtle scientific perception of the GDR system. The study gains additional importance from yet another point of view. It proves that by making use of both published materials and some methods developed by empirical political science, academic research can be carried out in a field that so far has been the domain of classified studies. As Herspring has shown, a careful and comprehensive analysis of published materials concerning the East German military improves our knowledge and demonstrates that scholarly studies can lead to meaningful results in this crucial field. This work, therefore, offers new prospects for political science by suggesting an incorporation of the military sector into political science research and by stimulating a discussion on some basic assumptions concerning the army in communist political systems. Thus, empirical political science in its efforts to build a more realistic model of communist rule undoubtedly can profit from Dr. Herspring's fine study.

CONTENTS

	Page
ACKNOWLEDGEMENTS	vi
FOREWORD Peter C. Ludz	vii
LISTS OF TABLES AND FIGURES	xiii
LIST OF ABBREVIATIONS	xiv
LIST OF EQUIVALENT MILITARY RANKS	xv
INTRODUCTION	xvi
Theoretical Framework	xvi
Methodology	xx
Review of the Literature and Sources	xxx
Anticipated Results	xxxiv
Notes	xxxv

PART I
TECHNOLOGY AND POLITICAL CONTROL—SOME EMPIRICAL INDICATORS

Chapter

1	TECHNOLOGY IN THE NATIONAL PEOPLE'S ARMY	3
	Notes	19
2	POLITICAL CONTROL IN THE NATIONAL PEOPLE'S ARMY	21
	Notes	39

Chapter		Page

PART II
THE EAST GERMAN MILITARY, 1949-72

3	A HESITANT BEGINNING: 1949-55	43
	Military Technology	45
	Political Control	47
	Observations	55
	Notes	56
4	THE POLITICIZATION OF THE NATIONAL PEOPLE'S ARMY: 1956-59	59
	Military Technology	61
	Political Control	68
	Observations	82
	Notes	84
5	THE PERIOD OF THE TECHNICIAN: 1960-63	93
	Military Technology	95
	Political Control	101
	Observations	112
	Notes	114
6	THE PERIOD OF CONSOLIDATION: 1964-67	120
	Military Technology	121
	Political Control	129
	Observations	141
	Notes	144
7	THE NVA EMERGES AS A MODERN MILITARY FORCE 1968-72	152
	Military Technology	154
	Political Control	160
	Observations	173
	Notes	175

Chapter	Page

PART III
CONCLUSION

8	POLITICAL CONTROL AND TECHNOLOGY IN A COMMUNIST POLITICAL SYSTEM	183
	Notes	189
APPENDIX: Selected Statistics		191
BIBLIOGRAPHY		194
INDEX		214
ABOUT THE AUTHOR		217
RELATED TITLES		218

LISTS OF TABLES AND FIGURES

Table		Page
3.1	Level of Technology in Period I, 1949-55	48
3.2	Level of Political Control in Period I, 1949-55	54
4.1	Level of Technology in Periods I-II, 1949-59	69
4.2	Level of Political Control in Periods I-II, 1949-59	81
5.1	Level of Technology in Periods I-III, 1949-63	102
5.2	Level of Political Control in Periods I-III, 1949-63	111
6.1	Level of Technology in Periods I-IV, 1949-67	129
6.2	Level of Political Control in Periods I-IV, 1949-67	142
7.1	Level of Technology in Periods I-IV, 1949-72	160
7.2	Level of Political Control in Periods I-V, 1949-72	172

FIGURE		
3.1	Technology and Political Control in Period I, 1949-55	55
4.1	Technology and Political Control in Periods I-II, 1949-59	82
5.1	Technology and Political Control in Periods I-III, 1949-63	112
6.1	Technology and Political Control in Periods I-IV, 1949-67	141
7.1	Technology and Political Control in Periods I-V, 1949-72	173

LIST OF ABBREVIATIONS

DGP	Deutsche Grenzpolizei	German Border Police
FDJ	Freie Deutsche Jugend	Free German Youth
GDR		German Democratic Republic
KVP	Kasernierte Volkspolizei	People's Police quartered in barracks
NVA	Nationale Volksarmee	National People's Army
Politorgane	Politische Organe	political organs
P S	Pferde Stärke	horsepower
SBZ	Sowjetische Besatzungszone	Soviet Occupation Zone
SED	Sozialistische Finheitspartei Deutschlands	Socialist Unit Party of Germany
SSD	Staatssicherheitsdienst	State Security Service
VP	Volkspolizei	People's Police

LIST OF EQUIVALENT MILITARY RANKS

GDR Army	U.S. Equivalent
Armeegeneral	General
Generaloberst	Lieutenant General
Generalleutnant	Major General
Generalmajor	Brigadier General
Oberst	Colonel
Oberstleutnant	Lieutenant Colonel
Major	Major
Haputmann	Captain
Oberleutnant	First Lieutenant
Leutnant	Second Lieutenant
Unterleutnant	—

GDR Navy	U.S. Equivalent
—	Admiral
Admiral	Vice Admiral
Vizeadmiral	Rear Admiral
Konteradmiral	Commodore
Kapitän zur See	Captain
Fregattenkapitän	Commander
Korvettenkapitän	Lieutenant Commander
Kapitänleutnant	Lieutenant
Oberleutnant zur See	Lieutenant, Junior Grade
Leutnant zur See	Ensign
Unterleutnant zur See	—

Note: The National People's Army includes the air force and navy as well as the army. The same ranks are used for border troops, air force, People's Police and State Security Service.

INTRODUCTION

> The training of the so-called pure specialist (Nur-Fachmann) was unreconcilable with both the political character of our army as well as its military demands. An officer must combine a high degree of political maturity, solid military, scientific and technical knowledge with the ability to pass on his knowledge and conviction and to lead and train socialist military collectives.
> ——Oberstleutnant Dr. J. Schunke, in
> <u>Mitteilungsblatt der Arbeitsgemeinschaft
> Ehemaliger Offiziere</u>

THEORETICAL FRAMEWORK

One effect of the increased importance of technology in communist political systems is its generation of questions concerning the types of individuals who occupy positions of leadership. Specifically, is it possible to develop individuals who are both "red" and "expert," or as George Fischer put it, a "dual executive"?

Fischer defines a dual executive as an individual who combines "two kinds of skills—economic and political."[1] This definition is utilized throughout this study with one modification: In place of economic skills, I will substitute technical expertise. Included in this definition is, of course, the assumption that an individual who possesses both technical and political skills will make use of them. It is conceivable, for example, for an individual to possess political skills but—as a result of his failure to participate in party activities—to remain an apolitical technocrat. In order to politicize him, the party must force him to actively engage in party life. In addition, it should be noted that the concept of a dual executive is an ideal type. Consequently, although it is unlikely that any individual will represent a perfect combination of technical and political skills, I think it is a useful tool for focusing attention on a communist party's attempt to combine these attributes in certain individuals.

Reliance on "pure technocrats" or "party hacks" could have serious ramifications for a communist political system. The price of placing individuals with little or no technical expertise in positions of authority would be technical backwardness. Focus on individuals who

---

The views and opinions expressed in this study are those of the writer and do not represent official State Department policy.

are technically qualified, but apolitical, could result in an eventual loss of party hegemony. Consequently, the system must develop individuals who, to a degree, are a blend of both worlds if it wishes to maximize political control and industrial progress.

Although some studies suggest that a dual executive type of leader is playing an increasingly important role at the highest political levels (i.e., the Central Committee, Secretariat, and Politburo),[2] it remains unclear whether it will be possible for the party to develop such individuals within various occupational groups. This is particularly true for occupational groups dealing with advanced technology. The pluralists, according to Fischer, argue that it is necessary to grant such groups social autonomy "so that they can act more or less on their own within one or more spheres of life."[3] A decision on the part of the party to permit such a development could be just as dangerous to its continued viability as admitting apolitical technocrats to the uppermost ruling circles. Individuals within these groups who feel no allegiance to the party on occasion might tend to follow the dictates of technological rationality rather than those of party dogma.

The basic question, then, is to what degree it is possible for the party leadership in a modern, communist political system to develop individuals who are both "red" and "expert" in occupational groups fulfilling technical tasks the party leadership deems necessary. Two aspects of technology—specialization and technological interdependence—complicate the party's task of developing dual executives.

Specialization forces an individual who wishes to acquire a skill to work within the context of a group on a full-time basis in order (1) to gain the knowledge necessary to perform the skill, (2) to consult with other members of the group on particular problems, and (3) to maximize his self-interest as a specialist in concert with other specialists. Forced to interact closely within a group context—particularly if the group tends to be isolated from the rest of society—the individual may develop a narrow definition of social responsibility. A physician may limit his activities to medical diagnosis and treatment while a chemist may feel his responsibilities go no farther than the laboratory. Since the party cannot accept such a narrow definition of social responsibility, its natural reaction would be to intervene in the groups' internal life in order to assure politicization according to party dictates. However, technological interdependence, with its emphasis on coordination and planning, stands in the way of such action.

A large technical organization resembles a complex machine. All its parts must be coordinated, its workings and maintenance well planned. A group using technology in the fulfillment of what the leadership perceives to be a need works similarly. The actions of hundreds of thousands of specialists must be coordinated. In addition, because of the growing amount of time needed for the production of goods and services, the allocation of resources must be planned. Interference in the group's internal affairs, even though restricted to one small part, may short-circuit the entire system and frustrate the group's efforts to fulfill its assigned need. Faced with an ever expanding universe of knowledge with which they must acquaint themselves in order to master their skills properly, group members will not be able to devote much time to the study of political subjects without sacrificing their continued mastery of technical expertise.

Thus, the political leadership finds itself increasingly confronted by an uncomfortable dilemma. It wishes to develop technically, in order to fulfill economic needs and maintain security. To achieve these goals, the political leadership must sacrifice its strict control over the internal affairs of the groups that produce the needed items. To do so, however, could mean that the leadership might one day end up with a group of apolitical specialists. As Barrington Moore, Jr. put it in another context, "strong accent on one is possible only in circumstances that are very different from those permitting stress upon the other."[4]

Based on the apparent incompatibility of technical development with a high degree of politicization of technical skill groups, it appears that a high level of technical development is possible only by abandoning any hope of creating dual executives within a technical skill group. The fundamental proposition advanced here is that, the greater the use of technology required by the group in fulfilling the goal desired by the political leadership, the less the party leadership will be able to interfere in the group's internal affairs and thereby affect the types of individuals who belong to the group. As a result, the party's chances of producing dual executives will be greatly diminished.

Among the countries of Eastern Europe, the German Democratic Republic (GDR) is of particular interest for a study of communist attempts to develop a dual executive in occupational groups utilizing a high degree of technology. To begin with, it is one of the most technically advanced countries in Eastern Europe. In addition, there is an abundance of primary source material dealing with the GDR in the West, in particular in the German Federal Republic.

Peter Christian Ludz's analysis of the SED (Sozialistische Einheitspartei Deutschlands, or Socialist Unity Party of Germany) bureaucracy stands as one of the most important studies of the affects of technology on skill groups in the GDR.[5] Modern technology, he suggests, has made it necessary for the SED to recruit a new type of individual—a technocrat—in place of the party hack so typical of the past. These individuals, who are particularly numerous in the economic sphere, do not pass through the same party schools as their predecessors did in the past. What is important is their "expertness."[6] Their "redness," although a consideration, occupies second place. As Ludz says in another context, "The political prerequisite for such a career is party membership. Further 'commitment' is, however, rarely required of trainees qualified in technology and economics."[7]

Thus, it would appear from Ludz's account that the East Germans have given up any attempt to create a dual executive. Nevertheless, it might be argued, party actions with regard to industrial managers are not necessarily representative of policy throughout the rest of society. A determination of the degree to which this policy is prevalent throughout the system is possible only after similar studies of other groups are completed.

A communist government considers few skill groups more important than the military. With a potential monopoly over the application of the increasingly technical and complex instruments of violence, as well as a tendency to isolate itself from the rest of society, the military presents a potential threat to the existence of the regime. Consequently, it can be assumed that any communist government will go to great lengths to assure as high a degree of control of the military as possible by politicizing it. As Samuel Huntington put it with regard to the Nazi experience, "an 'unpolitical' army is an intolerable anomaly in a completely totalitarian society."[8]

The specter of German militarism has haunted policy-makers in both East and West. Few, however, have more reason to fear a rebirth of an autonomous German military than SED party leaders, who in many cases suffered at its hands, and the Russians, who sustained 20 million fatalities as a result of the German invasion.[9] So it should come as no suprise that the Russians and the East German party leaders are prepared to take whatever steps necessary to assure that the East German military remains under complete party control.

To assure politicization of the military, while at the same time allowing for increases in technology, the East Germans adopted a concept Lenin made famous: the single leadership principle (Einzelleitung).[10] This concept is very close to the dual executive approach suggested by George Fischer, and the two terms will be used interchangeably throughout the remainder of this study. According to Heinz Hoffmann,* "the trusted principle of single leadership involves the unity of political and military leadership."[11] Thus the ideal officer of the NVA (Nationale Volksarmee, or National People's Army) is one who is both politically and technically qualified, as well as actively engaged in party activities and technical pursuits.

---

*All translations of German sources in this study are those of the author unless otherwise noted. In addition, it should be noted that a number of East German terms, such as Einzelleitung have a particular meaning in East Germany. In such cases the original word will be placed in parentheses. A similar practice will be followed

Recognizing their preference for a dual executive model for officers in the armed forces, the question still remains whether they can develop such an individual while at the same time creating a highly technical and competitive military. Is the military dual executive wishful thinking or a real possibility?[12] To use Huntington's term, is it possible for the SED to create a highly technical military while relying on "subjective" forms of civilian control?[13] What has been said up to this point suggests that it is not; the remainder of this study is devoted to an analysis of the SED's attempts to prove this proposition wrong.

Methodology

This study concentrates on the officer corps of the NVA.* At first glance, a definition of this unit of analysis appears a simple matter. On closer inspection, however, complications arise due to changes in the organizational structure and nomenclature of the armed forces of the GDR. In broadest terms, I will define the military as those societal groups that, on a full-time basis, specialize in the application of the more technical and complex instruments of violence, with the constitutional task of protecting the state from external enemies.[14]

The units that make up the East German military for the purposes of this study are:

In 1949-55**: The KVP (Kasernierte Volkspolizei, or People's Police quartered in barracks) and DGP (Deutsche Grenzpolizei, or German Border Police). The KVP's primary mission was defense against external enemies. Although the primary function of the DGP was securing the state's borders, it had tanks and other heavy weapons and so qualifies it as a military unit. The intention of combining the DGP with the KVP in case of external attack also was stated, supporting its identification as part of the military. In addition,

---

for words that have no special meaning in East Germany but are difficult to translate into English.

*Primary emphasis will be placed on the officer corps for three reasons. First, the level of military expertise will be higher. Second, almost all officers are career soldiers and thus can be expected to identify with the military more closely than enlisted personnel who usually serve for shorter periods of time. Third, as a result of the hierarchical nature of the armed forces, members of the officer corps usually are those who make the most important decisions.

**The date 1949 was selected as the starting point because it coincides with the founding of the GDR.

these two groups later were combined under the NVA, when it was formed. Examples of paramilitary forces not included are the Transportpolizei (transport police) and the VP (Volkspolizei, or People's Police).

In 1956-70: All military units that come under the administration of the NVA, including border troops, the navy, the air force, and the army.

In order to test the basic proposition advanced in this study, two concepts were constructed. The first is a conglomerate of 17 empirical indicators associated with the technological level existing within a military force. This concept will be referred to as "technology" and includes both individual characteristics indicating an individual's technical qualifications—such as educational level—and unit characteristics—such as the horsepower level—that show a member of the unit is engaged in a technical pursuit. A justification for the selection of each indicator, as well as an explanation, is provided in Chapter 1. The indicators of technology are:

1. Educational level required for entry into officers' training schools.
2. Length of officer training schools.
3. Percentage of total officers who have completed three years officer training.
4. Value of officer's education when compared with civilian degrees.
5. Percentage of total officers with mittlere Reife (tenth-class certificate).
6. Percentage of total officers with Abitur (final high school examination).
7. Percentage of total officers with Fachschulausbildung (technical education certificate).
8. Percentage of total officers classified as engineers or technicians.
9. Percentage of total officers with an academic degree.
10. Percentage of army regimental level commanders with an academic degree.
11. Length of time officers are obligated to serve.
12. Importance of technical qualifications for officers for promotion or retention in the service.
13. Existence of technical awards.
14. Number of occupational categories recognized by the military.
15. Number of specialized journals.
16. Number of books printed on specialized military subjects.
17. Horsepower level or PS level (Pferde Stärke).

The other concept consists of 15 empirical indicators that relate to the party's attempt to assure that its officer corps is politically qualified and actively engaged in party life. This concept is referred to as "political control" and includes control measures, such as the organizational level down to which the political officer is present, and measures to assure participation in party affairs, such as responsibility for political indoctrination. A justification for the inclusion as well as an explanation of each of these indicators is supplied in Chapter 2. The indicators of political control are:

1. Level down to which political officers are present.
2. Level down to which secret police officers are present.
3. Length of training period for political officers.
4. Prior military service of political officers.
5. Level down to which the Politorgane (political organs) are active.
6. Activity of the military party organization.
7. Percentage of officers who are party members.
8. Importance assigned to the political reliability of regular officers for promotion or retention in the service.
9. Responsibility for political indoctrination.
10. Responsibility for Massenarbeit (work with the masses).
11. Part-time ideological training.
12. Effectiveness of self-criticism.
13. Handling of disciplinary questions.
14. Handling of criminal offenses.
15. Hours per year spent on civilian types of projects.*

For the purposes of this study, five time periods were constructed. In setting up these time periods, two approaches were considered. The first was to divide by events. This method was rejected for two reasons. First, due to the paucity of secondary works available on the NVA, it was not possible to ascertain at the outset exactly which events were most significant for the development of

---

*The indicators of political control focus specifically on the party's control system within the military. Other areas of controversy between the party and the military common to the Soviet Union are not included either because they are not discussed, as in the case of the allocation of resources to the military, or because they are taken directly from the Soviet military, as in the case of tactics or strategy. Some indicators on which information was available are not included because the information was restricted to only one period. Among these are service by officers as enlisted men and civilian contacts, or Offentlichkeitsarbeit. Membership in the FDJ was not included because it was considered to be too similar to SED Party membership.

civil-military relations in the GDR. Second, since this study is aimed at observing long-term trends in the relationship between technology and the party's attempt to create a military dual executive, it was feared that focus on specific events, such as the building of the Berlin Wall, might give a false impression of what really was occurring. One legitimately might expect party efforts on the political side to increase at this time, but would that really be indicative of a long-term trend? Consequently, it was decided to construct the time periods so as to lessen the chance that any single event would dominate the average level of political control and technology at a given point.

To do this, a second approach was employed, that of equally dividing all the time periods—with the exception of the first and last periods. The first time period covers seven years rather than five, as is the case for periods II, III, and IV, for two reasons. Due to the scarcity of data for this period it would be very difficult to make any determination on the level of technology or political control if the period were limited to five years. In addition, unlike the subsequent periods which deal with the NVA, this period is concerned with similar, but in some important ways different, units—the KVP and DGP. A division of the first time period at the end of 1956 would have included the NVA in the same period with the KVP and DGP.

The last period covers six years because division of the 21-year period from 1956-72 into five perfectly equal periods seemed impractical. Division into three equal time periods was rejected because it would be difficult to detect a trend if only three time periods were utilized. The time periods used in this study are:

Period I	1949-55
Period II	1956-59
Period III	1960-63
Period IV	1964-67
Period V	1968-72

In order to index the levels of technology and political control, a method of combining these different types of data must be devised. Within the concept of technology alone, there are 17 different indicators. Some may easily be combined, but others are more difficult. For example, one may accept the fact that the percentage of officers possessing a certain level of education, perhaps the mittlere Reife, is comparable with the percentage of those possessing the Abitur. But problems arise when one attempts to combine this type of data with such indicators as the number of journals published or the existence of technical awards. While the need for a method that can be used to combine these indicators is obvious, its nature is not.

Three methods appeared most relevant insofar as the purposes of this study are concerned. The first would retain the data collected for the study in their original form. During each of the time periods, each indicator would be discussed and evaluated separately.

Although this type of approach may be quite useful for a study that utilizes a limited number of indicators, it presents problems when applied to the relatively large number used here. For example, an explanation of the relationship between an increase in the percentage of officers having an academic education and the number of journals published in a given period, in addition to an increase in the PS level, appears plausible. However, an explanation of how all 17 indicators fit together would exhaust the talents of even the most astute analyst because of the multiple interrelations that are possible.

In addition, the writer would be faced with the problem of keeping the analysis systematic, i.e., using the same system of weighting for each indicator in each period. The temptation, indeed, the complexity of the undertaking would be so great that there is little likelihood the analyst would able to maintain the same frame of reference throughout. He probably would lapse into intuitive explanations—such as "after looking at the indicators present, I conclude that the level of technology has increased." If one accepts—as does this study—the position that an analyst must be as systematic and as intersubjective as the data allow, then this approach is unsatisfactory for the purposes of the study and the nature of the data.

The second possible method for combining the data would be to classify each indicator in one of three categories—increase, decrease, no change. For example, if the level of an indicator of technology or political control increased when compared with the preceding period, it would be classified as showing an increase. For Pereiod I and where data for a preceeding are not available, the indicator will be classified by whether it showed an increase, decrease, or no change during the period under study.

Each of these categories then would be assigned a numerical score, with an increase appearing as +1, no change as 0, and a decrease as -1. The total number of points awarded in each period would be divided by the total number of indicators present in the period. Combination of all the indicators would result in an index of the overall change in the level of technology or political control achieved—i.e. whether it is increasing, decreasing, or remaining the same. The two concepts then could be compared over time to ascertain any relationship between them. For example, does political control increase as technology increases?

This approach has obvious advantages over the first one. First, it eliminates the need for the writer to descriptively compare every indicator with every other indicator during each period. Instead, he proceeds from the position that, since all indicators are indexes of technology and have the same value, an overall increase in a majority of the indicators signifies an increase in technology. Second, he uses the same frame of reference for evaluating each indicator during each of the periods under study.

Nevertheless, this method also seemed unsatisfactory. It lacked sufficient sensitivity to the degree of change that occurred on a number of indicators. Let us, for example, view the case of indicator 13, the handling of criminal offenses (see Chapter 2). During Period I, there was no change, during Period II an increase, and during Period III a decrease, while Periods IV and V showed no change. As a consequence this indicator would be scored as follows: Period I, 0; Period II, +1; Period III, -1; Period IV, 0; and Period V, 0. So the overall average for this indicator would be 0, signifying no change. This conclusion, however, gives a false picture of what occurred. It reflects only changes between periods, not degrees of change. Political control increased in Period II, but we do not know by how much. It decreased in Period III, but again we do not know by how much. As a result, since we are not sure how much it increased or decreased in Periods II and III, we are not certain if the readings for Periods IV and V are the equivalent of Period I.

The third method, which incorporates the advantages of the second method over the first, proved to be more sensitive to changes in the level of technology and political control. Rather than evaluate each indicator in terms of an increase, decrease, or no change, this method seeks to evaluate the degree of change and set up a cumulative scale facilitating determination of the level of each indicator. At the same time, it combines the indicators in order to obtain an index of the level of technology and political control during each period. It classifies each indicator present in a given period on the basis of high, medium, and low. Each category is assigned a numerical score: high = 3, medium = 2, and low = 1. In addition, it assigns each indicator equal weight. In order to obtain an average level of political control and technology, some relationship between the indicators must be established. A great deal of time and effort was devoted to making them as equal as possible. Nevertheless, it might become apparent in the course of this study that some indicators are more important than others. This, however, can be ascertained only after the data have been analyzed.

To illustrate the advantages of this system over those previously outlined, let us consider the way it measures changes on the same indicator discussed above—the handling of criminal offenses (see Chapter 2). During Period I regular military officers made the final decision in regard to criminal cases; this is classified as low. During Period II the party intervened, playing a major role in deciding how criminal offenses were handled; this is scored as high. In Period III a change allowed for equal participation of party and military officials; this is categorized as medium. Periods IV and V remain the same; consequently, they also are classified as medium. The scoring would be 1, 3, 2, 2, 2—or an average of 2. Thus one obtains a more sensitive overall reading that shows a medium level of political control, rather than no change. In addition, it more accurately indicates changes between periods and provides a better idea of the level of technology or political control in a period when the indicators are combined, as illustrated by the tables below, which show two hypothetical indicators over two periods.

Method II

	PERIOD I	PERIOD II
Indicator X	Same through-out period 0	-1
Indicator Y	Same through-out period 0	+1
Total	0	0
Average	0	0

Increase = +1; same = zero; decrease = -1.

Method III

	PERIOD I	PERIOD II
Indicator X	2	1
Indicator Y	1	3
Total	3	4
Average	0.7	2.0

High = 3; medium = 2; low = 1.

According to Method II, changes in the level of technology during Periods I and II cancelled one another, insofar as the two hypothetical indicators above are concerned. But according to Method III an overall increase in the level of technology occurred. The problem with Method II, as illustrated in the chart, is that it treats all increases and decreases as of equal magnitude. Method III, however, was sensitive to the different gradations of change.

Before proceeding to a detailed discussion of the mechanics of Method III, something should be said about the classification system of high, medium, and low. This system is not an absolute one. The reader should not get the impression that the boundaries of the indicators employed here could not be drawn differently under other circumstances. There is nothing to prevent the use of a different classification system with the same data in another study—this system is merely a means to an end.

The purpose of this system is to combine a number of indicators so that an <u>approximation</u> of the level of technology and political control can be made within each period. Thus it will be possible to test the proposed relationship between technology and political control in a state attempting to maintain party dominance while creating a highly technical military.

In order to explain how this method will assist the reader to observe the relationship between technology and political control in the East German military, it may be helpful to discuss the system of classification as it applies to each of the concepts separately. First, let us consider the case of technology.

As mentioned above, two different types of data are utilized in this study in evaluating the level of technology. One type of data is quantifiable. For example, the educational level of the NVA officer corps, i. e. 60 percent of all NVA officers possess an Abitur. The other type of data is not available in quantitative form but concerns equally important indicators—i. e., the importance assigned to technical awards. In accordance with the two types of data, two different approaches were utilized in converting it into the scale of high, medium, and low discussed above.

First, let us consider the method used to classify the quantitative data. Since comparative data of this type are not available from other communist military forces, it is necessary to view the NVA as a self-contained unit in evaluating the level of technology. In order to do this, I have decided to consider the <u>total</u> change in the percentage of officers possessing a specific characteristic over all five periods under study and to divide this figure by three, in accordance with the three categories of high, medium, and low (the only exception to this method is in cases where the data is in quantitative form but has natural dividing points). Those in the upper third will be viewed as indicative of high, those in the middle as medium, and those in the bottom third as low. For example, the total percentage of officers possessing academic education varies from a low of 2.6 to a high of 14 percent. As a result, one has a unit of analysis of 11.4 (14.0 to 2.6). Dividing by three, we obtain the figure of 3.8. Thus, the three categories would be as follows: low, 2.6 to 6.4 (2.6 + 3.8 = 6.4); medium, 6.5 to 10.2; and high, 10.3 to 14.0.

One may object to this method as arbitrary and mechanical, and indeed it is. Nevertheless, there are important reasons for selecting it. First, it insures that all indicators of this type are treated equally. Second, although it assures that each indicator will show a <u>high</u> level of technology in some period, this does not contradict the purpose of this analysis. The major goal of this study is to determine whether political control increases, decreases, or remains the same as the level of technology rises within the NVA, and not to ascertain the level of technology of the NVA within the world military community.

Indicators not available in quantitative form were handled by carefully considering the specific conditions surrounding each indicator and, based on that investigation, three categories were established corresponding to the classifications of high, medium, and low. For example, in viewing the importance of military education when compared to civilian institutions, it was found that three different categories developed over the years. First, graduates of military education programs were considered tradesmen and received little or no civilian recognition of their educational achievements. Next, the programs were raised to the status of a technical school where graduates obtained technical certificates on a par with comparable civilian institutions. Later, the value of military education was raised to the equivalent of that of a university. As a result, the categories established were low, medium, and high, respectively. The reader also may object to this type of classification as arbitrary. To a degree such a criticism is valid, although I submit less so than in the case of the quantifiable data. Nevertheless, it should be noted that an explanation of why the categories were selected is provided for each of the indicators.

Political control in communist armed forces has been the topic of several works, one of the best by Roman Kolkowicz.[15] Although most of these works deal with the Soviet military, the situation in the NVA is quite similar, perhaps because the NVA has relied heavily on Soviet experience.

Although such studies exist and were helpful in setting up the categories used here, the fact remains that, to my knowledge, a study similar to this one has never been undertaken on any communist military. This means that, as in the case of technology, many of the categories are constructed for the first time.

In setting up the categories of high, medium, and low for political control, the same procedure is followed as in the case of the nonquantifiable data under technology. After careful consideration of the conditions surrounding each indicator, a division into the three categories of high, medium, and low will follow. Assuming, as this study does, that the party wants to maintain as high a degree of political control as possible, it may be inferred that it will make use of the highest or strongest form of control considered tolerable at the time, particularly when authorities make comments to the effect that more political control is necessary.

As an example, let us consider the organizational level on which the political officer is present (the role of this indicator is discussed in detail in Chapter 2). The lower the level within the military hierarchy on which the political officer is present, the better he will be able to observe and report on the activities and opinions of his colleagues. The determination of the levels that should be considered high, medium, and low in this case is assisted by the structure of the military organization, which usually is broken down into three major units: the division and regiment, the battalion and company, and the squad and platoon. Consequently, for the purposes of this study, these categories are employed. Thus political control would be high if political officers are assigned down to the lowest organizational level, the squad and platoon; medium if down to the middle level, the company and battalion; or low if restricted to the middle level, the division and regiment. For each indicator of political control, I will provide a similar explanation of why each classification was selected.

In some cases, the level of the political control indicators remains the same over the entire period under study. This raises the question of whether the inclusion of such indicators is not a mere formality. I am of the opinion that it is not. It will be very important, I suggest, if this study shows that some indicators of political control remained the same despite increased technology (no indicator of technology remained the same throughout all the periods under study). It would suggest that, insofar as that particular indicator was concerned, the party felt not only that this means of control remained essential but also, and more important, that it was either not necessary or impossible to increase the level of political control as evidenced in this indicator. Such a finding would itself raise such questions as why this particular factor was considered important enough to be retained, or why it was not possible or necessary to strengthen it while other indicators varied.

One might suggest that a study of this nature would be far more useful if the averages derived for the technological level were correlated with those for the political level. Unfortunately, such a computation is not feasible. First of all, most statistical texts require the presence of at least 20 variables for a correlation analysis.[16] With the exception of one period, there is an average of 16 indicators of technology and 14 of political control in each period, which falls short of the suggested 20. Second, and more important, the categories employed here do not lend themselves to this type of analysis. The categories are artificial constructs employed to combine a number of varying types of data so that an approximation of the level of technology and political control can be obtained. To subject these categories to a very precise correlation analysis would apply them in a manner requiring standards they cannot meet and for which they were not designed.

Each indicator present in a period will be classified as high, medium, or low. After a value is assigned to each indicator of technology, or political control, this value will be converted to a corresponding score—3 for high, 2 for medium, and one for low. These figures then will be combined on a table and averaged. Indicators on which there is no information in a given period will be omitted from consideration for that period. Once all the averages for levels of technology and political control have been ascertained, they will be charted on a graph.

Each chapter is devoted to an analysis of data in a given time period and is divided into four sections. The first section includes a statement of the major events and trends visible in the society as a whole during the period. This provides the reader with background information, enabling him to fit the interaction of technology and political control into a broader perspective. The second section offers an analysis of the empirical indicators of technology, including a classification of each one according to the criteria outlined above. The third section is similar to the second but treats the subject of political control. The last section of each chapter includes a discussion of the overall trends visible during the period. Among the questions that will be asked are the following: Do the changes in the level of political control appear related to changes in technology? If technology does not seem to have played an important role, what other factors seem to be operative?

Review of the Literature and Sources

In light of the importance the Russians and East Germans attach to preventing the rise of a military establishment possessing a separate identity and manifesting attitudes that could deviate from those of the party, it is surprising indeed that Western scholars have virtually ignored the results of their efforts. Although a number of works of this nature dealing with the Bundeswehr have appeared,[17] the NVA is the subject of only one book-length study in the West.[18] Unfortunately, it is more descriptive than analytical.

The sources utilized in this study are primarily of East German origin, although Western material also was consulted. Many of these journals, newspapers, and books are being used for the first time in a Western analysis.[19] The major journals and newspapers include the following, the first five of which are not generally available in the West:

1. Militärwesen (Military science). This is the most important East German military journal dealing with military problems. Published primarily for army officers up to 1972, it occasionally also included articles by members of the other services and two or three articles a year by important political personalities. From 1957 to 1961 it was published six times a year and since 1961, monthly. In 1972 it was changed to incorporate the journals Marinewesen and Luftverteidigung. It now appears with three special sections in addition to articles of general interest; Section A with articles for the army, Section B for the air force, and Section C for the navy. All issues but one of this journal were available and consulted.

2. Marinewesen (Naval science). This journal dealt primarily with problems of interest to naval officers and was published by the navy. Articles by members of other branches were rare, except for those by the minister of national defense, an army general. It was published six times a year in 1962-64, nine times in 1965, and monthly from 1966 to 1971. It was incorporated into Militärwesen in 1972. All but four issues of this journal were consulted.

3. Luftverteidigung (Air defense). This journal dealt primarily with problems of interest to air force officers and was published by the air force. It was published four times in 1966, six times per year in 1967-68, and monthly from 1969-72. It was incorporated into Militärwesen in 1972. All issues of this journal were consulted.

4. Parteiarbeiter (Party worker). This journal is the organ of the Main Political Administration of the NVA. Almost all issues of this monthly journal during the period 1965-72 were consulted. Although it appears that this journal began publication in 1965, this could not be confirmed.

5. Der Ausbilder (The educator). This monthly journal deals primarily with problems associated with political and technical training. It began publication in 1972. All issues were consulted.

6. Der Kämpfer (The fighter). This newspaper is the organ of the East German militia. It deals primarily with military problems. Scattered issues were consulted.

7. Volksarmee (People's army). This newspaper, published weekly, is the main organ of the NVA for all services. It includes discussions of party decisions and military events as well as other information of interest to the average member of the NVA. The first five years (1956-61) it appeared under the title Die Volksarmee. All issues of this newspaper were consulted.

8. Neues Deutschland (New Germany). This is the central organ of the SED. It is important for its statements on military policy, which can be assumed to be highly authoritative. It is published daily. Scattered issues were consulted.

9. Zeitschrift für Militärgeschichte (Journal of military history). Although primarily devoted to a consideration of historical questions, it also is important for its inclusion of discussions of the proper role of the party in the military. It has been published monthly since 1961. The title of this journal was changed to Militärgeschichte in 1972. All issues were consulted.

10. Volkspolizei (People's police). Although devoted primarily to police questions, this journal is important for a consideration of civil-military relations in the GDR, particularly during the early period (1949-56), when it served as the main organ for the KVP. Scattered issues were consulted.

Other journals also were consulted, but only for specific articles since their contents as a whole were not relevant. Among the most important of these are Gefechtsausbildung (Combat training) and Rückwärtige Dienst (Supply service), neither of which is available in the West, as well as Militärtechnik (Military technology), Sport und Technik (Sport and technology), Mitteilungsblatt der Arbeitsgemeinschaft ehemaliger Offiziere (Information organ of the Society of Former Officers), Einheit (Unity), and Armeerundschau (Army panorama). In addition to these periodicals, journals, and newspapers, East German books covering military questions were consulted (see Bibliography).

Concentration on primary documents such as these raises a question as to their reliability. How certain can one be that the data they supply accurately reflect the real situation in the East German military? Although there is reason to question the reliability of any governmental documents, there are steps that can be taken to insure the highest degree of reliability.

First, one can choose documents primarily intended for internal consumption. The probability that the role of the Politorgane will be misrepresented in a document intended to inform military officers of the behavior expected of them is less than in one intended for external propaganda. This is particularly true insofar as military journals are concerned.

The degree to which Western governments accept East German data on their military forces also is an indication of reliability. This is particularly true of the West German government, which has done the greatest work in this area and until quite recently was quite hostile to the GDR. Where the data are not accepted by the West German agencies, it will be necessary to establish whether rejection stems from political motivation or real skepticism about the accuracy of the data. A comparison of long-range changes will be helpful in this regard. For example, an extreme change in educational level that is disputed by Western experts and, could not be accounted for on the basis of events within the East German military would be open to question.

A number of my colleagues, themselves students of the GDR, suggested at the outset of this study that I would find little if any disagreement between the party and the military even in the professional journals noted above. It was argued that differences of opinion, to the degree they exist, are settled privately. Such differences of opinion, I discovered, do exist, although they are not as openly expressed as in the West. But finding such disagreements requires patience and a great deal of attention to detail. The reader hoping to find statements by military officers to the effect that the party should meddle less in the military's internal affairs will be disappointed. Indeed, there is an absence of challenges on the part of the military to party interference in its internal affairs that are similar to those made by Marshall Zhukov in the Soviet Union.[20] Nevertheless, there are revealing differences between military professionals and political soldiers over the role of the party in the internal affairs of the military.* Often, statements by political officers decrying practices or attitudes not in accord with party preferences are most revealing. As Ellis Joffe stated with regard to the Chinese Communist Army:

> There are no articles written by members of the opposition which explicitly expound their views, and those articles and speeches which can be interpreted as taking exception to the position of the party high command are vaguely couched and tread a thin line between endorsing the party's policies and criticizing them. There are, however, many articles and pronouncements which condemn the views and actions of the professional officers in no uncertain terms, and these condemnations, coupled with the campaigns to curb professionalism are the best barometer of party-army tensions and the source of our knowledge on the issues which divide them.[21]

An example of a complaint by an East German political officer may illustrate what I am suggesting: "The social science (gesellschaftswissenschaftliche) study programs must help enable the officer to master the ideological contents of class oriented (klassenmässige) education as well as the many-sided and often difficult problems of military life."[22] The introduction of such policies, combined with

---

*In the simplest terms, a political soldier is one who concerns himself primarily with political matters while a regular soldier is one concerned basically with what traditionally are referred to as military questions.

statements complaining about the tendency of officers to give precedence to military activities rather than political ones,[23] indicates that there is a tendency by professional soldiers to ignore political factors and, further, that even after policies were introduced to correct this situation, the lack of interest in political subjects continued.

ANTICIPATED RESULTS

The significance of a finding that an increase in the level of technology is associated with a decrease in the level of political control exerted over the military in a communist system would be significant because it would offer important support for the thesis put forth by Ludz.[24] If the party is unable to prevent an increase in group identity and common attitudes in a group as important as the military, then these forms of control may be even less compatible with a modern and highly industrialized society than hitherto suggested.

On the other hand, a finding that political control and technology are not related would be important for a number of reasons. First, it would question the conventional wisdom that suggests the two are incompatible. Further, it would indicate that, although the party may not have been interested in highly politicized technocrats in the economic sphere, it retained the potentiality for developing such individuals. Certainly, if it can create a dual executive in the military there would not seem to be any reason why it could not develop such individuals in other parts of the political system if this was felt necessary. Such a finding also would be important for an understanding of civil-military relations in communist political systems. It would suggest, for example, that the party is firmly in the saddle and that there is little danger—in the GDR, at least—of the rise of an apolitical military. Whether this is also true for other communist political systems is, of course, open to question. In any case, such a finding would provide food for thought.

The first part of this study is devoted to a discussion of the indicators of technology and political control that were constructed for analysis. It also explains why the dividing line between high, medium, and low was set at at a particular point for each indicator. Although Part I will be helpful for those who are unfamiliar with the usage of these indicators in the East German context, the general reader who is primarily interested in substantive information about the development of the NVA or in the findings of this study may wish to skip this part. The second and main section provides a detailed analysis of each indicator present during the period under study. In addition, careful consideration is given to the relationship between technology and political control. The Conclusion considers some of the ramifications of this study, not only for the GDR but for an understanding of civil-military relations in other technically advanced communist political systems.

NOTES

1. George Fischer, The Soviet System and Modern Society (New York: Atherton, 1968), p. 14.

2. Examples from the SED include such individuals as Günter Mittag, a member of the Politburo and the Central Committee Secretary for Economic Affairs; Werner Jarowinsky, a candidate member of the Politburo and Central Committee Secretary for Trade and Supply; Georg Ewald, a candidate member of the Politburo and a specialist on agricultural matters; and Central Committee members Günther Klieber and Walter Halbrit. See Melvin Croan, "East Germany," in Adam Bromke and Teresa Rakowska-Harmstone, eds., The Communist States in Disarray, 1965-1971, (Minneapolis: University of Minnesota Press, 1972), p. 87. See also Fischer, The Soviet System and Modern Society, pp. 47-64; R. Barry Farrell, "Top Political Leadership in Eastern Europe," in R. Barry Farrell, ed., Political Leadership in Eastern Europe and the Soviet Union, (Chicago: Aldine, 1970), pp. 94-100. Note the increasingly important role of education and political reliability. Gehlen notes the increased importance of education for members of the Soviet apparatchiki who are also members of the Central Committee. See Michel P. Gehlen, "The Soviet Apparatchiki," in Farrell, ed., Political Leadership, p. 144. See also Carl Beck, "Career Characteristics of East European Leadership," Farrell, ed., Political Leadership, p. 192; Michel P. Gehlen and Michael McBride, "The Soviet Central Committee: An Elite Analysis," in Roger Kanet, ed., The Behavorial Revolution and Communist Studies, (New York: The Free Press, 1971), pp. 106-7.

3. Fischer, The Soviet Union and Modern Society, pp. 13-14. See also his excellent discussion of writers from the pluralist school in his Introduction, pp. 8-12. See also Frederic Fleron, "Toward a Reconceptualization of Political Change in the Soviet Union: The Political Leadership System," Comparative Politics, I, 2 (January 1969), 232.

4. Barrington Moore, Jr., Terror and Progress, U.S.S.R. (Cambridge, Mass.: Harvard University Press, 1954), p. 196.

5. Peter Christian Ludz, Parteielite im Wandel (Cologne and Opladen: Westdeutscher Verlag, 1968).

6. Ibid., pp. 60-70.

7. Peter Christian Ludz, The German Democratic Republic from the Sixties to the Seventies (Cambridge, Mass.: Harvard University Press, 1970), pp. 22-23.

8. Samuel Huntington, The Soldier and the State (New York: Vintage, 1964), p. 116. See also Roman Kolkowicz, "Interest Groups in Soviet Politics," Comparative Politics, II, 3 (April 1970), 470.

9. Jesse Clarkson, A History of Russia, (New York: Random House, 1963), p. 706.

10. For the origin of this term in Lenin's writings, see Vladimir Lenin, "Die nächsten Aufgaben der Sowjetmacht," in Lenin, Ausgewählte Werke, Vol. II (Berlin-Ost: Dietz Verlag, 1959), pp. 385, 387. In citing East German books published in East Berlin, the West German practice of listing East Berlin (Berlin-Ost) will be utilized to differentiate them from works published in West Berlin.

11. This statement is from 1962. However, it is representative of official statements throughout the course of this study. Armeegeneral Heinz Hoffman, "Zu neuem Erfolg in Ausbildungsjahr 1963, dem Jahr der VI. Parteitages," Militärwesen (December 1962), p. 1807.

12. As of the Eighth Party Conference in 1971, no members of the SED Politburo also were military officers on active duty. Three officers were members of the Central Committee and one was a candidate member. None of these individuals could be classified as a dual executive, however. These members of the Central Committee are Armeegeneral Heinz Hoffmann, the minister of National Defense and a veteran of the Spanish Civil War; Generaloberst Heinz Hessler, deputy minister of National Defense, chief of the Main Staff, and apparently Hoffmann's heir apparent; and Admiral Waldemar Verner, chief of the Main Political Administration and notoriously lacking in technical qualifications. The candidate member is the former political officer, Generalleutnant Herbert Scheibe, leader of the Section for Security Questions in the Central Committee, and Verner's heir apparent.

13. Huntington, The Soldier and the State, p. 83.

14. This definition differs from that suggested by Lasswell's "experts in the management of violence." See Harold D. Lasswell, "The Garrison-State Hypothesis Today," in Samuel Huntington, ed., Changing Patterns of Military Politics (New York: The Free Press, 1962), p. 51. The term "management" suggests that military officers are specialists not only in the application of violence but also in the policy-making process.

15. Roman Kolkowicz, The Soviet Military and the Communist Party (Princeton, N.J.: Princeton University Press, 1967). See also Raymond L. Garthoff, Soviet Military Doctrine (Glencoe, Ill.: The Free Press, 1953); Ellis Joffe, Party and Army: Professionalism

and Political Control in the Chinese Officer Corps, 1949-1964, (Cambridge, Mass.: Harvard University Press, 1967).

16. Johan Galtung, Theory and Methods of Social Research (London: Allen and Unwin, 1967), p. 60.

17. Erich Waldman, The Goose Step Is Verboten (Glencoe: The Free Press, 1964); Rolf R. Bigler, Der Einsame Soldat (Frauenfeld: Verlag Huber, 1963). See also the three-volume work edited by Georg Picht, Studien zur gesellschaftlichen Situation der Bundeswehr (Witten and Berlin: Eckert-Verlag, 1965-66), as well as Wido Mosen, Eine Militärsoziologie (Neuwied and Berlin: Luchterband, 1967), Wido Mosen, Bundeswehr—Elite der Nation? (Neuwied and Berlin: Luchterband, 1970).

18. Thomas M. Forster, NVA—Die Armee der Sowjetzone (Cologne: Markus Verlag, 1966-67). In addition there are some references to the NVA in book-length studies, the most extensive being a chapter in David Childs, East Germany (New York: Praeger Publishers, 1969). See also Ernst Richert, Die DDR Elite (Hamburg: Rowolt, 1968), pp. 86-88.

19. The importance of such journals as an indication of problems in the military establishment cannot be overemphasized. As one writer noted, "In many respects . . . its [the journal's] function is clear. It is an instrument of efficiency and control, a sort of impersonal and complex command. In short it tells the officers what they need to know." Maury Feld, "The Military Self-Image in a Technical Environment," in Morris Janowitz, ed., The New Military (New York: Wiley, 1967), p. 176 (emphasis in original). See also Morris Janowitz, "Organizing Multiple Goals: War Making and Arms Control," in Janowitz, ed., The New Military, pp. 21-22.

20. For an analysis of the struggle between the Party and the military in the Soviet Union during Zkukov's tenure as Defense Minister, see Roman Kolkowicz, The Soviet Military and the Communist Party (Princeton: Princeton University Press, 1967), pp. 121-38.

21. Joffe, Party and Army, pp. 46-47. See also Ludz, Parteielite im Wandel, pp. 123-24 in regard to the GDR.

22. Oberstleutnant E. Nowak, "Das Niveau der gesellschaftswissenschaftlichen Weiterbildung verbessern!" Militärwesen, March 1966, p. 354.

23. Ibid., pp. 347, 353.

24. Ludz, Parteielite im Wandel, pp. 324-27.

PART

I

**TECHNOLOGY AND
POLITICAL CONTROL—
SOME IMPIRICAL
INDICATORS**

CHAPTER 1

TECHNOLOGY IN THE NATIONAL PEOPLE'S ARMY

In order to measure the level of technology in the NVA during each of the time periods encompassed by this study, 17 indicators of technology were constructed. In addition, each indicator was divided into three categories: high, medium, and low. The remainder of this chapter is devoted to a consideration of each indicator as well as an explanation of why the dividing lines between the categories of high, medium, and low were drawn at particular points for each indicator.

The first of the 17 indicators developed to measure the level of technology in the NVA concerns the nature of special training received by officers. The technical problems of the contemporary world no longer can be met by an officer possessing the equivalent of a high school education. This increased reliance on higher education is evident in the American military. In 1956, for example, 50 percent of all U.S. Army officers were college graduates. By 1961 the percentage had risen to 75 percent.[1] It therefore, would seem reasonable to assume that, the higher the educational level of military officers, the more technical the military organization will be.

The East German educational system requires an individual to attend school for a specific number of years before starting to work as a laborer or entering a trade. The number of years of basic school attendance required indicates the importance placed on basic educational background and in some instances the intelligence of individuals entering a profession. Since all individuals commissioned as NVA officers in recent years must have attended a training school, the entrance requirements of these institutions are highly significant.

Therefore, the first indicator utilized to reveal the educational level of military officers focuses on the level of education required for entry into officer training schools. The following schema is employed in its evaluation:

High: Abitur or completion of twelfth grade required for admittance to officer training schools.
Medium: Completion of the tenth grade required for admittance to officer training schools.
Low: Completion of the eighth grade or less required for admittance to officer training schools.

The education provided through the eighth grade is very basic and, until the mid-1960s all youths in the GDR were required to continue their schooling through this level (with longer, special schools for the physically and mentally handicapped). Acceptance of officer candidates with only eight years of basic education or less would reflect the minimal standards of the community and therefore would be classified as low.

Educational reforms throughout the 1940s and 1950s created polytechnical high schools that offered ten years of education to all children. By 1965 all youths were required to complete the tenth grade under normal conditions. A requirement that all officer candidates possess the tenth grade certificate after 1965 would be less significant than prior to this date. Nevertheless, the fact that the military no longer would accept individuals who, for whatever reason, did not complete the tenth class shows they felt this higher educational level essential for officer candidates expected to deal with the complex problems of a technical military. Therefore, it is categorized as medium in the schema utilized here.

A small percentage of youths, the "intellectual upper crust" as John Dornberg labels them,[2] continues on through the twelfth grade or attends technical institutes offering an education equivalent to an American junior college and earns an Abitur. This in turn qualifies them to enter a university. Thus, a requirement that all officer candidates must possess an Abitur would reflect a great desire for academic training and intelligence that probably would be needed only for a profession requiring a high degree of technical knowledge. It would place entrance into a military officer training school on a par with acceptance to a university and force the military to draw its candidates from the same small portion of the population as civilian universities.[3] Accordingly, it would be considered high on the classification scale.

Closely related to the educational requirements for entering an officer training school is the number of years an officer is required to attend training school before being commissioned. This serves as the second indicator of technology. In light of the expense involved in the maintenance of instructional facilities, as well as the man-hours lost while officer candidates are in school, it can be assumed that the military would not send an individual to school any longer than was felt absolutely necessary to enable him to carry out the tasks assigned. Accordingly, the longer the period of training for an officer candidate, the higher the level of technology will be. Evaluation of this indicator follows the schema below:

High: Officer candidates are required to attend school for three years or longer.
Medium: Officer candidates are required to attend school for two years.
Low: Officer candidates are required to attend school for less than two years.

    An individual who attended an officer school for less than two years would be acquainted with only the most basic aspects of military life. One might expect that at least six months would be devoted to familiarization with military life, thus leaving only about a year for the study of technical subjects. Consequently, it would be considered indicative of a low level of technology.
    Raising the length of officer training schools to two years would provide the military with more time to devote to the inculcation of technical expertise. Nevertheless, this increased time available for technical training would appear insufficient to insure mastery of complicated subjects, particularly in light of the fact that the officer training schools exceed this time span in almost all other modern military organizations. It therefore would be classified as medium.
    A three-year period would enable the military to provide the officer candidate with a basic education in most aspects of technology. Although he could not be expected to be an expert in all phases of military technology, the young officer at least would have the opportunity to receive a basic introduction to technical practices. As a result, it is classified as high.
    Associated with the length of officer training schools is our third indicator of technology—the percentage of the officer corps that has completed what the military considers a necessary minimum of advanced training. In recent years the East German military, has considered the necessary minimum to be three years, and in some cases four.[4] It may be assumed that, since a three- or four-year education requires the allocation of a greater amount of funds than would a shorter period, the NVA will attempt to insure that a high percentage of its officer corps attends a training school for this length of time if it is felt necessary to enable a large portion of officers to deal with more complex technical problems. Consequently, it may be assumed that, the greater the degree to which the military has found it necessary to rely on officers having completed at least a three-year training period, the higher the level of technology will

be. In evaluating this indicator, the following schema is employed:

High: Between 56.9 and 80 percent of all NVA officers attended training schools for at least three years.
Medium: Between 33.8 and 56.8 percent of all NVA officers attended training schools for at least three years.
Low: Between 10.7 and 33.7 percent of all NVA officers attended training schools for at least three years.*

    The fourth indicator of technology is the value attributed to an officer's education in the society as a whole. Recognition by the educational authorities that an officer's training corresponds to that of a civilian institution would mean that individuals leaving the services would qualify for skilled civilian jobs. Overevaluation of the military officer's education would present problems for the civilian society since individuals who left military service would be able to assume positions for which they were not qualified. Consequently, civilian authorities could be expected to oppose any overestimation of the value of military education.
    The higher the civilian community evaluates military education, the more complex it can be assumed to be, and the higher the level of technology will be. In evaluating this indicator, the following schema is employed:

High: Officer education is equated with a civilian university education.
Medium: Officer education is evaluated lower than a university but higher than a "nonskilled" occupation.
Low: Officer education is evaluated as equivalent to any other occupation not requiring special education beyond basic school.

    If an officer's education fails to qualify him for a civilian occupation requiring anything more than completion of basic school, the skills he gained in the military could be assumed to lack both depth and quality. Such a narrow scope of competence could not cope with the varied problems an officer could be expected to face in any but a military possessing a low technological level. It therefore is scored as low.
    Recognition of an officer's training as equivalent to that provided by a technical school (Fachschule) would indicate that the officer had

---

    *These categories, like many of those that follow, are constructed in accord with the plan outlined in the Introduction. Consequently, no justification is provided here.

received additional academic education. If, for example, he were classified as an engineer* and upon leaving the service could find civilian employment in his area of specialization, such as electronics, this would testify to his engineering qualifications. Thus, the indicator will be evaluated as medium.

Placing a graduate of an officer training school on the same level with a university graduate would indicate a high degree of respect for the quality of the officer's education. Possession of a diploma opens the door to most higher positions in Germany, and this level of education probably would be provided only for officers in an army requiring a high level of technical competence. It therefore will be scored as high.

The next six indicators deal with the educational level attained by the East German officer corps. In particular, they focus on the SED's attempts to raise officers' education to a level commensurate with that required of a modern technical military.

The first indicator concerned with the educational level attained by the NVA officer corps, and the fifth indicator of technology, deals with the percentage of officers who achieved as their highest level of education the mittlere Reife (literally, middle level or middle development). The mittlere Reife corresponds to the tenth class. Although possession of the tenth-grade certificate was a minimum educational standard for officers in the German army prior to 1945,[5] this was not the case in the NVA, particularly in its early years.[6] As the need for more technically competent officers increased, the SED set out to assure that as many officers as possible would attain this level of education. Consequently, the higher the percentage of officers who hold this certificate, the higher the level of technology will be. The following schema is utilized in evaluating this indicator:

High: Between 36.1 and 53.9 percent of all NVA officers possess the mittlere Reife.
Medium: Between 18.1 and 36 percent of all NVA officers possess the mittlere Reife.
Low: Between 0 and 18 percent of all NVA officers possess the mittlere Reife.

The next educational level to be considered is closely related to the preceding one—it is the proportion of officers holding an

---

*It is not necessary for an individual to attend a university in the GDR in order to be classified as an engineer. Instead, he can attend a specialized technical school to qualify to perform less complex jobs than those handled by an engineer who graduated from

Abitur.* Entrance into many Fachschulen (technical schools) and all universities or Fachhochschulen (technical universities), requires the possession of an Abitur. As a consequence, the military must raise the percentage of its officers who possess the Abitur if it hopes to send them to schools that impart education of a highly technical nature and prepare them to work as highly trained specialists. Since it can be assumed that the military would not attempt to raise the percentage of officers possessing such an education unless it perceived a need for such an education, the higher the percentage of those possessing an Abitur, the higher the level of technology will be. The following schema will be employed in evaluating this indicator:

High: Between 27.6 and 37.0 percent of all NVA officers possess an Abitur.
Medium: Between 18.2 and 27.5 percent of all NVA officers possess an Abitur.
Low: Between 18.1 and 27.5 percent of all NVA officers possess an Abitur.

As modern technical equipment is introduced into the armed forces, it becomes necessary for the military to recruit and train officers who have a general technical education. This does not mean that all such individuals will be trained as technicians in areas specific to the military.** In addition to technicians competent to deal with problems associated with such equipment as rockets, it will be necessary to develop officers who understand the technical basis of such subjects as dietetics, library science, and pedagogy. A military dietician, like his civilian counterpart, must be able to deal with modern food processing equipment. A political officer must understand the mechanics of modern library science if he hopes to present the appropriate material to his charges. He also must possess an understanding of the equipment and techniques associated with modern pedagogy if he is to be a successful instructor. As a result, the

---

a university. A university-trained individual can be distinguished by the title Diplom-Ingenieur, or Dipl. Ing.

*Although this indicator may appear very similar to the first one, it covers a larger portion of the NVA officer corps, including officers who have responded to the NVA's encouragement to obtain the Abitur if they did not hold one when they entered the service.

**Although officer training schools were considered Fachschulen during part of the time period covered by this study, this indicator includes those officers who attended civilian Fachschulen as well, a common situation during the early years of the NVA.

more specialized the equipment employed, the greater the need to send individuals to Fachschulen or special technical schools.

In the GDR, Fachschulen generally last three years.[7] Since the military can be assumed to send individuals to such schools only if it feels a need for the skills they will learn, one can argue that the higher the percentage of those who attended a Fachschule, the higher the level of technology will be. The following schema will be used in evaluating this indicator:

High: Between 60.4 and 75.2 percent of all officers have attended a Fachschule.
Medium: Between 45.7 and 60.3 percent of all officers have attended a Fachschule.
Low: Between 31.0 and 45.6 percent of all officers have attended a Fachschule.

In addition to a basic technical background, a modern military requires individuals trained as military engineers and/or technicians. This category includes individuals trained in such areas as the development and maintenance of rockets. As General Heinz Hoffmann remarked:

> ... a modern army—and ours is a modern army—is in need of a highly qualified officer corps. This is clearest in the Soviet army, where two-thirds of the officers in the rocket troops (Raketentruppen) are engineers. We have also taken this development into consideration. Hundreds of engineers and technicians have finished their education in the last two or three years. A large number of other officers are educated as technicians and engineers at our officer schools. If that does not fully satisfy our needs for military-technical cadre (Kader) it should be noted (so zeigt sich doch) that we are in the process of educating an even larger number of specialists for the army.[8]

Since the military can be assumed to educate officers as military engineers or technicians only if it perceives a need for such training, this may be considered our eighth indicator of technology: The higher the percentage of officers who are military engineers or technicians, the higher the level of technology will be. The following schema will be used in discussing this indicator:

High: Between 11.9 and 17.0 percent of all NVA officers are military engineers or technicians.

Medium: Between 6.8 and 11.8 percent of all NVA officers are military engineers or technicians.
Low: Between 1.7 and 6.7 percent of all NVA officers are military engineers or technicians.

Three to four years of education at an officer training school—even when it is primarily devoted to the study of technical subjects—often is insufficient to enable an officer to carry out his tasks effectively in a highly technical modern military. As a consequence, the military sends selected officers on for advanced degrees.*

In the NVA, officers may attend the Friedrich Engels Military Academy or a university in the GDR. They also may attend an equivalent institution in the U.S.S.R. Their studies normally require from three to four years to complete unless they continue on for a doctorate, in which case studies may last for another two or three years. Not only is the military deprived of the officers' services during this period but it also pays for their education as well as their salaries during the period of study. The military would commit resources for advanced training, one might suggest, only if it perceived such education as very important. As one West German writer put it, "He who sits on the school bench is not available as a combat soldier, must be replaced by another, and needs a teacher as well."[9]

In this study, NVA officers' attendance at such schools will be viewed in two different ways. These two approaches supply our ninth and tenth indicators of technology.

The first approach concerns the percentage of NVA officers possessing an advanced degree. In light of the costs and loss of time involved in sending an officer to such a school, one might suggest that the higher the percentage of officers who have an advanced degree, the higher the level of technology will be. The following schema will be utilized to measure this indicator:

High: Between 11.6 and 16.0 percent of all NVA officers have advanced degrees.
Medium: Between 7.1 and 11.5 percent of all NVA officers have advanced degrees.
Low: Between 2.6 and 7.0 percent of all NVA officers have advanced degrees.

---

*The curriculum of officer training schools roughly approximates that provided by U.S. service academies. Therefore, especially in recent years, an East German officer who is a graduate of one of these schools can be considered to have earned a B.S. or B.A. similar to that earned by his American counterpart.

The second approach deals with the percentage of army regimental-level commanders who have advanced academic degrees. Lest the reader think this indicator is a repetition of the previous one, it should be noted that, of all sections of the military, the army ground forces are traditionally the least affected by technical advancements. Consequently, this measure, which includes all army officers holding command positions at the regimental level, is a significant indicator of technology. If a high percentage of officers possesses advanced education in this least technical branch of the armed forces, it suggests that, at least insofar as command responsibilities are concerned, the military feels an advanced degree indispensable for an officer at this level. As a result, it would seem logical to suggest that the higher the percentage of army regimental-level commanders possessing advanced degrees, the higher the level of technology will be. The following schema will be used to measure this indicator:

High: Between 54 and 80 percent of all army commanders at the regimental level or higher possess advanced academic degrees.

Medium: Between 28 and 53 percent of all army commanders at the regimental level or higher possess advanced academic degrees.

Low: Between 2 and 27 percent of all army commanders at the regimental level or higher possess advanced academic degrees.

Traditionally, the military has relied upon large numbers of civilian draftees and reservists to fill its ranks in wartime. But as the pace and extent of specialization required by technological advance increases, this alternative to a large career officer corps is disappearing rapidly, particularly in the more technical areas. Since the start of World War II, all American military command positions (brigadier general or rear admiral and above) have been filled by career officers who have spent 20 or more years as part of the military establishment.[10]

One might object that, although this was true for top positions, civilians have carried out many important functions requiring specialized talents during and following a war. Although this is true, the possibility of utilizing such individuals appears to be decreasing.

The longer time needed to train a military officer affects the ability of civilians to step into active duty swiftly enough to satisfy manpower and leadership requirements. As Morris Janowitz put it: "The adequacy of the short-time specialist has been declining, as junior officers must be trained for longer and longer periods before they can be effective."[11]

In World War II it was possible to train a civilian engineer for a year and put him in a responsible position aboard a submarine. The expertise necessary to adequately carry out a similar task on a modern atomic-powered Polaris submarine does not sufficiently parallel skills utilized by civilian professionals to make possible rapid interchangeability of positions. Therefore, even a civilian engineer would have to undergo extended and expensive training to meet the Navy's needs. While they are still in school, the war may come to a disastrous end as a result of the state's inability to mobilize its forces rapidly.

To lessen this problem, officers normally have been trained and provided with a couple of years of experience and then returned to civilian life in reserve status, ready to answer the call for able leaders if a crisis should arise. Yet the increased length of time required for training also is undermining this possibility. The amount of training and experience an individual can accumulate in the number of years normally spent in the service by officers who are not making the military a career gives them no more than a basic working knowledge of their area of endeavor. Such an officer's competence is inferior to that of a career officer who has gained more experience and training over a longer period of service.

The limited expertise possessed by an officer as he reenters civilian life rapidly deteriorates into obsolescence in the face of onrushing technology. In a short time, many of the complex components of a modern submarine may be replaced by new models. One reserve meeting a week or an annual two-week cruise is not sufficient to keep the reserve officer abreast of such changes.

One indicator of the level of technology in the military, then, can be found in the length of time officers are required to serve. The longer the obligatory period of service, the more likely the individuals entering the service are to make the military a career. The power concentration represented by a large professional officer corps makes it unlikely that the formation of such a corps would be encouraged by long periods of service unless technological requirements played an important role. This factor will be evaluated as follows:

High: Military officers must obligate themselves to serve for periods of eight or more years.
Medium: Military officers must obligate themselves to serve for periods of four to seven years.
Low: Military officers must obligate themselves to serve for periods of less than four years.

Officers obligated to serve actively for less than four years would feel a minimal degree of pressure to remain in the service at the close of their tours of duty. Probably they still would be young enough to enter civilian careers with relative ease or to continue their education. Their contacts with civilian friends would not be impaired significantly and their adjustment to civilian social and business life would be less difficult. Such officers could have received only a small amount of specialized training or experience. A military following such a practice most likely would require little expertise among the majority of its officers and would be recorded as having a low level of technology on the schema listed above.

A period of service lasting from four to seven years requires a much greater commitment on the officer's part. Many civilian career opportunities may be lost because of the length of service. Nevertheless, it still is possible to launch a successful civilian career after such an interval. Officers could be expected to complete fairly extensive training programs during a service period of this length and to gain a fair amount of experience as well. These factors would seem to indicate a military system with a medium level of technology, and are scored accordingly.

Before an individual would agree to remain in the military for a period of eight or more years, he would have to plan seriously to make the service his career. After eight years his family and financial obligations probably would make starting a new career exceedingly difficult. His attachment to military practices and relationships would be insured. Such an officer probably would have spent a great deal of effort learning special skills of little use in civilian life. A decision to walk away from a profession in which he had invested so much time and effort would have to be based on very strong reasons. A military requiring officers to make this type of commitment most likely would feel a great need for highly skilled experts to handle advanced technological requirements. It therefore would be scored as high on the schema for this indicator.

The twelfth indicator of technology involves the importance of technical qualifications in the promotion and retention of officers in the service. A military service dealing with the problems of modern technology will tend to place increased emphasis on the technical qualifications of its officer corps. Technical competence will play an increasingly important role in deciding who is promoted and retained in the service. Officers who might otherwise be highly qualified will not be promoted or retained if the military perceives their technical qualifications as too low.

Consequently, one may propose that the greater the degree to which technical qualifications are considered important for promotion and retention in the service, the higher the level of technology will be. The following schema will be used in evaluating the importance of technical qualifications:

High: A high degree of technical competence is a prerequisite for promotion and retention in the service.
Medium: Technical competence is an important consideration for promotion and retention in the service.
Low: Technical competence is one of a number of factors considered for promotion and retention in the service.

As long as technical qualifications are just one of a number of factors involved in promotion and retention in the officer corps, an officer can remain weak in this area and retain his position or even earn promotions on the basis of such other factors as strong leadership ability or excellent political qualifications. Such qualifications probably would correspond to a low need for technical skill in a military in which technology played a minor role; it is therefore scored as low.

Raising technical qualifications to the "important consideration" level reduces the possibility that an individual lacking technical qualifications can remain or advance within the officer corps. Such a measure would reflect a military in which few activities could be carried out without technical skills, and it is recorded as medium on the above schema.

The requirement that individuals be technically qualified would indicate a high degree of technology. Individuals failing to meet this standard would be denied promotion or dropped from the service, indicating that, regardless of their desirability from other standpoints, the military could find little or no use for them without technical skills.

Another indicator can be found in the issuance of awards to officers and men for specific technical capabilities. One purpose behind the issuance of such awards is to encourage individuals to perform difficult and needed tasks. Awards may be for difficult duty assignments, heroic actions, or specific skills. Consequently, if the military issues awards to its members for technical competence, it must feel a need for them.

It can be assumed, then, that the greater the degree to which awards are given for technical expertise, the higher the level of technology will be. The following schema will be employed in considering the importance of this factor:

High: Awards are given in the form of occupational titles useful in both the civilian and military worlds for those technically qualified.
Medium: Medals are awarded to those technically qualified.
Low: Special notation is made of those who are technically qualified.

Special notation of those who are qualified involves nothing more than the reading or publication of an announcement that a certain individual is qualified to perform a specific task or, more likely, an entry to this effect in his service record. This aids the military in locating individuals with special qualifications, if needed, but provides only limited incentive for the attainment of such skills.

Despite its apparent unimportance to civilians, the awarding of medals carries a great deal of importance within the military and the issuance of medals for technical competency adds significant incentive for such achievement. Such an award would reflect a medium level of interest in attracting and recognizing skilled individuals.

The issuance of an occupational certificate such as that of Master (Meister) is very important for a member of the armed forces because it means that, upon leaving the military, he may return to civilian life assured of recognition for skills acquired in the military. Since such certificates require long study and training periods demanding sacrifices from both the individual and the military, it may be considered an indication of a high level of technical expertise.

The fourteenth indicator concerns the number of occupational categories recognized by the military. In order to deal with the problems of modern warfare, the military establishment has developed a number of occupational subdivisions, each of which deals with a specialized type of warfare. For example, an army 50 years ago might be composed of five branches: the infantry, cavalry, artillery, supply, and staff corps. An officer joining the army would specialize in one of these branches and remain there until he reached general/flag rank,* becoming an expert in that particular area. Increases in technology have resulted in a larger number of specialized occupational branches within the military.[12] This means that the commander of these troops faces greater difficulty in coordinating their actions. Commanders could be expected to resist any unnecessary specialization on the part of their subordinates because of the additional work such narrowness creates. Every addition of a major new branch to the military's organizational structure, therefore, could be expected to reflect a strong need for specialization caused by technological requirements. Hence, the larger the number of major organizational units recognized by the military, the higher the level of technology will be. This indicator will be evaluated as follows:

---

*The term "general/flag rank" is an American military term. It refers to military officers above the rank of colonel or navy captain who, because of their rank, are either generals or, in the case of the navy, admirals warranting a flag. Thus, a rear admiral would have a flag with two stars, a vice admiral, one with three stars, etc.

High: The military recognizes 33 to 47 major occupational branches.
Medium: The military recognizes 17 to 32 major occupational branches.
Low: The military recognizes 0 to 16 major occupational branches.

Specialization creates a need for the military expert to consult other military specialists if he is to fulfill his assigned task. An artillery specialist is dependent on consultation with specialists in armor and infantry, as well as air observers and radar technicians to maximize the utility of his weapons. Consultation with these specialists is needed to assure that the right amount of firepower is provided in the right place at the right time. Failure to consult with such specialists might seriously jeopardize a mission.

One indicator of this need for consultation, and the fifteenth indicator of technology, is the existence of military technical journals. Although some space in such journals is used to instruct officers about the proper line to follow on civil-military relations or related issues, a large portion usually discusses either technical issues directly or the effect of technology on various aspects of military life, such as ideological indoctrination. In my analysis of East German military journals, I found about three-fourths of the articles to be related either to technology directly or to related issues. One journal, Militärtechnik (Military technology) is devoted almost exclusively to technical issues. Such journals are published, I submit, to enable individual officers to benefit from the experience of others. In a sense, they promote collaboration among officers by encouraging the exchange of ideas on particular topics.

A journal provides a widely available source of specialized information from which an officer can readily supplement his own education and experience. The need for such a source of information increases as the technical level of the military increases, driving individual officers into ever more limited fields of specialization and increasing their dependence on learning from the experience of others in order to develop a broader view of military problems. The number of such journals published could be expected to correspond to the demand for such an interchange of information in the military. As a result one can propose that the more specialized military journals published, the higher the technical level of the military will be. This indicator will be evaluated using the following schema:

High: Eight or more special military journals are published.
Medium: Four to seven special military journals are published.
Low: Three or fewer special military journals are published.

The existence of up to three journals means that the problems treated in these journals are of a general nature and of interest to all military specialists. Consequently, it suggests that the specialized nature of the problems faced by the individual officer are low.

An increase in the number of special military journals from four to seven would create approximately one journal for each of the major branches of the service and indicate that the problems concerning military officers have become more specialized since the generalized journals no longer suffice. For example, a journal dealing with naval problems might be introduced. Although naval problems might have been treated in the past by a general journal, the number of articles it devoted to the subject would be limited and they probably would be written so that an army officer also could understand them. Now, however, in response to a higher level of technology, a naval journal could devote its pages to a more specialized audience, supply more articles suited to its particular interests and needs, and indulge in a degree of specialized terminology important to the "cognoscenti" but incomprehensible to a more generalized readership.

A further increase in the degree of specialization could raise the number of special military journals above eight, with each service publishing more than one journal. Naval warfare, for example, might become so complex that two different journals appear, one for engineering officers and another for deck officers. Sustaining so many journals would indicate a high need for intercommunication and, as mentioned above, suggests a high level of technology.

Just as a technically advanced military is in need of specialized journals to inform its members of the latest developments in military technology, it also must print books explaining the operation of such equipment. This is the sixteenth indicator of technology. The greater the number of books published on specialized military subjects, the higher the level of technology will be. The following schema will be employed to measure this indicator:

High: Between 96 and 111 books on military technology are in use during a given period (since some books are withdrawn and others published to replace them, the total number in use at the close of a period is used).
Medium: Between 80 and 95 books on military technology are in use during a given period.
Low: Between 56 and 79 books on military technology are in use during a given period.[13]

The degree to which a military unit is mechanized is an important indicator of technology. If more machines are utilized, there will be a greater need to apply systematic knowledge to the solution of practical tasks. One means of noting the degree of mechanization in a military unit is to measure the horsepower (Pferde Starke or PS) present.* The higher the level of horsepower, the greater the use of complex machinery will be. As a result, the PS level serves as the seventeenth indicator of technology. The following schema will be utilized to measure the PS level:

High: The PS per soldier equals 30 or more.
Medium: The PS per soldier exceeds 20 but is less than 30.
Low: The PS per soldier exeeds 10 but is less than 20.

    Ten PS per soldier, according to an East German source, means that for every 100 soldiers, there exists one tank, four trucks, and two jeeps.[14] At this level, the problems involved in maintenance and operation would be minimal. Hence it is considered low.
    Twenty PS per soldier, according to the same source, means that the number of vehicles has doubled. At this point, for every 100 soldiers there are two tanks, seven trucks, three jeeps, and three motorcycles.[15] With a PS of this level, the military is being forced not only to modify its battle order but also to supply an increased number of specialists to deal with the operation and maintenance of machines. Consequently, this level is evaluated as medium.
    Thirty PS per soldier means that for every 100 soldiers, there are three tanks, ten trucks, four jeeps, and six motorcycles.[16] This would mean first of all that a large number of individuals are assigned to the operation and maintenance of equipment. Second and equally important, it would mean that military tactics and strategy are affected as a result of greater reliance on more complex machinery. The soldier not only would be required to know traditional military skills but also to perform them under conditions of mechanized warfare. As a result, the time devoted to training on complex equipment would be increased. Therefore, 30 PS will be scored as high.
    Well aware of the dangers presented by a technically competent but apolitical military, the party has developed a number of measures to ensure that the military officer is skilled in political subjects and participates in party activities. The form these political control measures have taken is the subject of the next chapter.

---

    *The German term Pferde Stärke or PS cannot be directly converted into the American term horsepower. Although the term itself is directly translatable, the numerical values assigned to the term in the United States and Germany differ.

NOTES

1. Kurt Lang, "Technology and Career Management in the Military Establishment," in Morris Janowitz, ed., The New Military (New York: Wiley, 1968), p. 54.
2. John Dornberg, The Other Germany (New York: Doubleday, 1968), p. 311.
3. For a discussion of the East German educational system by a West German specialist, see Hartmut Vogt, Bildung und Erziehung in der DDR (Stuttgart: Kleh, 1969).
4. Four years of training are required for pilots and flight engineers as well as naval officers. See Oberst Leuscher et al., Taschenbuch Militärpolitik und Wehrpflicht (Berlin-Ost: Deutscher Militärverlag, 1967), p. 345.
5. See for example, Werner Baur, "Deutsche Generale: Die militarischen Führungsgruppen in der Bundesrepublik und in der DDR," in Wolfgang Zapf, ed., Beiträge zur Analyse der deutschen Oberschicht (2nd rev. ed., Munich: R. Piper, 1965), pp. 118-19.
6. Of the KVP officer corps, 79 percent possessed only a "Grundschule" (basic education) at the time of the establishment of the NVA in 1956. See Oberstleutnant Dr. K. Ilter, "Die sozialistische Offizierspersönlichkeit: Probleme und Gedanken zum Bild des sozialistischen Offiziers," Militärwesen (November 1967), p. 1546.
7. Bundesministerium für Gesamtdeutsche Fragen, ed., A bis Z (Bonn: Deutscher Bundesverlag, 1969), p. 183.
8. Armeegeneral Heinz Hoffmann, "Wie erreichen wir in der Armee den wissenschaftlich-technischen Hochstand?" Militarwesen, February 1963, p. 172.
9. Heinz Kluss, "Mehr Bildung für Soldaten," Die Zeit, August 13, 1971, No. 33, p. 44.
10. Morris Janowitz, The Professional Soldier (New York: The Free Press, 1964), p. 57. In addition, the majority of these individuals were academy graduates.
11. Ibid., p. 56. See also Morris Janowitz, The Military in the Political Development of New Nations (Chicago: Phoenix, 1964), p. 116; Samuel Huntington, The Common Defense (New York: Columbia University Press, 1961), p. 436.
12. A West German sociologist, for example, reports that specialization in the West German air force has caused an increase of 200 occupational categories in recent years. In addition, he notes a similar increase in other branches of the West German military establishment. See Wido Mosen, Eine Militärsoziologie (Neuwied: Luchterhand, 1967), pp. 15-16. Although he does not state the exact years over which he makes this comparison, Mosen seems to be comparing the West German air force of 1963-64 with the German

air force prior to 1945. Increased usage of technology is also forcing communist military forces to create more positions for specialists. See, for example, Marshal Grechko's rather frank remark to this effect in "Reliably Defend What Has Been Created by the People," Sovestskiy Voin, No. 1 (January 1972), pp. 2-5.

13. The list of books utilized for this indicator is taken from Thomas A. Forster, NVA—Armee der Sowjetzone (Cologne: Markus Verlag, 1966-67), pp. 300-6, 313. Books on other subjects such as novels (Schöneliteratur), history (Militärgeschichtswissenschaft), military politics (Militärpolitik), and military theory (Militärtheorie) were not included. In comparing the bibliography found in this work with that compiled by other authors, it was found that Forster's work is inclusive, although it cannot be ruled out that some books were omitted. The categories are constructed in accordance with the plan outlined in the Introduction, so no justification is provided here.

14. "Kurz und Knapp," Volksarmee, No. 9 (1969), p. 7.
15. Ibid.
16. Ibid.

CHAPTER 2

POLITICAL CONTROL IN THE NATIONAL PEOPLE'S ARMY

In order to measure the level of political control in the NVA during each of the time periods encompassed by this study, 15 indicators of political control were developed. In addition, each of the indicators was divided into three categories—high, medium, and low. The remainder of this chapter considers each of these indicators and explains why the dividing lines between the categories of high, medium, and low were drawn at particular points for each indicator.

The first indicator of the level of political control in the East German military treats the organizational level within the military down to which political officers are assigned. The lower down in the military hierarchy political officers are present, the better able they will be to observe and report on the political skills and activities of those around them and the greater the party's control will be. The schema below shows the consideration given this measure:

High: Political officers are assigned down to the lowest organizational units of the military structure, i.e., squad and platoon.
Medium: Political officers are assigned down to middle level organizational units, i.e., company and battalion.
Low: Political officers are assigned only to high level organizational units, i.e., regiment and division.

The organizational level down to which political officers are assigned reflects not only their number but also the closeness with which they can observe members of the military. If every small unit contains a political officer, no member of the military organization will be able to escape his notice. The political officer will have much closer contact with members of the military and will be in a better position to be aware of officers' opinions and actions. It would be very difficult for a political officer in the military to behave purely as a technical specialist—he would have to carefully consider his political behavior as well. Such close surveillance would provide a high degree of political control.

Political officers assigned down to middle-level organizational units will lose contact with members of the military lower in the hierarchy. Responsible for covering the activities of so many more men, their reports will become more selective and general and middle-level officers probably will receive most of their attention. Although the regular officer will not be able to be oblivious to party activities, he is in a far better position to avoid confrontation with the political officer simply because there are fewer around. Such a system provides for a medium level of political control.

Once political officers are limited to the higher reaches of the military hierarchy, their contact with the vast majority of the organization becomes tenuous. Only major anti-party actions can be included in their reports, and their focus centers on major military figures. Since the regular officer would come into contact with the political officer only on rare occasions, unless he were a member of a high level staff, the regular officer would have an easier time avoiding ideological confrontations. Political control then would be low.

The use of the secret police to spy on officers traditionally has been a basic instrument of communist political control. Individuals manifesting attitudes not in accord with those of the party can be identified and quietly eliminated. In addition, because of the large network of spies the secret police employs and because of the anonymity of the spies, an officer must watch every word he utters, lest one false step be taken as representing a subversive attitude.[1]

As in the case of the first indicator, the lower in the military organizational structure secret police officers are assigned, the greater the level of political control will be.* In evaluating the effect of the placement of secret service officers, the same scale

---

*A secret police officer will undoubtedly make use of informants much as political officers do. As a result, he might have operatives present down to the lowest level. Nevertheless, since his presence might be restricted to a higher level, he would not be in a position to check on the accuracy of the information supplied by his informants. A secret police officer present on a lower level, on the other hand, would be responsible for fewer individuals and in a better position to check on the actions not only of his operatives but of his informants as well.

will be used as that outlined for the organizational level down to which political officers are assigned (indicator one). Consequently, neither the schema nor the justification utilized to evaluate it will be repeated here.

The third indicator of political control concerns the political officer's qualifications. The better qualified the political officer is, the better he can be expected to perform his duties. This is particularly true in the area of ideological instruction.

The successful dissemination of political ideology in a modern army possessing a high overall level of education relies heavily on the ability of the political officer to raise party dogma from a litany of memorized questions and answers to a conceptual framework that, although it supplies a basic Weltanschauung, does so in a form enabling the individual to relate to the contemporary technical world in a relevant manner. This means the political officer must know more than the basic catechismal answers to questions posed by those in his jurisdiction. If, for example, an officer possessing the equivalent of a college education questions the relevance of the Berlin Wall, an answer that it provides a defense against the West will not suffice. The answers to such questions must go beyond the often repeated responses and deal with the problem on a level commensurate with the questioner's educational background. Failure to do this means that, although the political officer may be listened to and obeyed, the ideology he represents may be ignored or considered irrelevant and time-consuming.

In addition to a sophisticated knowledge of the subject he presents, the political officer must be acquainted with the most modern techniques and methods for imparting this knowledge. As the educational level and technical competence of his audience increases, he is faced not only with the problem of knowing his own subject better but also of presenting it in such a manner that he is able to overcome any hostility or lack of interest on the part of his audience.

One of the most important sources of the political officer's education in the area of Marxism-Leninism, as well as the techniques for presenting it, is the specialized schooling he receives in the military for that purpose. In general, one may suggest that the longer this training lasts, the more competent the political officer will be, both in terms of knowledge of the subject and in terms of its presentation. As a result, the third indicator of the level of political control will measure the length of training afforded political officers as follows:

High: Political officers in any given period receive more than two years of education in a special political officer training school.

Medium: Political officers in any given period receive from one to two years of education in a special political officer training school.

Low: Political officers in any given period receive one year or less of education in a special political officer training school.

    A training period of one year or less is barely long enough to supply the individual with a very basic understanding of party ideology and operation. The individual must supplement the basic introduction to Marxism-Leninism he received in civilian schools with advanced training if he is to present his subject to his technically oriented comrades in a manner they will find relevant. One year or less provides barely enough time to introduce him to the basic elements of pedagogy as well as Marxism-Leninism. Consequently, it is considered representative of a low level of political control.

    A training period of one to two years would raise the level of the political officer's education appreciably. He would have time not only to expand his basic knowledge of Marxism-Leninism but also to devote considerable time to techniques and methods. It therefore is considered indicative of a medium level of political control.

    If more than two years of training is required, the individual will have time to do basic and advanced work in party ideology as well as in methods and techniques. He also will be able to receive training in the field on how to conduct himself and carry out his tasks. Thus, his theoretical education will be supplemented with practical experience.

    Overcoming the gulf that often seems to separate the political officer from his military counterpart is very important if the party hopes to create a dual executive. As long as the gap remains, the military officer may tend to view political skills and activities as tasks for the political officer and of little concern to him. One means of handling this problem is to select as political officers individuals with prior military service. This would mean political officers would have a higher level of technical expertise as well as a greater understanding of the difficulties faced by the regular officer. In addition, the regular officer will tend to perceive the political officer and the doctrines he represents as less alien. Accordingly, the fourth indicator concerns the time individuals are required to serve in the regular military before training to become political officers. The following schema will be utilized to analyze this indicator:

High: The majority of new political officers entered training to become political officers or received commissions as political officers after more than 18 months of regular military service.

Medium: The majority of new political officers entered training to become political officers or received commissions after 18 months or less of regular military service.

Low: The majority of new political officers entered training to become political officers or received commissions as political officers directly from civilian life.

If political officers are selected and developed from among individuals who have more than 18 months in the regular military, their understanding of the difficulties faced by the regular officer in dealing with problems associated with a highly complex military could be expected to be quite advanced. They almost certainly would have attended an NCO technical school. The regular military officer, having assured himself that the political officer has a good understanding of his problems, might be quite receptive to the political officer's ideas. A high level of political control would then exist.

A political officer who enters special training after serving in the regular military for 18 months or less, the normal length of service for draftees, could be expected to have at least a rudimentary knowledge of regular military life. As a result, although his technical expertise might be limited, he probably would have more understanding of the problems faced by a regular officer than would, for example, someone who came directly from the civilian world. Consequently, 18 months or less of prior service will be considered indicative of a medium level of political control.

Individuals who enter the political officer training school directly from civilian life can be expected to have little or no appreciation of the problems faced by the regular officer. Their understanding of the technical aspects of the military also will be low. The hostility a regular officer can be expected to feel toward such individuals would be high. The gulf between political and military officers would be wide and the resultant level of political control, low.

The SED, like other ruling communist parties, established a number of instruments within the armed forces to assure their loyalty. Two aspects of this control structure have been mentioned thus far: the political officer and the secret police or SSD (Staatssicherheitsdienst) officer. It is now appropriate to mention two other instruments of control, as they serve as the fifth and sixth indicators of political control. They are the organization and effectiveness of the Politorgane (political organs) and the military party organization.*

---

*The term Politorgane is a general expression referring to the political organizations in the NVA. It includes all units of the party

Before discussing how the fifth indicator—the organizational level down to which the Politorgane are active—will be operationalized, it may be helpful to include a discussion of the structural components of the Politorgane.[2] The highest body in the Politorgane is the Politische Hauptverwaltung or Polithauptverwaltung (Main Political Administration), which functions as a department of the Central Committee of the SED. It is the task of the Main Political Administration to supervise all political work in the NVA. Included in this supervisory task are the following areas of special concern:

> Controlling the setting of goals in the NVA, the political schooling of NVA members, party schooling of SED and FDJ members, strengthening of combat morale, supervision of the carrying out of orders, concurrence (Mitwirkung) in all personnel affairs and supervision of cadre political (Kaderpolitischen) personnel records.[3]

To assist the Main Political Administration in carrying out this task, it is provided with two important commissions: the Party Control Commission (Parteikontrolkommission or PKK) and the Party Revision Commission (Parteirevisionskommission or PRK). The Party Control Commission, the most important of the two, works very closely with both the Central Party Control Commission of the SED and the SSD. Among its areas of responsibility are the following:

> 1. Handling of all party proceedings against party members in positions of command or similar positions, as well as members of the Politorgane.
> 2. Supervision of subordinate PKK.
> 3. Supervision of the maintenance of the party statute.
> 4. Supervision of the carrying out of party resolutions.
> 5. Maintenance of the general line of the party.[4]

---

control structure in the NVA with the exception of the party organization itself. In terms of this indicator, however, neither the SSD officer nor the political officer are included since they are separate indicators. Any information on the activities of these officers that is not within the scope of indicators one and two will be mentioned under this indicator.

The party organization within the military, although maintaining close relations with the civilian party organization, is administratively separate.

The Main Political Administration and the two commissions are represented at lower levels by subordinate organizations.* The following chart shows the levels on which the Politorgane is present when fully developed.5

Central Committee of the SED
↓
Deputy of the Minister, National Defense
Chief, Main Political Administration
↓
Leader, Political Administration,
Military "Bezirk"
↓
Leader, Political Section,
Division Level
↓
Deputy of the Commander for Political
Work, Regiment Level
↓
Deputy of the Commander for Political
Work, Battalion Level
↓
Political Deputy of the
Company Chief

Very little has been written about the activities of the Bezirk or district level. However, there apparently is a large unit present, including both the Control and Revision committees. As on the division level, the political section reportedly is composed of 15 officers. The positions to which these officers are assigned include:
1. Leader of the political section
2. Deputy leader of the political section
3. Head instructor for party work
4. Head instructor for agitation and propaganda
5. Head instructor for political schooling
6. Head instructor for political schooling of the troops

---

*This description is for 1966-67. Thus, although it includes the level down to which the political officer is present it does not mean that this was the case throughout the entire period studied. The level down to which the political officer is present was handled separately for two reasons. First, it is a subject frequently discussed in works dealing with political officers. Second, information was available on it for all five periods studied.

7. Chairman of the Party Control Commission
8. Chairman of the Party Revision Commission
9. Assistant for youth questions (FDJ)
10. Instructor for youth work (two officers)
11. Instructor for political cadres
12. Instructor for party information
13. Instructor for cultural work with the masses
14. Instructor for personnel documents.[6]

Six political officers are engaged in political work at the regimental level. One, the chief, is deputy to the regimental commander for political work. The other five are assigned to such tasks as chief officer for agitation and propaganda, chief officer for cultural work with the masses, club leader and librarian, SED secretary, and FDJ secretary.

At the battalion level there are four political officers present: the deputy of the battalion commander for political work, head of propaganda, SED secretary, and FDJ secretary.

At the company level, only one officer is present. He assists the commander in all aspects of political work.

Such a structure is important only to the degree to which it is employed. Consequently, the operationalization of this indicator focuses on the degree to which these organs are active as a political control mechanism. The higher the degree to which they are actively engaged in political work, the higher the level of political control will be. The following schema is employed to test this indicator:

High: The Politorgane are very active. They do not wait for an unfriendly act; preventive maintenance is employed.* The Politorgane structure is very tight.
Medium: The Politorgane are actively engaged in preventive maintenance, but they tend to respond to unfriendly acts as much as act in advance to prevent them. The Politorgane structure is fairly tight.
Low: The Politorgane tends to be more responsive than active. Its organizational structure is loose.

A situation in which the Politorgane merely respond would indicate that apolitical regular officers can avoid being detected as

---

*The term "preventive maintenance" refers to the practice of not waiting for harmful attitudes to show up in the form of political-military conflict. Instead, the party adopts the attitude that it is better to force individuals to commit themselves, maintaining a high level of control by preventing the rise of individuals harboring unacceptable attitudes.

such by watching what they say in the presence of members of these organs. A loosely organized structure would mean that a regular officer who failed to actively participate in party affairs would have a good chance of not being reported or, more likely, not being punished since reports initiated at one level could easily be sidetracked and never reach the officers responsible for taking action on them. Therefore, such Politorgane would indicate a low level of political control.

If the Politorgane engage in preventive maintenance, the chances that an officer who perceives himself primarily as a technician can conceal his feelings are decreased. Now the individual who feels military officers should not be forced to participate in political activities will be forced to express his opinion; although he may succeed in avoiding detection, the probability of a slip will increase since he will be confronted with the situation more frequently. A better organized structure will decrease the chances that unfavorable reports will be forgotten. Thus, these conditions are considered to signify a medium level of political control.

With the Politorgane engaged in preventive maintenance on a full-time basis, the possibility for an officer to avoid acquisition of political skills or participation in political activities will be reduced drastically. Every time a military specialist turns around, he will be confronted with the presence of party control machinery. A very tight structure means that every utterance will not only be reported but recorded as well, possibly to be used against the officer at some future date. It is, therefore, indicative of a high level of political control.

The second major aspect of the party control structure introduced above is the military party organization. Before discussing how activities by the military party organization will be operationalized as an indicator of political control, it may be helpful to include a description of this organization. The military party organization existed on four levels in 1966-67: the Bezirk (or district) level, where a party circle (Partei Kreise) is present; the regiment level (Regimentsparteiorganisation), where a regimental party organization is present; the battalion level, in the form of basic organizations (Grundorganisation); and in some cases, below the battalion level by party groups (Parteigruppen) which may have only three or four members.

The party organization is the framework within which the individual party member interacts. He must attend lectures, engage in self-criticism, accept criticism, express his opinions, and participate in other activities that make it difficult for him to remain apolitical.

An active party organization affects the level of political control in two ways. The first involves the necessity for the individual to participate in party activities. The more active the party organization is in forcing the individual to interact within its framework, the better able it will be to observe the actions of individual military officers and thereby either propose the introduction of programs to counteract "specialist only" attitudes or, where necessary, recommend reprimands and/or dismissals. Second, it may affect the internal operation of the military unit. The greater the degree to which the party organization is able to play a role, not only by forcing the individual to participate in its activities but also by influencing the conduct of military affairs—through consultation with commanding officers, passing on promotions for military officers, and participation in political indoctrination—the greater will be its ability to prevent the rise of individuals who manifest apolitical attitudes. Consequently, the more active the party organization is in these areas, the higher the level of political control will be. The following schema is used to test this indicator:

High: Individuals who are party members are required to participate in all military party activities down to a very low level. The military party organization participates in almost all military-political decisions, except those involving combat operations.

Medium: Individual military officers are required to participate in party activities, although the level down to which they must participate is not as low as in the preceding case. The military party organization participates in some military-political decisions.

Low: Individual military officers are required to participate in military party activities. Failure to do so may be common, however, and is not strongly punished. The military party organization plays a very limited role in military-political decision-making.

If a military officer has the option of attending or not attending party activities, with the only penalty perhaps a verbal admonition, he will be able to avoid in large measure those activities at which he would run the greatest risk of revealing his views. Similarly, if the influence of the party organization is restricted to the point where it is only one of many groups influencing military-political affairs, it is possible for individuals who view themselves primarily as technicians to say so with only limited danger to their careers. As a result, this type of party organization activity is classified as indicative of a low level of political control.

Requiring an officer to attend all party organization activities means it will be impossible for him to avoid situations in which he may be forced to express his opinions on various subjects. But the effect of forced participation in party activities will de diluted if the

organization is a large one, like the Grundorganisation.[7] If this
organization does not meet more than once a month, an officer might
avoid disclosing his views by carefully preparing for the few occasions
when he would be required to speak.

Participation by the party organization in some political-military
decisions would restrict the ability of the technically oriented military
officer to see his views become reality in daily practice. But the
powers of the party organization to prevent this also might be limited.
Its influence might extend only to specific areas, perhaps political
education and leave policy. This would mean, of course, that military-
technical attitudes might prevail in other areas. As a consequence,
this situation will be classified as indicative of a medium level of
political control.

If officers must participate in all party activities down to the
very lowest level—the party groups (Parteigruppen)—the individual
is continually forced to interact with other party members (a party
group may be organized down to the squad level, where there may
be only two or three members, one of whom is the secretary). Thus,
he has less chance to hide attitudes not in accord with those desired
by the party. He also may be required to attend party group meetings
three to four times a month, in addition to the monthly basic organization meeting. This further increases the amount of party interaction in which he is required to engage.

By permitting the party organization to participate in almost
all political-military decisions, with the exception of those relating
to actual combat, the political authorities would make the party
virtually omnipresent. An officer who did not take political factors
into consideration might well find himself in trouble. These increases
in the party organization's influence result in a high level of political
control.

A seventh indicator of political control is the percentage of
officers who are members of the SED. Membership in the East
German Communist party is important for two reasons. First
although there are five parties in East Germany, according to the
Party Statute adopted at the Sixth Party Conference in 1963, the
SED is the only one allowed to organize within the military.[8] So if
members of the armed forces belong to any political organization,
it is the same one. This eliminates any danger that opposition to the
ruling SED might develop as a consequence of allegiance to another
party within the military.

Second, SED membership enables the party to keep a close watch
on the actions of its members. Party members are subject to
scrutiny of not only their public lives but their private lives as well.
Close surveillance of their actions through party activities makes
it more difficult for them to hide attitudes hostile to the party, as

discussed above. The greater the degree to which party membership is required of military officers, or the higher the percentage of military officers who are party members, the higher the level of political control. The following schema will be used in evaluating the importance of party membership:

High: 90 percent or more of all officers are SED party members.
Medium: 75 to 89 percent of all officers are SED party members.
Low: Less than 75 percent of all officers are SED party members.

If fewer than 75 percent of all officers are party members, at least one out of four officers can avoid contact with the party through membership. Since the training and education of a modern military officer requires long periods of time and large outlays of money, the military has a great deal invested in its officer corps. The political authorities could find that the individual most qualified for a specific task is not a party member. With one of every four officers not a party member, the probability that such a situation will arise remains high.

Raising the percentage of officers who are party members above 75 percent decreases the likelihood that the political authorities will be forced to rely on individuals in important positions who are not party members. But if two out of every ten officers are not party members, such a situation still may arise. Consequently, this level of membership is considered to represent a medium level of political control.

An increase in the percentage of military officers who are party members to 90 or above leaves only a remote chance that the political authorities will find themselves forced to utilize an individual who is not a party member. It therefore is considered to represent a high level of political control.

The party also may require special political qualifications for promotion or retention in the military. In order to be advanced to the next higher rank, political reliability may be very important. This subject forms the eighth indicator of political control.

The greater the role that political qualifications play in the promotion or retention of military specialists, the less opportunity there will be for an individual who sees himself as primarily a military technician to advance or remain in the service. To get ahead, he must not only pass exams but also participate in political activities. This process is bound to erode his view of himself as a military specialist who is merely a soldier doing a technical job. The following schema will be employed to determine the importance of political qualifications:

High: Political qualifications are one of the most important considerations for promotion and retention in the service.
Medium: Political qualifications are very important for promotion and retention in the service.
Low: Political qualifications are one of a number of factors considered for promotion and retention in the service.

    As long as ideological qualifications are one among many factors in the decision on whether to promote or retain an officer, he can afford to remain weak in this area if he excels in others. His identification with the military could develop to a fairly high level. Such a requirement probably would correspond to a low level of political control.
    Raising ideological qualifications to the strongly recommended or very important level reduces the possibility that an individual not well versed in the party line and approach could remain, much less advance, in the military. Few officers would dare risk neglecting the political aspect of their duties. A medium level of political control would be indicated.
    Making political qualifications one of the most important factors in promotion or retention places a very high premium on ideological knowledge. No officer, no matter how skilled nor how needed, could make the military a career unless he also devoted considerable attention to ideological matters. The ascendancy of ideological purity over technical achievement would be guaranteed. Identification primarily as a technician would be strongly challenged. Political control of the military would be high.
    One primary prerequisite for the development of a military dual executive is to assure the participation of regular officers in political activities. An officer who remains aloof from such activities will be able to stress the technical nature of his task. One area of political activity that has always played an important role in communist armed forces is political indoctrination. Traditionally, regular officers have resisted involvement in this process, feeling it a task better left to the political officer. The party, on the other hand, may wish to involve the regular officer in this process, perhaps by making him responsible for it. If he is responsible, it will be hard for him to ignore it or to fail to give it its proper place. Those who do not handle political indoctrination properly may be forced to seek another career. The question of who is in charge of political indoctrination supplies the ninth indicator of political control. The following schema will be used to measure this indicator:

High: The military officer bears full responsibility for political indoctrination.

Medium: The military officer and the political officer share responsibility for political indoctrination.
Low: The political officer bears full responsibility for political indoctrination.

When the political officer bears full responsibility for political indoctrination, the regular military officer can avoid any contact with this "political" task. Problems in this area do not concern him unless they affect the unit's combat readiness. Such a situation will tend to reaffirm his and society's view that he is a military technician.

Dividing the responsibility for political indoctrination between the political officer and the regular officer forces the regular officer to exercise and demonstrate a degree of competence and concern on political matters—in this case, ideological indoctrination. If a problem arises concerning the effectiveness of political indoctrination, he can be held equally responsible with the political officer. So if he wants to make the military a career, he will give increased attention to the substance, if not the techniques, of political indoctrination to assure that it is satisfactory.

Placing full responsibility for political indoctrination on the military officer makes him a technical officer who is also a political officer—in essence, a military dual executive in this area. Such an individual would have to know almost as much about the techniques of ideological indoctrination as he did about military tactics and strategy.

Closely related to responsibility for political indoctrination is responsibility for Massenarbeit (work with the masses), the tenth indicator of political control.

Work with the masses consists of special lectures, films, outings to factories, museums and other places of interest, and meetings with civilian organizations as well as Soviet and other socialist military units. A military officer who considers himself primarily a technician would resist involvement in such activities, just as he would oppose accepting responsibility for ideological indoctrination. Forcing him to participate in work with the masses would have much the same effect as responsibility for indoctrination. Because the nature and effects of involvement are so similar, the same schema and justification will be employed here as in political indoctrination.

Closely related to responsibility for political indoctrination and work with the masses is the amount of time devoted to part-time ideological training, the eleventh indicator of political control.

Officers and men may be required to complete courses of instruction, such as correspondence courses, that deal with ideological questions. The important factor here is how much time the military specialist must devote to such courses. The more time a regular officer is required to spend studying ideological problems, the greater the party's opportunity to force him to consider and become proficient in party ideology as well as military technology. If such courses exist, how much time is devoted to them? The following schema will be employed to discern the importance of this indicator:

High: Three or more hours per week are devoted to part-time ideological instruction.
Medium: More than one but less than three hours per week are devoted to part-time ideological instruction.
Low: One hour or less per week is devoted to part-time ideological instruction.

When one considers that in a week (168 hours) the average East German officer may put in 60 hours of work, (six days per week, 10 hours per day) and 56 hours of sleep, leaving him only 52 hours to relax and take care of his other needs, the significance of these hours becomes clearer. Unless he wants to give up his free time or his day off, an officer devoting 3 hours per week to course work must plan to study a half-hour every work day and also take care of such needs as doing his laundry, cleaning his room, and preparing his uniforms—no little amount of effort after a 10-hour work day. Thus, a large share of his free time could be considered tied up with ideological matters. The likelihood he will develop a "specialist only" attitude is sharply decreased. Thus, spending 3 or more hours per week on part-time ideological instruction courses is considered indicative of a high level of political control. Spending from 1 to 3 hours a week would have less effect, and thus is considered a medium level of political control. One hour or less of study a week could quite easily be undertaken. The subject matter would not be very extensive and its effect on the military officer probably would be slight. Hence, the level of political control is evaluated as low.

The procedure of self-criticism, long a basic tool in the party's handbag of control mechanisms, provides the twelfth indicator of political control. Walter Ulbricht describes the purpose of this procedure as follows:

> Criticism and self-criticism are essential parts of this socialist relationship; they are one of the forms of mutual help and cooperation. Criticism and self-criticism have the goal of bringing the collective of working people (Werktätigen) closer together; wherein mistakes and bad habits which endanger the collective and dissipate its strength can be overcome; wherein false deeds and conceptions can be corrected; and wherein it will be possible

that the goal of all members of the collective possessing correct opinions and actions may be achieved.[9]

The form that criticism and self-criticism take is important for an understanding of why this method often is opposed by members of the military. Roman Kolkowicz described it as follows:

> Essentially, it is a method by which Party members confess sins against the Party and demand that their comrades do the same. This ritual is usually performed at Party meetings, where rank, positions, and seniority are relatively unimportant, and all participants, especially among the younger Party members, are encouraged to criticize publicly any actions of those present which do not meet the standards or interests of the Party.[10]

Any officer who fails to give the appropriate credence to political factors could thus be brought to task by anyone, including the most junior private. Although this is a very effective control mechanism in the hands of the party, it also can be damaging to military efficiency. For this reason it has long been opposed by military specialists.[11] A commanding officer may well ask himself what a young recruit knows about the importance of devoting spare time to the study of technical, rather than political, subjects.

The greater the degree to which self-criticism is effectively employed, the less able a regular military officer will be to build up an identity primarily as a technician and thus, the greater the level of political control will be. A military commander can affect the effectiveness of self-criticism by intimidating others from voicing criticism. He need not resort to disciplinary measures, which might be too obvious, but instead can make life uncomfortable for those voicing criticism of which he disapproves by assigning them undesirable duties, denying them certain assignments, or withholding privileges.

It can be assumed that if the effectiveness of self-criticism is undermined by such tactics by commanders, this problem will be emphasized in articles on self-criticism activities in the military. Hence, the less mention there is of this problem, in general, the more effectively it would appear that self-criticism is working. The following schema will be employed to determine the importance of this indicator:

High: The majority of articles on self-criticism make no mention of the problem of military officers suppressing criticism.

Medium: The majority of articles mention the problem but treat it as an occasional difficulty, not widespread within the military and not threatening the effectiveness of self-criticism overall.
Low: The majority of articles stress the problem as one of major proportions, widespread among officers and seriously harmful to the effective use of self-criticism.

As mentioned above, the amount of discussion and stress given this problem in published articles can be considered roughly proportional to the degree it hampers the effective employment of self-criticism. If the majority of articles discussing it fail to mention the problem, it could be considered of minimal concern. Self-criticism probably operates effectively and the level of political control probably is high. A problem of military suppression of criticism described in the majority of works as existing but not causing major harm would indicate medium concern and a medium level of political control. A low level of political control would be compatible with a situation in which self-criticism practices are seriously undermined by widespread suppression of criticism by military commanders, as indicated by frequent references to this problem and its extensive proportions.

The handling of disciplinary questions traditionally has been a prerogative of the military commander. By controlling disciplinary questions, the commander is able to enforce compliance not only with military regulations but with military attitudes as well. Anyone who has served in the military is well aware of a superior's ability to invent an infraction of regulations, if necessary, to punish someone for opinions with which he disagrees. Consequently, the question of who controls the disciplinary process becomes very important in a military organization. The Soviet Communist Party, for example, has been aware of this situation and on occasion has taken the power to enforce discipline into its own hands in the form of "comrades' courts."[12] The question of who controls the disciplinary process is the thirteenth indicator of political control.

The greater the degree to which discipline is controlled by the military itself, the greater will be its ability to enforce compliance with a military point of view. Control of discipline by the party would have the opposite effect and facilitate political control of the military. This indicator can be assessed as follows:

High: Political representatives and organs alone handle disciplinary questions.
Medium: Regular military officers and regular military organs and political representatives and political organs share equally in the handling of disciplinary questions.

Low: Regular military officers and regular military organs make the final decisions on disciplinary questions, with the political representative and political organs reduced to an advisory role.

If disciplinary actions are controlled solely by political representatives and organs, political values will predominate. Punishment of a regular officer for giving too much attention to political indoctrination, for example, would be practically impossible. Although a military commander might be able to collect sufficient proof on other grounds to initiate disciplinary action, he would have a difficult time proving his case without his true motivation emerging.

If discipline requires agreement by the regular officer and the political representative, more sympathy for military considerations on the part of the political officer might exist. If he took unreasonable positions and refused to work with the commander, he would soon be removed by the Politorgane. A commander's attempt to enforce his views would probably generate less opposition and a medium level of political control would be indicated.

Once the role of political representatives and organs is reduced to a mere advisory position in disciplinary cases, a military commander has much greater freedom to ignore political considerations. A low level of political control then exists.

Closely associated with the handling of disciplinary questions is the handling of criminal offenses. This subject supplies the fourteenth indicator of political control. Criminal offenses are distinguished from disciplinary offenses in that they involve court proceedings because the offense is usually much more serious. The question in this case is who has the primary role in determining guilt as well as the type and length of punishment. As with disciplinary questions, military authorities, if they are in charge, are in an excellent position to suppress views they consider too "political." Consequently, the greater the degree to which the military controls criminal proceedings, the greater will be its ability to enforce compliance with its own views. The same schema and justification will be used on this indicator as for disciplinary questions, with nonmilitary personnel and organs replacing political representatives and organs in the schema.

The fifteenth and final indicator of political control proposes that, the more time the military specialist is required to spend on civilian types of projects, the less exclusively military his skills and experience will be and the less likely he will be to identify himself as primarily a military technician. In evaluating the importance of this indicator, the following schema will be used:

High: The military specialist spends an average of one-fourth or more of his working time carrying out civilian types of projects.
Medium: The military specialist spends an average of one-eighth to one-fourth of his time carrying out civilian types of projects.
Low: The military specialist spends an average of less than one-eighth of his time carrying out civilian types of projects.

A military man who regularly devotes one-fourth of his working time to civilian types of projects is spending considerable time on projects not directly related to his specialty. He is forced to deal with individuals who are not members of the military more than one of every five days. He is forced to go beyond the framework of his technical environment to develop skills to deal with people and projects unknown in the service. Spending so much time on such projects, he would be hard-pressed to identify himself as solely a military technician. Political control of the military would be high.

Devoting from one-eighth to one-fourth of his working time to civilian types of projects would mean less adaptation of the officer's skills into civilian forms. Military tasks would take up an overriding portion of his time, and his association with civilians and identification with extra-military activities would be reduced. The likelihood that he will identify himself primarily as a military technician would increase. A medium level of political control would be indicated.

Military men engaged in civilian work for less than one-eighth of their working time probably would be participating in sporadic or special projects such as helping with the harvest or flood relief. They could engage in such activities with minimal effect on their primary identity as military technicians. Consequently, the level of political control would be classified as low.

I have tried to show that a communist political leadership must decide between emphasizing an individual's "redness" or his "expertness." The necessity for such a decision increases as the conduct of war becomes more technical and complex. The next section of this study analyzes how the East German leadership has reacted to this dilemma.

NOTES

1. For a discussion of the role of the secret police in this regard, see Merle Fainsod, How Russia Is Ruled (rev. ed; Cambridge, Mass.: Harvard University Press, 1967), pp. 494-95.
2. The description is taken from two West German sources, Thomas A. Forster, NVA—Die Armee der Sowjetzone (Cologne:

Markus Verlag, 1966-67), pp. 87-91; Ulrich Rühmland, ed., NVA, Nationale Volksarmee der SBZ in Stichworten (Bonn: Bonner Druck- und Verlags-gesellschaft, 1969), pp. 67-68.

3. Forster, NVA—Die Armee der Sowjetzone, p. 87.

4. Ibid., p. 88.

5. This chart is a partial reproduction of one in Bundesministerium für Gesamtdeutsche Fragen, ed., A bis Z: Ein Taschen—und Nachschlagebuch über den anderen Teil Deutschlands (11th rev. ed.; Bonn: Deutscher Bundes Verlag, 1969), p. 485.

6. Forster, NVA—Die Armee der Sowjetzone, p. 90.

7. The basic organization, based on 1969 sources, is present down to the battalion level. Bundesministerium für Gesamtdeutsche Fragen, A bis Z (1969), p. 485. According to another source, the average Grundorganisation has about 50 members, although this figure refers to civilian party organizations. Eckart Förtsch, Die SED (Stuttgart: Kohlhammer, 1969), p. 47. If this is also true for the military, then it is possible that an individual who views himself primarily as a military technician could go undetected as long as the Grundorganisation activities were limited primarily to monthly meetings, as they appear to be—at least in the civilian organizations.

8. See "Statut der Sozialistische Einheitspartei Deutschlands," Protokoll des VI. Parteitages der SED (Berlin-Ost: Dietz Verlag, 1963, Vol. IV, p. 434.

9. Walter Ulbricht, "Der Kampf um den Frieden für Sieg des Sozialismus, für die Nationale Wiedergeburt Deutschlands als Friedliebender Demokratischer Staat," Prokotoll der Verhandlungen des V. Parteitages der Sozialistischen Einheitspartei Deutschlands (Berlin-Ost: Dietz Verlag, 1959), Vol I, p. 111.

10. Roman Kolkowicz, The Soviet Military and the Communist Party (Princeton, N.J.: Princeton University Press, 1967), pp. 94-95. For a description of the role of self-criticism in the Chinese Communist Army, see Alexander George, The Chinese Communist Army in Action: The Korean War and Its Aftermath (New York: Columbia University Press, 1967), pp. 94-105.

11. Kolkowicz, The Soviet Military and the Communist Party, pp. 167-71.

12. Ibid., p. 149.

PART II
THE EAST GERMAN MILITARY, 1949-72

CHAPTER

3

**A HESITANT
BEGINNING:
1949-55**

A cloud of uncertainty enveloped the establishment of the German Democratic Republic, in 1949. Unsure of the West's intentions with regard to Germany, the Soviets still hoped for the creation of a united but neutralized German nation. Consequently, they hesitated to act in a manner that might provoke the West into binding the newly founded Federal Republic into the Western alliance system, making neutrality and reunion with the Soviet Zone impossible.[1]

In few areas was the caution and uncertainty of Soviet policy more evident than in the organization of the East German armed forces. Although paramilitary forces had existed covertly since 1948[2] and overtly since 1952,[3] they were in no way comparable with the national armed forces so often associated with a sovereign nation.

From the Soviet point of view, the creation of national armed forces, as desired by the East German political leadership, would have contributed significantly to making the division of Germany permanent. As one writer put it:

> Nevertheless, the Soviets did not accede to the SED leadership's demand for the establishment of national armed forces (Nationale Streitkräfte); perhaps Moscow wanted to keep the possibility of an all-German policy open by not agreeing to this request.[4]

Contrary to West German assertions, creation of paramilitary forces in the GDR had little to do with any East German or Soviet desire to create the basis of a modern military force. Instead, remembering the role a hostile German military had played in the persecution of communists and socialists both during and prior to the war, the SED leadership resolved to create a military force that would protect it from any threat in the future, regardless of the source. In addition, it was aware that the majority of the East German population was less than sympathetic to its cause. A military force offered an excellent opportunity to remove young men from family and peer group influences that might be hostile to the party, and place them in an environment where at least a feeling of neutrality if not sympathy toward the system could be inculcated.[5]

Symptoms of Soviet uncertainty appeared in the areas of both technological development and political control of the armed forces that emerged between 1949 and 1955 in the GDR. Technologically, restraint guided the allocation of resources and time to the military. What would have been the sense of devoting much time and money— both very precious commodities—to the creation of a modern military force if it might later be disbanded? It would be better to wait and see.

The educational level of most individuals who became officers in the KVP (Kasernierte Volkspolizei or People's Police Quartered in Barracks) was abysmally low. But little effort was expended to correct this situation. This is not to suggest that the Russians were oblivious to the need for military technicians to operate the equipment they supplied to the East Germans. But instead of investing time and money in educating these individuals, they decided to rely on the services of former Wehrmacht officers who were sympathetic or at least neutral toward their cause. As Ernst Richert noted:

> On the whole, this opportunity did not lead to the entrance of a significant number of former Nazis into positions of authority in the SBZ/DDR administration. The only exception concerns the establishment of the DDR armed forces, which in the beginning to a considerable degree, was in the hands of high Wehrmacht officers who either deserted or were re-educated.[6]

In addition, the KVP was forced to rely on outdated World War II equipment and arms, which sharply curtailed its need for officers with a high degree of technical expertise. Here, too, the Russians gave no indication of any desire to upgrade the KVP by giving it modern equipment. This decision was to come later, well after the decision to create a modern military had been made.

In the realm of political control, the policy adopted during this period reflected that prevalent in the remainder of the GDR: namely, to neutralize hostility toward the regime. Recognizing the difficulty of "converting" individuals who had been socialized during or prior to the Hitler period, the SED leadership set out to prove that its interests and those of most citizens were compatible. For officers in the armed forces this meant that, despite the presence of such political controls as political officers and party organizations, there was no attempt like those common in later periods to remove individuals not politically qualified or not active in the party. The concept of a military "dual executive" was a matter for consideration at some future date.

To obtain deeper insights into the nature of the military force the Russians and East Germans built in the GDR and the political controls they created to combat hostility toward the regime during this early period, a more thorough inquiry is required. The indicators of military technology and political control developed earlier will guide this investigation and facilitate comparison with other periods.

MILITARY TECHNOLOGY

Seven of the 17 indicators of military technology developed for this study appeared as early as Period I. The first of these, the length of officer training schools, varied during the period.

At the beginning of the period (1949), officer training schools required attendance for nine months.[7] A year later, an East German source noted the extension of the term to two years, stating, "the officer schools of the NVA and HVS, on which a reorganization is being carried out, will go over to a two-year period of study."[8] By the end of the period, the length of study at an officer training school had increased again, this time to three years.[9]

At first glance, it would appear that this indicator warrants a classification of high since by the close of the period the length of time an officer candidate spent in training was three years. But merely viewing the number of years an individual attends these schools can be misleading. Instructors devoted only two years of this time to actually training students to become officers. They used the other year to provide students with a basic education so they could do the work required in the regular officer training period. As one observer suggested:

> These cadres are so underqualified that in spite of the increase of the training period from one to two to an average of three years, the first year must be considered a loss (Ausfall).[10]

Consequently, the length of time devoted to training officer cadets is considered here as two years and classified as medium.

The second indicator present in this period is the value of an officer's education compared with that offered at civilian institutions. Only one source provided an evaluation of this indicator during the first period. It is a book written by a former East German political officer who defected to West Germany, Heinz Godau. Even with the heightened caution called for in evaluating the credibility of a defector, Godau's account in this case appears reliable. On matters on which more information is available, other sources—both East and West—tend to substantiate his reports.

Although Godau does not directly discuss the value of an officer's education in East German society during this period, he does discuss a number of officers who left the KVP, either voluntarily or involuntarily, and because of their lack of a skill, were forced to take jobs requiring little or no training.[11] Since the training received by these individuals was rudimentary and of value only within the military, it will be classified as low for this period.

The third indicator present measures the percentage of officers whose highest level of education is the mittlere Reife. Figures for this indicator during Period I once more come from a single source—an East German article dealing with questions of military history. According to the authors, only 0.1 percent of KVP officers possessed the mittlere Reife as their highest level of education.[12] This exceedingly low level can be explained in part by the fact that the vast majority of junior officers were recruited from poorly educated social groups and very often had had their education interrupted by the war. Furthermore, as mentioned above, the Russians had decided not to invest a large amount of time and resources in raising the educational level of the KVP officer corps. In accordance with the schema outlined above, this indicator is listed as low.

The fourth indicator is the percentage of the officer corps possessing the Abitur. The same East German article again served as the sole source for the figures employed here. The article gives the percentage of officers in the KVP who had attained the Abitur as 2.2 percent, lower than in the NVA at its inception.[13] By subtracting this figure from the known percentage of officers with an Abitur at the inception of the NVA (this figure will be discussed in Chapter 4), one obtains a figure of 8.8 percent, qualifying it for classification as low.

The length of time an officer is required to serve on active duty is the fifth indicator present. A Western source providing the sole mention of this indicator states that officers of the KVP were required to serve for seven years during this period; they could obligate themselves to serve longer, but this was the minimum amount of time for which they could sign up.[14] The indicator is evaluated as medium.

The number of specialized journals utilized within the military also could be ascertained for this period. Apparently, there was only one journal devoted strictly to military questions—the journal entitled Volkspolizei (People's police). Another journal, Der Kampfruf (Call to struggle), was intended primarily for the KVP. But although I consulted a number of issues, I could not determine the journal's exact purpose. Whether one decides that one or two journals existed, this indicator still is classified as low in accord with the schema established.

The last indicator in this period concerned the PS level in the East German military. Although no source encountered supplied a direct statement on the PS level, it is possible to arrive at an estimate by using a number of sources. According to one East German source, the PS level at the beginning of World War II was about 12 PS and by the end of the war it had reached approximately 15 PS.[15] David Childs, in discussing the KVP as of 1954, remarks that its equipment and weapons were known to be antiquated, suggesting that they consisted primarily of items left over from World War II.[16] Thus, it would seem reasonable to conclude that the PS level of the KVP during this period was approximately 15. A PS level of 15, according to the schema worked out above, is indicative of a low level of technology.

Further analysis of military technology in this period requires a determination of the overall level of technology. Entering the appropriate numerical values of the indicators in Table 3.1 provides this measure.* As suggested at the beginning of this chapter, the level of technology for Period I (1.3) is rather low.

POLITICAL CONTROL

Turning to the level of political control in the first period, a wider range of the indicators outlined could be identified than was the

---

*Some may object that seven indicators is an insufficient number upon which to base an overall average for the period. This would certainly be true if one were attempting to run correlations, but I do not believe it presents a serious problem here. Although data are lacking, the available information suggests that almost every missing indicator, if present, would provide a low level of technology, thus confirming the results achieved here.

TABLE 3.1

Level of Technology in Period I,
1949-55

Indicator	Period I
1. Entry education	—
2. School length	2
3. Three-year course	—
4. Educational value	1
5. Mittlere Reife	1
6. Abitur	1
7. Fachschulausbildung	—
8. Engineers or technicians	—
9. Total academic education	—
10. Regimental academic education	—
11. Length of service	2
12. Technical qualifications	—
13. Technical awards	—
14. Occupational categories	—
15. Journals	1
16. Books	—
17. PS Level	1
Total	9
Average	1.3

Note: 1 = low; 2 = medium; 3 = high; — = no information.

case with technology. Of the 15 indicators of political control constructed for this study, information on 14 appeared during Period I.

The first indicator present in this period treats the organizational level down to which the political officer is present. Only one source, Heinz Godau, discussed the subject. In viewing the activities in which a political officer is engaged, Godau notes that the political officer was active down to the company level.[17] Although he participated in meetings and other activities below the company level, he was assigned to the company commander's staff and was held responsible for political activities at that level. Consequently, this indicator is classified as representing a medium level of political control.

The second indicator concerns the organizational level down to which secret police officers are assigned. One source was utilized, a West German source judged reliable because of its accuracy in areas where other studies substantiated its findings. According to this source:

> The organization of the MfS in the KVP is represented on the Army level by five liaison officers, and on the Regiment and independent (Selbstständiges) battalion levels by one liaison officer and one enlisted rank.[18]

The term independent battalion refers to battalion strength units that operate independently, such as chemical troops. In the main, however, the SSD—or at this time SfS—officers were restricted to the regimental level. Accordingly, it is classified as indicating a low level of political control.

The third indicator of political control measures the amount of training required for political officers. At the beginning of Period I, the normal training period was four months.[19] By 1952, it had increased to a full year.[20] Further extension of the political officer's schooling to an average of two years was an important component of the reorganization carried out in 1953.[21] The length of training of political officers in this period therefore reflects a medium level of political control.

The fourth indicator deals with the prior military service of political officers. At the beginning of the period, emphasis rested on recruiting party members from factories and then sending them to political officer schools.[22] Thus, they came directly from civilian life and, upon graduation, assumed their duties in a regular military unit.

This approach soon proved impractical as the political officers were unable to deal with questions of military technology. Consequently, a greater effort was made to recruit KVP officers with a military background. Although prior military service was not an absolute requisite, Godau gives the impression that it was desired.[23] The only source listing figures states that more than 50 percent of all political officer candidates came from the ranks of regular KVP officers during this period.[24] Since at least half of the political officer candidates can be considered to have served at least a year in the military, including training time, this indicator is evaluated as signifying a medium level of political control.

The fifth indicator treats the activity and structure of the Politorgane. Throughout this period, the Politorgane were loosely organized. At the beginning, military control and administration functions came under the direction of political-cultural organs

(Polit-Kultur).[25] The Main Political Administration described in Chapter 2 did not exist at this time. The political-cultural organs appear to have consisted of a number of administrative units, all under the control of the Central Committee. This situation changed in 1952 when political-cultural organs were replaced by political administrations.[26] The creation of the Collegium (Kollegium) in 1953 instituted a further important alteration. This body, which was to meet once or twice a month, assumed the task of making certain that not only military directives but also political ones were being followed.[27] At this time the Collegium represented the closest thing to a centralized political organ in the armed forces.

This situation changed again in 1954 with the issuance of the Statute for the Political Organs, Party and Youth Organizations of the People's Police Quartered in Barracks of the German Democratic Republic.[28] These regulations established a political administration that operated with the authority of a section of the Central Committee. It was responsible for controlling and directing party and FDJ (Freie Deutsche Jugend, or Free German Youth) organizations. No mention is made of how active this organ was at the time. But later statements regarding its "strengthening" strongly indicate that it still did very little, carrying out its control functions only on a periodic basis. Because of the loose organizational structure and inactivity of the Politorgane in the period, this indicator will be listed as indicating a low level of political control.

The sixth indicator deals with the activities of the military party organization, which concerned itself primarily with the construction of a party organization during this period. As a result, it largely abdicated an active role in the enforcement of control measures. It was necessary to create a party that would evoke neutral if not loyal sentiments from members of the East German military. Only after this was done could it begin to become an effective force in the battle to build unquestioned loyalty toward the new state.

One method the party used to accomplish this task was the recruitment of individuals who could serve as examples that, it was hoped, non-party members would admire and follow.[29] In addition, individuals who belonged to the party received constant encouragement to excel in the performance of their tasks.[30]

This does not mean that the party was uninterested in establishing the military party organization as an effective control mechanism during this period. Based particularly on subsequent developments, it appears the party felt this was about as far as it could push the matter at this time. As a result, although the party requested members to participate in party activities, there is very little evidence that failure to participate was penalized. Also, there is very little evidence to indicate that the military party organization played an active role in military-political decision-making. In fact, based on information to be presented in Chapter 4, any authority the party organization possessed appears to have been more formal than real. Consequently, this indicator will be classified as signifying a low level of political control.

The seventh indicator of political control concerns the percentage of officers who are party members. The only figure located for this period, 74 percent, comes from an article by East German military historians.[31] The relatively small percentage of officers who were party members—in light of later developments—appears to reflect the East German policy at the time of leaving military experts alone as long as they performed their assigned tasks satisfactorily and were not hostile to the regime. The schema established above reflects the relative unimportance assigned to party membership in this period. Accordingly, this indicator is classified as signifying a low level of political control.

The eighth indicator of political control focuses on the importance assigned to the political reliability of military officers. One factor that seems to stand out in this period is the separation between political and military officers. Military officers received encouragement, of course, to attend political lectures and prepare themselves politically. Significantly, however, their attendance at lectures or successful completion of examinations demonstrating a specific level of ideological competency was not required. In fact, if one attempted to ascertain which factor weighed most heavily in considering whether to retain or promote an officer, it would appear that all factors--technical competency, leadership ability, and political reliability—were of equal importance except at the very highest ranks where political considerations were very important.[32] Hence, a technically competent officer with leadership ability might gain promotions even though he was weak politically.[33] Consideration of political reliability as one of a number of factors in deciding promotion and retention in the service corresponds to the category of low in the schema for this indicator outlined earlier.

The ninth indicator deals with the responsibility for political indoctrination. As mentioned above, a definite separation of responsibilities marked this period. The military officer concerned himself with military questions and the political officer with political ones. This division pervaded political indoctrination as much as other areas. Considered a political function, political indoctrination fell into the sphere of the political officer. The political officer was assigned as a deputy to the military officer, who assumed the command role. Although military specialists might occasionally deliver lectures, the political officer normally performed this chore and bore primary responsibility for a successful program.[34] This does not mean that the military officer was exonerated of all responsibility if the quality of political indoctrination was determined inadequate. If, for example, the political officer could prove, as Godau says happened, that he failed in his objective because of opposition from the military commander, the commander would be held responsible.[35] In the main, however, political indoctrination remained the responsibility of political officers. As a result, the gulf between the political and technical aspects of the military "dual executive" loomed large. This is indicative of a low level of political control.

The tenth indicator present in this period deals with responsibility for Massenarbeit. This indicator is very closely related to the preceding one and shows the same trend. The military officer has formal responsibility but the political officer bears primary responsibility. The following comment illustrates this point:

> The evaluation of the results of Stalin's statement (Aufgebot) must serve as a decisive warning for the political-culture organs to upgrade political work, for in that way they better technical work as well.[36]

Significant in this quotation is the clear designation of the political-culture organs as the perpetrators of better political work. It makes no mention of the actions or responsibilities of regular military officers, and one can only surmise that their role in political work was marginal. As in the case of responsibility for political indoctrination, the clear division between political and technical work is evident. In accord with the schema developed above, this indicator is classified as indicating a low level of political control.

The eleventh indicator of political control concerns the amount of time devoted to part-time ideological study. Although no information on this indicator appeared in East German sources, two West German articles discussed it. They agree that an average of two hours per week was devoted to part-time ideological training.[37] One must not forget that the group of men with whom the East Germans were dealing either knew very little about Marxism-Leninism, as was the case of many former Wehrmacht members, or possessed superficial knowledge at best, as was the case of many from working-class backgrounds who, although enthusiastic, lacked ideological training as well as military competency. Consequently, it is not surprising that much time was devoted to part-time ideological training. On our schema, two hours of ideological study is indicative of a high level of political control.

The twelfth indicator of political control deals with the effectiveness of self-criticism. Only one source offered information on this topic for this period. Since this East German source is not

for general distribution but only for restricted internal use in the
GDR, its reliability would seem high. The practice of criticism and
self-criticism seems to have been both ignored and suppressed.
This source contends:

> It is not accidental that . . . in such sections there was
> no sign of criticism and self-criticism, and in fact, in
> some cases criticism and self-criticism was suppressed
> with administrative measures.[38]

The reasons for this situation are not difficult to ascertain.
Many officers perceived themselves primarily as military specialists.
And, as noted above, the East German government also tended to
view them in this way. Consequently, it is not suprising that military
officers would resist the interference of individuals they considered
incompetent into their areas of expertise. This situation indicates
a low level of political control.

The thirteenth indicator of political control treats the handling
of disciplinary matters. As one of the effects of the policy of leaving
military specialists alone as long as they did not exhibit opposition
to the party, the military superior continued to perform the functions
traditionally assigned to him. In the case of disciplinary questions,
this meant the party played a relatively minor role—unless, of course,
the question at hand was of direct concern to the party. As one
source put it:

> The superiors of all levels (Leitungsebenen) receive
> authority over disciplinary matters through the orders
> which enable them to significantly promote the education
> of those placed under them to conscious discipline and
> order.[39]

The Disciplinary Regulations (Disziplinarordnung) of the KVP (DV-
10/6) formalized this decision to leave disciplinary questions in the
commanders' hands.[40]

Allowing the military to maintain authority in this area made
it possible for the party to avoid the danger of a drop in military
efficiency brought about by forcing the military specialist to work
under conditions for which he was neither prepared nor trained. He
was a military technician; consequently, he was the one primarily
concerned with disciplinary questions. The separation between the
military and political aspects of the "dual executive" is evident. It
indicates a low level of political control.

The fourteenth indicator concerns the handling of criminal
offenses which, like disciplinary problems, remained in the hands of
military specialists. As one East German expert said:

Up until the extension of the penal code (Strafrechtsergänzungsgesetzen) came into force on February 1, 1958, the DDR Penal Code did not contain a special military criminal code (Militärstrafbestände) which protected military discipline and combat readiness, so that acts which were against very basic military relationships could only be handled through disciplinary measures.[41]

In view of the preceding indicator, the meaning of this situation is obvious—the military commander remains in a position of authority and can punish those who commit criminal acts as he sees fit. Accordingly, it is considered indicative of a low level of political control.

As in the case of technology, it is necessary to chart the figures assigned the indicators of political control in order to determine the average level of political control for the period under study (see Table 3.2). These figures yield an overall average level of political control of 1.4.

TABLE 3.2

Level of Political Control in Period I,
1949-55

Indicator	Period I
1. Political Officer Level	2
2. Secret Police Level	1
3. Training Length	2
4. Prior Service	2
5. Politorgane	1
6. Military Party Organization	1
7. Party Membership	1
8. Political Reliability	1
9. Indoctrination	1
10. Massenarbeit	1
11. Part-Time Training	3
12. Self-Criticism	1
13. Discipline	1
14. Criminal Offenses	1
15. Civilian Projects	—
Total	19
Average	1.4

Note: 1 = low; 2 = medium; 3 = high; — = no information.

OBSERVATIONS

The introduction to this study suggested that, as the level of technology increases, that of political control will decrease. The results reported in this chapter for Period I are shown in Figure 3.1.

The low priority the Russians and East Germans assigned to the development of a modern technical military is reflected in the figure of 1.3. At least technically, this military force does not resemble the camouflaged modern military force some West Germans warned of. Rather, it appears to be a highly neglected component of society that would have been hard-pressed to operate modern military equipment under peacetime conditions, let alone during wartime. In fact, it is possible that information on more of the indicators of technology would have lowered the figure of 1.3 even further. Such a possibility exists especially in the case of indicators 1, 3, 7, 9, and 10 because discussions of these indicators during later periods constantly refer to the fact that they have increased. By determining the level of these indicators in the next period, it will be possible to obtain some idea of how low they really were during Period I. In any case, the technical half of the military dual executive left much to be desired at this point.

The level of political control also was low and shows minimal concern on the part of the Russians and East Germans for developing a military officer who was both "red" and "expert." They apparently were satisfied with attempting to produce a neutral officer corps.

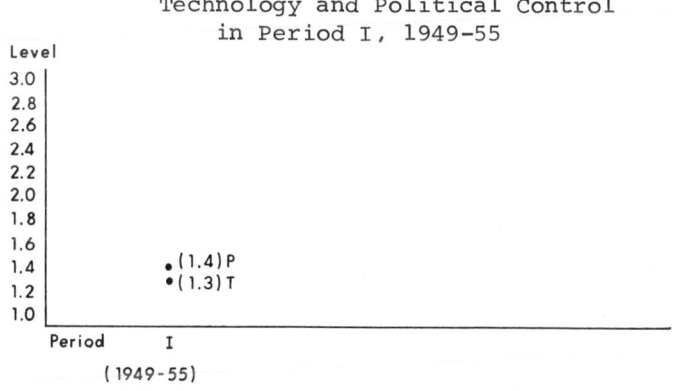

FIGURE 3.1

Technology and Political Control in Period I, 1949-55

Note: P = political control; T = military technology.

In fact, in a number of areas such as responsibility for political indoctrination and work with the masses, the involvement of regular officers was minimal. In other areas, such as self-criticism, the party seldom stopped regular officers from suppressing political activities. In addition, the party did little to interfere in discipline or the handling of criminal offenses, both of which the regular officers perceived as of concern to only the professional military officer, not the party. In only one area was party activity high—the time spent on political indoctrination. Much of this, however, can be attributed to unfamiliarity on the part of many officers with the SED's goals and values. To be neutral, the officers needed at least to understand the party's aims and ideas.

If the fundamental proposition advanced at the beginning of this study is accurate, the political side of the dual executive should decrease as the technical one increases. Whether this actually occurs is a question that will be answered by the analysis of events in subsequent time periods.

NOTES

1. Ernst Richert, Das Zweite Deutschland: Ein Staat der nicht sein darf (Hamburg: Fischer, 1966), p. 8; Ernst Richert, Die DDR Elite (Hamburg: Rowolt, 1968), pp. 13-14. See also Jean Edward Smith, Germany Beyond the Wall: People, Politics . . . and Prosperity (Boston: Little, Brown, 1969), pp. 199-240.
2. Thomas A. Forster, NVA—Die Armee der Sowjetzone (Cologne: Markus Verlag, 1966-67), p. 34.
3. Autorenkollektiv des Deutschen Instituts für Militärgeschichte, Zeittafel zur Militärgeschichte der Deutschen Demokratischen Republik, 1949 bis 1968 (Berlin-Ost: Deutscher Militärverlag, 1969), pp. 33-34, 49-68.
4. Hermann Weber, Von der SBZ zur DDR, 1945-1968 (Hanover: Verlag für Literatur und Zeitgeschehen, 1966), p. 67.
5. The writer is indebted to Heinz Lippmann for these observations.
6. Richert, Das Zweite Deutschland, p. 140. For the situation in other parts of the society, see Thomas Baylis, "The New Class in East German Politics" (unpublished Ph.D. thesis, University of California, 1964), p. 42.
7. "Blaue Uniform mit Roten Schlips," Deutsche Zeitung und Wirtschaftszeitung, No. 94 (November 25, 1950), p. 4.
8. Autorenkollektiv, Zeittafel . . . 1949 bis 1968, p. 23.

9. Die Kasernierte Volkspolizei in der sowjetischen Besatzungszone Deutschlands (Bonn: Bundesministerium für Gesamtdeutsche Fragen, 1955), p. 30; "Sowjetzone . . . Kasernierte Volkspolizei: Ein langgezogenes Hurra," Der Spiegel, IX, 6, (1955), 13-18.

10. Die Kasernierte Volkspolizei i. d. SBZ, p. 30. See also Generalmajor F. Dickel, "Die Notwendigkeit einer allseitigen wissenschaftlichtechnischen Qualifizierung des Offizierskorps der Nationalen Volksarmee," Militärwesen, July 1961, p. 871.

11. Heinz Godau, Verführter, Verführer, Ich war Politoffizier der NVA (Cologne: Markus Verlag, 1965), pp. 140-45.

12. Karl Greese and Alfred Voerster, "Probleme der Auswahl und Förderung des Offizierskader in der NVA (1958-1963)," Zeitschrift für Militärgeschichte, V, 1 (1966), p. 36n. According to another source, in 1952 87 percent of all officers had not gone beyond elementary school (Grundschule). See Dr. J. Schunke, "Zur militärischen Bedeutung Lenins," Mitteilungsblatt der Arbeitgemeinschaft Ehemaliger Offiziere, July 1970, p. 14.

13. Greese and Voerster, "Probleme der Auswahl und Förderung des Offizierskader in der NVA (1958-1963)," p. 36n.

14. "Zu Befehl, Genosse Hauptmann!", Parole, V, 5 (1955), 6.

15. K. Erhart, "15 Jahre Nationale Volksarmee: Wachsam und Bereit," Volksarmee, November 1971, p. 8.

16. David Childs, "The Nationale Volksarmee of East Germany," German Life and Letters, XX, 3 (1967), p. 195.

17. Godau, Verführter, Verführer, p. 55.

18. Die Kasernierte Volkspolizei i. d. SBZ, p. 23.

19. "PK-Hochschule beendete den 2. Lehrgang," Volkspolizei, September 10, 1950, p. 9.

20. Godau, Verführter, Verführer, pp. 25-43.

21. "Die Ausbildung der Polit-offiziere für die Volkspolizei," Parole, V, 1 (January 15, 1955), p. 4; Werner Holgert, "Die Ausbildung der Polit-offiziere für die KVP," SBZ Archiv, V, 54 (1954), p. 341. In some cases, the length of the school was three years, although this appears to have been restricted to those officers coming directly from civilian life, with the first year devoted to acquainting them with the basics of military life.

22. Holgert," Die Ausbildung der Polit-offiziere für die KVP," p. 341.

23. Godau, Verführter, Verführer, p. 24.

24. Holgert, "Die Ausbildung der Polit-offiziere für die Volkspolizei," p. 341.

25. Autorenkollektiv, Zeittafel. . . 1949 bis 1968, pp. 13, 19.

26. Ibid., p. 35.

27. Ibid., p. 41.

28. Ibid., p. 43.

29. Ibid., p. 24.

30. See, for example, the 1953 letter of the Central Committee to "Members and Candidates of the SED in the Armed Forces of the DDR," mentioned in Ibid., pp. 49-50.

31. Greese and Voerster, "Probleme der Auswahl und Förderung des Offizierskader in der NVA (1958-1963)," p. 34.

32. "Offiziersversammlungen—Ein Instrument zur Erziehung der VP-Offiziere," Volkspolizei, VI, 21 (1951), pp. 6-7.

33. One must not exaggerate this situation. Officers who openly challenged the party or were otherwise hostile toward it were dismissed immediately.

34. Karrasch, "Entwicklung eines festes Staatsbewusstseins— Eine Aufgabe der PK-Organe," Volkspolizei, III, 10 (May 25, 1950), p. 4; Chefinspekteur der VP Herbert Grünstein, "Die Aufgaben des PK-Organe der Volkspolizei im neuen Jahr," Volkspolizei, IV, 2 (January 25, 1951), p. 1; Godau, Verführter, Verführer, p. 112.

35. Godau, Verführter, Verführer, p. 131.

36. "Noch bessere Anleitung durch die PK-Organe," Volkspolizei, IV, 15 (August 1, 1951), p. 7; Karl Maron, "Alle Kräfte für die Erhöhung der Kampf- und Schlagkraft der Volkspolizei," Volkspolizei, VIII, 1 (1955), p. 17.

37. "Die militärische Aufrüstung in Sowjetzone Deutschlands," PZ Archiv, I, 6 (1950), pp. 2, 9; "Blaue Uniform," Deutsche Zeitung und Wirtschaftszeitung, No. 94 (November 25, 1950), p. 4.

38. Grünstein, "Die Aufgaben des PK-Organe der Volkspolizei im neuen Jahr," p. 2.

39. Autorenkollektiv, Zeittafel... 1949 bis 1968, p. 25. See also Übel, "Verbesserung der Kaderarbeit—das Gebot des Stunde," Volkspolizei, V, 9 (1952), pp. 5-6; Willi Fischer, "Die richtige Anwendung des Disziplinarordnung—ein wesentlicher Hebel zur Festigung der Disziplin," Volkspolizei, V, 9 (1952), pp. 7-8.

40. Autorenkollektiv, Zeittafel... 1949 bis 1968, p. 48.

41. Alfred Hartmann, Die Abgabe von Straftaten an den Kommandeur zur Behandlung nach der Disziplinarvorschrift der Nationalen Volksarmee DV-10/6 (Berlin-Ost: Deutsche Militärverlag, 1968), pp. 22-23.

CHAPTER 4

THE POLITICIZATION
OF THE NATIONAL
PEOPLE'S ARMY:
1956-59

By 1956 the Russians had decided that the unification of Germany could not be effected on grounds they considered acceptable. Consequently, they acceded to East German requests for the establishment of national armed forces and on January 18, 1956, the East German Volkskammer (People's Chamber) passed the Law on the Establishment of the National People's Army and the Ministry of National Defense (Gesetz über die Schaffung der Nationalen Volksarmee und des Ministeriums für Nationale Verteidigung).[1]

In terms of technology, the establishment of permanent national armed forces initiated a broad program aimed at creating modern naval, air and ground forces. The East Germans began purchasing new and more modern equipment, establishing more schools for training officers and enlisted men and placing more emphasis on either obtaining officers with better educational backgrounds or convincing them to upgrade their education.

The organization of a permanent military force equipped with modern weapons raised the question of how civilian authorities should handle the military. Should they tighten or loosen political controls? Should the officer corps be retained? If the goal was to maximize technical development, then they might be well advised to leave political considerations aside and focus on technology. While the East German leadership pondered such questions, an event occurred that would shake their techniques of control to the very core: the Hungarian uprising.

If East German party leaders learned nothing else from the Hungarian experience, they absorbed the lesson that individuals and groups not expressly with them might some day decide to act against them. To avoid such an occurrence, they decide to strengthen the relationship between the party and the rest of society. As Walter Ulbricht put it at the Fifth Party Conference:

> The party drew a lesson from the counter-revolutionary uprising (Putsch) in Hungary. As a result of the Hungarian events our members recognized more clearly the necessity of the Marxist-Leninist strengthening of the party, the decisive struggle against revisionism and opportunism and the need for closer ties by the party with the workers' class and the masses (Volksmassen).[2]

This recognition of the need for closer ties between the party and the rest of society precipitated a number of important reforms. Only those directly affecting the armed forces will be treated here.[3]

A number of Hungarian officers had sided with the rebels. For a political leadership like that of the GDR, which had a weak hold on the population and relied to a large degree on Soviet troops for its continuance in office, these events seemed to clarify one point: All officers who were not loyal supporters of the regime would have to be dismissed; the party would no longer sanction political neutrality.

The party leadership recognized that it would have to develop a much more intensive and effective means of guaranteeing a reliable officer corps (a number of methods utilized to keep the officer corps in line such as increased pay and better living conditions will not be discussed here because it is felt that they are of only marginal concern for the purposes of this study). As a result, although technical factors were by no means ignored, politicization of the officer corps became the hallmark of this period.

Willi Stoph, minister of national defense at the time and head of the NVA with the rank of colonel-general, took note of this need for increased politicization of the armed forces when he stated:

> Particularly damaging was the attitude in some cases that the task could be solved purely from the standpoint of a specialist (Fachmann). It is understandable that this non-Marxian attitude which is comparable to managerialism (Managertum) must lead to serious mistakes in practical work. The members of our party relentlessly uncover such weakness in the work which remains and thereby do away with the bureaucratic obstacles which result from it.
>
> A number of officers are behind in the level of consciousness. For this reason, it is our task to structure the political education (Erziehung) more effectively because the preparedness of our troops is dependent upon it.[4]

As a result of this concern over the development of political consciousness within the military, a set of instructions was issued in 1957, followed by a resolution by the Politbüro in 1958 that increased the role of the party in internal military affairs.[5]

Although concerned primarily with ensuring a politically reliable officer corps, the SED party leadership also sought to lay the foundation for a modern technical military. How it went about this task is discussed below.

MILITARY TECHNOLOGY

All 17 indicators of technology were present during this period. The first indicator deals with the educational level required for entry into officer training schools. At the time of the establishment of the NVA in 1956, an individual seeking to attend an officer training school needed to possess at least the eighth-class certificate.[6] This educational requirement was soon raised, however. According to a new set of instructions that appeared in 1959, an officer candidate had to have "the eighth-class basic school as well as have completed trade school, or one year's experience in socialist production, or at least one year's service as a soldier."[7] In addition, before the individual could gain admission to the final examination, he had to have the mittlere Reife or tenth-class certificate.[8] Although this meant the officer candidate needed the tenth-class certificate before graduating, he did not need it at the time of entry. This is important, because it meant that those who did not possess the certificate would have to devote a part of their time to subjects not directly related to military technology. As a result, the overall technological level of their education suffered. Therefore, this indicator is still classified as low.

The second indicator considered is the length of officer training schools. Fully aware of the need for highly skilled cadres to deal with modern weapons systems, the East German authorities lengthened the time required before commissioning soon after the National People's Army was founded. They adopted this policy during September and October 1956, announcing that the training period," lasts in the main three years, in some schools with a predominately technical character, four years."[9]

According to one West German source, this time period was shortened in the fall of 1957 to two years.[10] Whether or not this occurred is difficult to ascertain. The East Germans do not mention it, and in view of the significance of such a change, their failure to do so casts doubt on the matter. Based on their normal practice, they would have noted such a change five or six years later to show how far they had advanced or what difficulties they had surmounted. In any case, the next East German reference to the length of officer training schools appeared in 1959 at the close of this period and specified the normal term as three years.11 Thus, regardless of whether there was a change in 1957, the term was three years at the close of the period and thus warrants classification as high.

The third indicator of technology deals with the percentage of officers who completed a three-year officer training school. The first figures available for this indicator appear in 1956. The most frequently quoted figure is 10.7 percent.12 Gunther Schulz, an East German military historian, places it at 9.3 percent.13 One other source gives the figure as 12 percent, but this appears to include individuals who graduated from civilian technical schools.14 The first source was utilized here because the variation introduced by the other was not sufficient to affect the results of this study.

Within two years, East German authorities had succeeded in raising the percentage of officers who had graduated from a three-year officer school to 23.5 percent.15 But although the percentage of the East German officer corps having a three-year education more than doubled during the period, it still fails to qualify for more than a rating of low.

The fourth indicator, which treats the value of an officer's education when compared with civilian institutions, reveals that during Period I officer schools provided training useful only within the military service. Employers hired individuals leaving the military only as semiskilled workers. A resolution of the Presidium of the Council of Ministers in 1958 (Beschluss des Präsidiums Ministerrates der DDR von 28 November 1958) changed this policy.16 This resolution made officer training schools technical schools (Fachschule) and placed them on a par with other technical schools in GDR. As one source put it:

> The certificates awarded are equal to those awarded by technical schools (Fachschule) in the GDR. They entitle the individual, in case of transfer to the reserve, to placement in a corresponding function in the state and economic apparatus and social organizations for which graduation from a technical school is required.17

Thus, the level of this indicator increased and it is reclassified as representing a medium level of technology.

The fifth indicator of technology concerns the percentage of officers who possessed the mittlere Reife as their highest level of education. The first figures available for this period are for the year 1956. Four sources were available and all agreed that 10 percent of the total officer corps possessed the mittlere Reife.18 The only other mention of a figure for this period appeared in 1958. According to this source, the percentage for the total officer corps increased threefold from 1958 to 1962.[19] Knowing the level in 1962, one can calculate the level for 1958 as approximately 12 percent. Although the percentage of officers possessing the mittlere Reife increased during this period, it proved insufficient to change the classification of this indicator, which remained at low.

The sixth indicator of technology focuses on the percentage of officers who possess the Abitur. Figures for this indicator first appear in 1956. There are a total of five sources and although some variation among the figures exists, none differ more than one percentage point, which is not significant for the purposes of this study. The generally accepted figure is 11 percent.[20] One source lists it at 10 percent,[21] another as 10.8 percent.[22]

To obtain the only other set of figures for this period, calculations similar to those just discussed in regard to the mittlere Reife were utilized. Sources claim the percentage of officers possessing the Abitur increased between 1958 and 1962 one and a half times and provide the figure for 1962 as 18.5 percent.[23] The percentage derived for 1958 would thus be 13 percent.

Although the percentage of officers possessing the Abitur increased not only over the first period but during the second one as well, again the gain was too small to warrant a change in classification and this indicator again is listed as low.

The seventh indicator of technology involves the percentage of officers who graduated from a technical school. Only one set of figures provides data on technical school graduates during this period, but since the author supplying it agreed with the other writers quoted for the two previous indicators, he appears reliable. He claims 31 percent of the NVA officer corps had graduated from a technical school by 1965.[24] The schema for this indicator classifies this figure as low.

The eighth indicator of technology deals with the percentage of the total officer corps composed of engineers or technicians. The first figure for this indicator lists it at 1.7 percent for the year 1956.[25] Three sources agree on this figure, attesting to its reliability. Figures from 1958 show an increase to 5 percent.[26] Although this change represents a major increase in the percentage of officers who were engineers or technicians, it is not high enough to warrant a classification of medium. Accordingly, it will be listed as low.

The ninth indicator deals with the percentage of officers possessing the equivalent of a university-level education. The only figure available for this period is for 1956 and is given as 2.6 percent.[27] To catch up on the educational prerequisites needed to create a modern technical force, the East Germans relied heavily on the Friedrich Engels Military Academy, discussed below, along with study at certain specialized schools in the Soviet Union to educate selected individuals at the academic level. Despite efforts launched during this period, this indicator remained at a low level.

The tenth indicator of technology deals with the percentage of army regimental-level commanders with an academic education. Only one figure is available for this period for 1957. According to Heinz Hoffmann, whose figures are usually reliable, 2 percent of army regimental-level commanders had completed a university-level course of study.[28] This figure is important, particularly in view of the changes that were to occur during the next period. Since these changes were built on a foundation laid during this period, a discussion of the major cornerstone of this foundation—the founding of the Friedrich Engels Military Academy in Dresden—is in order.

The Friedrich Engels Military Academy opened on January 5, 1959. Its purpose was to train officers for command positions at the regimental level or higher.[29] According to Walter Ulbricht, the academy divided this training into four areas:

> Political—to help these officers better recognize the leading role of the party, historical—to impart to them a better understanding of the revolutionary tradition of the NVA, theoretical—to help them better understand the principles of military science, and technological—to enable them to make use of this theoretical knowledge in practice.[30]

The role set for the academy was to be a major one because, according to an instruction issued in 1959, after the founding of the academy, graduation from it was a prerequisite for command at the regimental level:

> The qualification of individuals as regiment commanders, political deputy at regimental level, and similar positions as well as higher positions takes place by studying at the military academy.[31]

Prior to this time, a special school in Dresden, founded in 1956, trained officers for battalion and regimental command.[32] This school does not appear to have been on a par with the academy as no academic degrees were awarded. The percentage of officers who attended this school is unknown. Officers being prepared for general/flag rank positions usually attended academic institutions in the Soviet Union from which they received degrees.[33]

As the 2 percent figure shows, the number of such individuals was limited. Persons who are to be promoted to the rank of general or admiral continue to attend the general staff academy of the Soviet armed forces for two to three years.[34]

The length of study at the military academy in Dresden varies from three to five years depending on the area selected.[35] Individuals attending the academy can earn a diploma in one of three areas: military science, engineering, or social sciences.[36] In addition, selected individuals can remain at the academy to study for a doctorate. Although in the beginning only officers from the army gained admittance to the academy, naval and air force officers soon were added.[37]

The East Germans were unprepared for many of the problems that the establishment of a modern military academy entailed. One was providing qualified instructors. In fact, at the time of its establishment the academy could boast of only one officer who had finished the requirements for the title of professor (promoviert).[38] Only 8 percent of the instructors possessed a diploma.[39] In response, a crash program was initiated to develop better qualified instructors:

> In the course of the following years—along with the training of the officers and the carrying out of further educational plans (or courses, Weiterbildungslehrgängen)— the main task was raising the overall qualifications of the teaching staff (Lehrkörper) and mastering the basic problems of the revolution in military science for the further development of the military academy.[40]

Insofar as this indicator is concerned, these changes had not yet borne fruit. The 2 percent figure from 1957 leads to a classification of low.

The eleventh indicator pertains to the length of time officers are obligated to serve. Period II shows an increase in the required term of service over the preceding period. Well aware of the need for long-term service by officers in order to build up a modern military, the East German authorities quickly lengthened to 10 years the time a commissioned officer is required to serve.[41] In this way, they maximized their training resources. Rather than attempting to impart what education they could to a transient officer corps, they focused on a group of officers with a low rate of attrition. In accord with the schema devised earlier, this indicator signifies a high level of technology.

The twelfth indicator of technology involves the importance assigned to a military specialist's technical qualifications. Although it is difficult to say how important this factor was for an officer's career at this time, the emphasis being placed on upgrading the overall educational level of the officer corps suggests that it was not unimportant. Nevertheless, it appears that technical qualifications were only one of a number of factors considered in determining whether an individual should be promoted or retained. For example, in discussing the need for increased attention to technical qualifications, Heinz Hoffmann complained that too often time-in-grade served as the primary criterion for promotion.42 This situation warrants a classification of low.

The thirteenth indicator of technology deals with the existence of technical awards. The first mention of available technical awards came in 1958 when commanders received authorization to award a specialist's insignia to men serving under them who had distinguished themselves by special competence in a technical area. As one writer put it:

> The commander is given a greater possibility with the introduction of the specialist's insignia (Dienstlaufbahnabzeichnen) to praise the work of the specialist and place greater demands on them in terms of the performance of their duty.43

The awarding of insignia still falls short of the issuance of medals to distinguish an individual as not only competent but among the best in his field. Accordingly, this indicator is classified as low.

The fourteenth indicator deals with the number of occupational branches recognized by the East German military. Although unable to find a statement of the exact number existing at this time, I was able to devise a substitute method of obtaining this information. With the introduction of specialist's insignia, a series listing and picturing the insignia for the various occupational branches appeared in the East German military newspaper. Although no claim of completeness accompanied this presentation, there appears no reason to doubt its comprehensiveness. During this time, 26 occupational specialities were recognized.44 The 26 categories and their American equivalents are:45

1. Truppen Nachrichten Einheiten — troop communications unit
2. Aufklärer — scout
3. Panzer — armor
4. Nachrichten — communications
5. Sanitätsdienst — medical service
6. Kraftfahrer und Traktoristen — driver
7. Funkortung — radio locator
8. Artillerie — artillery
9. Waffen Geschütz und Optikermeister — artillery technical service
10. Feuerwerker — ordnance technician
11. Funk (navy) — radio operator
12. Fernmeldedienst (navy) — communications

13. Motor-mechanik (navy)	mechanic
14. Taucher (navy)	diver
15. Sperrdienst (navy)	net or torpedo defense service
16. Torpedo (navy)	torpedoman
17. Artillerie (navy)	gunner's mate
18. E-technik (navy)	electronics technician
19. Pionier (navy)	engineer
20. Navigation (navy)	navigation
21. Ortung (navy)	position finding
22. Signaldienst (navy)	signal service
23. Fallschirmjäger	paratrooper
24. Musiker	musician
25. Flugzeugmechanik	airplane mechanic
26. Kanoniere der Luftverteidigung	air force gunner

In accordance with the schema devised earlier, 26 occupational categories indicate a medium level of technology.

The fifteenth indicator of technology involves the number of specialized journals printed. Upon the establishment of the NVA, a newspaper directed to all members of the military Die Volksarmee (People's Army) was created. Although this would appear to be an addition over the previous period, it was not; with the inception of Die Volksarmee, the bulk of the material formerly printed in Volkspolizei shifted to the new publication. Volkspolizei was converted to a specialized journal for certain groups under the minister of the interior. Along with Die Volksarmee, a second journal aimed primarily at the individual soldier was founded—Armee Rundschau (Army panorama). Thus, by the end of the first year of this period, two specialized journals existed. The next year brought the first issues of what became the most important journal in the East German military, Militärwesen (Military science). These were the only three journals published during this period, so this indicator still is classified as low.

The sixteenth indicator concerns the number of books published on military subjects. During this period, a total of 65 books were published,[46] a large number of them translations of Soviet military texts. Under the schema established earlier, these books fall within the classification of low.

The last indicator of technology deals with the PS level. This period saw a significant increase in the PS per soldier within the NVA. By the founding of the NVA in 1956, the PS per 100 soldiers had risen to 20 in comparison with 15 PS in Period I.[47] This equipment, however, although superior to that possessed by the KVP, was still comparatively primitive. As one article pointed out:

In 1956, the tanks, which were the backbone (Hauptstosskraft) of the motorized infantry divisions and the tank divisions, were relatively primitive. A high percentage of tanks were combat vehicles of the older design of type T34/76, or they were compensated for by self-propelled guns.[48]

As the same writer pointed out, however, this situation soon changed with the introduction of the T54 in 1957.[49] This equipment and other advanced weapons systems served to raise the PS level to 25.4 by 1958, the last year in this period for which figures appeared.[50] As a result of this increase in PS level, the classification of this indicator changes from low to medium.

In order to obtain an average level of technology for period II, the value assigned each of the indicators was entered on Table 4.1. The small rise in technology during Period II to 1.4 probably would have been more striking if additional figures had been available to provide a more accurate and probably lower measure of the first period.

POLITICAL CONTROL

Of the 15 indicators of political control constructed for this study, 14 were present during Period II. The first, dealing with the organizational level down to which the political officer is present, was discussed by only one source. It specified that political officers were assigned down to the company level.[51] The indicator is classified as indicating a medium level of political control.

The second indicator treats the organizational level down to which a secret police officer is present. According to the two Western sources, one from 1956 and one from 1957, that provide data on this indicator, the SSD is assigned to the same level in Period II as in Period I—the regimental level.[52] As in the preceding period, this indicator is classified as low.

The third indicator, the length of training for political officers, marks the first change of an indicator of political control from Period I. One of the first steps East German officials took upon establishing the NVA was to lengthen the training period required of political officers from two to three years.[53] In fact, the East Germans not only increased the training period to three years but also opened a new school in Berlin-Treptow.[54] In this way, they hoped to raise the quality of political officers. Another reference to the length of political officer training schools appearing the following year, 1957,

TABLE 4.1

Level of Technology in Periods I-II, 1949-59

Indicator	Period I	Period II
1. Entry education	—	1
2. School length	2	3
3. Three-year course	—	1
4. Educational value	1	2
5. Mittlere Reife	1	1
6. Abitur	1	1
7. Fachschulausbildung	—	1
8. Engineers or technicians	—	1
9. Total academic education	—	1
10. Regimental academic education	—	1
11. Length of service	2	3
12. Technical qualifications	—	1
13. Technical awards	—	1
14. Occupational categories	—	2
15. Journals	1	1
16. Books	—	1
17. PS level	1	2
Total	9	24
Average	1.3	1.4

Note: 1 = low; 2 = medium; 3 = high; — = no information.

also says they lasted three years.[55] Since a three-year training period is indicative of a high degree of political control according to the schema outlined above, it is so classified.

The prior military training of political officers provides the fourth indicator of political control. The decision made during the last period to concentrate more heavily on individuals with prior military service as political officer trainees gained strength during this period. For example, Colonel Grunberg, chief of the Political Administration of the NVA, issued instructions stating that "cadres from the best and most active soldiers and NCOs from units are to be selected and sent to the political officer training school."[56] Although it is not possible to say with accuracy how long individuals selected to attend the political officer school had been members of the military, they probably had served an average of one year. Soldiers, for example, might be selected after three to four months of basic training. NCOs, on the other hand, normally have been members of the military for one to two years before reaching that rank. As in Period I, the indicator is classified as medium.

The fifth indicator of political control deals with the activities of the Politorgane. The Political Administration was taken over from the KVP and continued to carry out its control and investigative functions during this period.[57] According to one source, the Politorgane conducted inspections by participating in meetings, but all indications suggest this occurred only periodically.[58]

In 1958 the above-mentioned instructions for political work were introduced in the NVA based on the resolution passed by the Politbüro. The most important aspect of these instructions was the increased responsibility they gave to the Politorgane for political work. According to these instructions, for example:

> The Politorgane are the leading organs of the SED for political work in the NVA. . . .
> The Politorgane are responsible to the Central Committee and the subordinate political organs for its actions as the leading party organ.[59]

One of the most interesting aspects of this instruction is that, despite the talk of increasing the authority of the Politorgane, the investigative activities of the Politorgane appear to have remained limited.[60] For example, Dölling, head of the Political Administration, in an article published a year after introduction of the instructions, disclosed that the Political Administration had carried out only four brigade-level inspections during the preceding year. He states:

> For example, the Political Administration carried out four brigade-level investigations (Brigadeeinsätze) within the period of a year, each of which lasted six to eight weeks, during which was shown how the work should be carried out and how changes could be effected.[61]

The primary change these instructions brought about was the strengthening of the power of the Politorgane over the issuance of directives concerning political work in the NVA. In addition, it gained the authority to supervise political materials utilized in the NVA.[62]

Therefore, important changes occurred in this indicator when compared with the preceding period. In addition to gaining formal authority over all political work within the NVA, the Politorgane assumed a structure very similar to that discussed in Chapter 2. Nevertheless, this structure, although a strengthening of the

Politorgane, was not tightly organized. The reasons for this will become clear in discussion of subsequent periods as the East German Party leadership attempted to improve the situation. In addition, the limited number of investigations in which the Politorgane participated suggests that, although more active than in the preceding period, Politorgane actions appear as much aimed at responding to unfriendly acts by particular units as directed toward preventing unfriendly acts. Consequently, this indicator will be classified as indicating a medium level of political control.

The sixth indicator concerns the activities of the military party organization. Changes in the military party organization occurred in two areas during this period: One was structural and the other dealt with the influence of the military party organization on military-political decisions.

One of the first structural changes involved the establishment of party groups (Parteigruppen). The East German party leadership appears to have decided that the basic organization was not sufficiently effective as a tool for guiding party members. If the commander ignored party activities, it was not surprising that many of his subordinates did also. The basic organization existed down only to the regimental level at this time. Thus, one could avoid <u>close</u> contact with the party. In fact, according to one East German officer writing in 1957, the activities of political workers were often limited to conferences and discussions.[63] In addition, the frequency of party meetings was often low. One writer, for example, pointed out that in 1957 only 50 percent of the required number of party meetings were held by party organizations that did not require approval of party reports (Berichtswahlversammlung).[64] One reason for this failure by the party to reach military specialists operating at lower levels may well have been the tendency of some military commanders to ignore the party, introducing instead the policies they found most desirable.[65]

During this period, party groups were organized down to the company level—and, if necessary, all the way down to the squad level.[66] The primary task of these groups, according to one East German source, was to exert increased influence on non-party members:

> The party group has the task of discussing the policy and resolutions of the party with non-party individuals (Parteilosen) and to constantly and unrelentingly struggle against all appearance of petit bourgeois (kleinbürgerlichen) thoughts and actions as well as against weakness and mistakes in military education and training and the appearance of hostile ideologies.[67]

By expanding its activities down to this level, the party organization, through its secretary,[68] was now able to report on the actions of party members as well as non-party specialists.

One primary concern of the instructions introduced in 1957 on the relationship between the military party organization and the functioning of the military unit was to attempt to overcome the gulf separating regular military officers from participation in party activities. Cooperation was lacking prior to this time. As one East German officer said:

> <u>Up to now</u>, the party organization was seen by the commander in our army as a supportive organization. The leading role and responsibility of the party was recognized everywhere to be sure, good decisions were also reached; however, in practice, it was often different. Each worked for himself; collective cooperation was not always present.[69]

The instructions sought to change this situation by instituting closer consultation between the party—in particular through the party secretary—and the regular military officers.[70]

Political education was to serve as one area for such cooperation.[71] Exactly how much influence the party organization succeeded in exerting is difficult to say. Although apparently it did take on a larger voice in this area, later complaints about its modest role suggest that its powers were limited.

In one area, however, the important area of promotions, the influence of the party organization does appear to have increased at this time. Previously the party, although endowed with formal power over promotions, seldom made use of it. As one author stated, "when the party leadership gave its approval, which was usually the case, it was very often formal."[72]

The 1958 resolution discussed above sought to change this situation. First, it made it very clear that those promoted must be politically reliable and receive the approval of the party organization:

> Only those officers can be sent to qualification courses (Qualifikationslehrgängen) at educational establishments and academies who possess a genuine perspective in the sense of the demands placed on a commander of the people's army of the workers' and peasants' state (Arbeiter- und Bauernmacht) and for which the approval of the respective party organization or party leadership is on hand.[73]

As a result, according to one writer, before an individual could receive consideration for advancement or even gain assignment to a school that might prepare him for advancement, he had to win the approval of the party organization.[74]

In viewing this indicator during period II, the party organization obviously assumed a greater degree of importance than it possessed in period I. The military party organization did participate in some military and political decisions, the most obvious example in this case being the promotion policy. Nevertheless, the power of the party organization was limited, as will become evident in discussion of subsequent periods when the party organization assumed a greater role. In addition, the party organization now extended down to a lower organizational level. Yet during this period the party continued to place emphasis on the setting of examples by party members.[75] Actual control functions—such as forcing members to attend meetings or closely watching all their actions—still were absent. Later periods will show that the party organization was capable of considerable tightening up in this area. As a result, it will be listed here as indicating a medium level of political control.

The seventh indicator of political control measures the percentage of officers who are SED members. At the time of the founding of the NVA in early 1956, 79.5 percent of all officers belonged to the SED.[76] Although this figure amounts to a 5.5 percent increase over the preceding period, the East German leadership still appeared to consider it insufficient. By the end of the year, the percentage had climbed quickly to 86 percent.[77] This figure apparently proved more satisfactory, at least in the short run, for there were no further increases by the close of the following year.[78]

The rise in party membership to 86 percent during this period represented a significant change in comparison with period I. The schema developed above classifies 86 percent as indicating a medium level of political control.

The eighth indicator of political control deals with the importance assigned to the political reliability of officers for promotion or retention in the service. This period marked an important change in the way the party viewed a regular officer.

Up to this point, as Chapter 3 indicated, regular officers were viewed basically as experts in the application of force. Insofar as the political reliability of military specialists was concerned, the party took the approach that those who were not against it were for it. Very little attempt was made to force military officers to become skilled in or engage in political pursuits.

As a result, many officers tended to ignore politics whenever possible. After all, if it was not necessary to engage in such activities, why waste valuable time on what many officers considered irrelevant to their main task?

Shocked by the actions of the Hungarian army in 1956, the party attacked this mentality in 1957 by emphasizing that a military officer is above all a political functionary. As one source put it:

> The essence of the first task is that comrade officers may not only be permitted to be administrators of things or good specialists, but <u>in the first place</u> are political leaders, who are devoted to the party, and must be tempered (gestählte) comrades. The party organization must help bring this about.[79]

The party soon went beyond pronouncements about military officers' political responsibilities. For example, in 1958, accompanying the "Regulations by the Politbüro on the Role of the Party in the NVA," criticism was leveled not only at the general tendency to separate politics from expertise but also at some specific officers who continued to consider themselves primarily military experts, leaving political work to political officers. As one East German officer put it:

> The practice shows, however, that political and military training have been separated from one another, that some comrade officers believe that they are military "specialists" (Fachleute) and that political work, the education of their subordinates, is the task of the political officer. This tendency was strengthened because the party organization exerted so little influence on military training and education.
> In the resolution of the Politbüro, the demand was stated decisively that each officer must, in the first place, be a political functionary who carries out his work on behalf of the party.[80]

The SED leadership adopted two methods of particular interest in its attempt to ensure political activism by regular officers. These methods were work by officers in industry and service by officers as enlisted men.[81] Walter Ulbricht introduced both these policies on the occasion of the opening of the Friedrich Engels Military Academy in Dresden.

In order to give officers a proper appreciation of the socialist basis of their society, the leadership announced that officers who had never participated in the productive process would be afforded the "opportunity" of serving a certain amount of time in industrial or agricultural work.[82] As one source explained, stressing the political basis of this work:

Experience in socialist production is seen as the basis for
a quick further development of socialist consciousness,
class-oriented (klassenmässigen) relations to the soldiers
and NCOs as well as a close tie to the workers' class and
other working people (Werktätigen).[83]

    Work by officers in agriculture or industry was not in itself new.
Indeed, comments appeared on a number of occasions suggesting that
even generals helped in such work.[84] The innovation in this policy
involved removing an individual who had always viewed himself as a
military specialist from his military environment and requiring him
to function for perhaps six months in a factory as a simple workman.
While he worked in this capacity, his superior and the party secretary
at his civilian place of work evaluated his performance. Failure to
show the proper enthusiasm for his tasks, however menial, or for
party activities might mean that the officer would not be allowed to
continue his service as an officer after finishing his productive service.[85]

    The relationship between officers and soliders presents an important problem, Ulbricht announced.[86] What better way was there
to overcome it, he said, than by forcing officers to become familiar
with their men's backgrounds not only by doing industrial or agricultural work but also by serving a term as enlisted men. According to
the details of this plan, "all generals and officers who are physically
able to do so will serve in a unit for a time of at least four weeks a
year as a soldier."[87] Further details of this plan are not available,
and it is not clear to what degree or for how long the leadership implemented this policy. But the important point for this study is that
the plan presented the regular officer with a situation not unlike that
existing under the policy that provided for officers to work in factories
and farms. Not only the officer's military superiors but political ones
as well would observe his actions. As an officer, he might avoid confrontations in which he would be required to defend his political views,
by taking refuge in his rank. But there would be little chance of utilizing rank as a refuge if he were forced to serve as an enlisted man.
Failure to give evidence of a proper understanding of party policy
might result in permanent reassignment to the enlisted ranks.

    One problem the party encountered in its attempt to raise the
level of officer political activity was the commanders' tendency to
avoid providing detailed analysis of the level of their subordinate
officers' political consciousness. Instead, they often preferred to
limit comments on a subordinate's political reliability to a one-sentence statement. According to one source, the following is typical:
"The comrade is class-conscious and faithful to the party and government of the DDR."[88] Such a statement makes impossible any comprehensive evaluation of the individual's political reliability.

Despite the commanders' reluctance to comment in detail on the political reliability of subordinates, there is little question that the importance of political qualifications for promotion or retention increased during this period. Indeed, insofar as this indicator is concerned, political reliability now appears more important than technical competence: The political half of the military dual executive was of primary importance. Because of these developments, this indicator is classified as signifying a high level of political control for Period II.

Responsibility for political education serves as the ninth indicator. At the time the NVA was founded, the policy of separation of political and military activities common during the preceding period still prevailed. In fact, according to some complaints published in Die Voksarmee, regular officers, feeling that political activity interfered with the efficient functioning of their military organization, obstructed party work. As one writer complained:

> At present, a part of our commanders view the party organization as an unneeded attachment (Anhängsel) with the result that in various forms, the orders and regulations in some units obstruct party work.[89]

If the regular officer had been responsible for political activities like political indoctrination, he probably would have opposed them less vehemently.

This situation began to change during 1957. The instructions issued in that year assigned increased importance to the party organization in the political indoctrination of members of the military.[90] The roles of both the regular officer and the party organization were changed. As one East German general commented:

> In the future, the commander himself will have to make better efforts to work together with the political representative and thereby make certain that the complete attention of the party organization is directed toward improving both the political-ideological and moral education as well as the combat readiness of our units.[91]

Changes discussed during 1957 were realized in 1958 with the issuance of the "Instructions for Work in the Party Organization of the SED in the NVA." These instructions made the military specialist— who had always been responsible for the military performance of his unit—officially responsible for its ideological level as well. One writer noted:

> The commander must view ideological work as his very
> own work, he must assign all responsible officers with
> the conduct of particular indoctrination periods (Schulungs-
> stunden) . . . and evaluate the place of each officer with
> respect to political schooling as a measure of his attitude
> toward Party resolutions.[92]

Although the regular officer was given formal responsibility for political indoctrination, this does not mean that others were not involved. Indeed, any failures in this area reflected not only on the military officer but on the political officer as well.[93] For example, the political officer handled the actual lectures himself. He selected the topics and designed the lectures in close consultation with the commander. Thus, blame or praise for the way political indoctrination was handled accrued to both. The gap between the political and technical sides of the military dual executive had lessened. In addition to reducing friction between the military and political sides of the command, this change resulted in greater tolerance for military factors in political lectures and activities. As a result of the change in responsibility for the conduct of political indoctrination, an increase in the level of political control occurred. The indicator is classified as medium in accord with the schema outlined previously.

The tenth indicator of political control concerns the responsibility for Massenarbeit. Commanders became responsible for political Massenarbeit earlier than for political indoctrination.* A directive issued by the Ministry of Defense on September 10, 1956, placed responsibility for the effectiveness of Massenarbeit directly in the commander's hands.[94]

In this case, as in political indoctrination, the commander shared responsibility with the political officer. The commander supervised a staff of political officers detailed to assist him in this area. As one political officer commented:

> Not all commanders are in a position to com-
> petently lead cultural work (Kulturarbeit). For that pur-
> pose, they need the assistance of an expert. The task of
> the cultural functionary (Kulturfunktionäre) is for that

---

*It is of course possible that responsibility for political indoctrination was passed on to the commander earlier than indicated in the preceding discussion. But all appearances suggest that, although it existed on paper, the Einzelleitung or single leadership principle was never strongly enforced in the military in terms of indoctrination until 1958 and in Massenarbeit until 1956.

reason to help the commander to lead the cultural work properly. Each club leader, before he complains about insufficient support on the part of the commander, should check to what degree he himself has assisted the commander in setting up the proper preconditions for leadership (Leitungstätigkeit) in the area of cultural work as well as put forth suggestions for improving the work.95

The result of this change in responsibility for Massenarbeit was much the same insofar as this period is concerned. It meant the regular officer was forced to take into consideration and deal with such political activities as Massenarbeit. As a consequence, it was more difficult for him to ignore political activities if he hoped to make the military a career. And since he was forced to deal in the political area, the chances he would identify himself primarily as an apolitical military technician lessened. The level of political control increased to medium since both the political officer and the regular officer played important roles in this area.

The eleventh indicator of political control present during this period involves the effectiveness of self-criticism (no information was available on part-time ideological indoctrination for Period III). Up to 1958, self-criticism, although present as shown in the first period, existed more in principle than in practice. The introduction of the Politbüro resolution concerning the role of the party in the NVA altered matters. In fact, this resolution focused considerable attention on self-criticism. It stated:

> The party organizations have the right in party meetings to judge critically the results of education and training, the condition of combat readiness and the duty-related activities of all officers as well as to make suggestions for improvement of the work. The basis of the unconditional carrying out of an order is not thereby affected; however, the results of the orders carried out must be examined.96

Although this process became more important from the party's standpoint during this period, available information suggests its promotion enjoyed little success. One writer took note of the problem when he said, "The mass initiative (Masseninitiative) of army members could not be developed quickly enough since criticism and self-criticism in many cases were suppressed by superiors."97

As a consequence, although the foundation for increased self-criticism was laid, effective use of it would have to be left for later periods. So this indicator is again classified as low.

This brings us to the twelfth indicator present during this period, the handling of disciplinary questions. Insofar as disciplinary questions are concerned, Period II represents a continuation of the policy followed during Period I, with minor variations. In 1957 a disciplinary code was adopted in the NVA.[98] Under this code, the military superior decided what punishment, if any, to give individuals who committed infractions against military discipline. The regular officer's authority in disciplinary questions is evident in the following quotation:

> In order to avoid mistakes which continue to occur frequently in the application of disciplinary actions, the respective commander must show the young officers that before they make use of disciplinary measures, they should talk with the individual concerned so that future mistakes can be avoided.[99]

The important factor to note in this quotation is that the military superior decide what punishment, if any, is to be applied. This does not mean the individual involved has no recourse if he feels himself wrongly punished. Indeed, an appeal process existed.[100] But other military authorities rather than the party or civilians would handle such appeals. This is not to suggest that the party did not play a role in disciplinary matters. But its task was more a supporting one to assist the commander than a consultant one. According to one article in the East German military newspaper Volksarmee:

> It is therefore the duty of the party organizations and party groups to fight for the carrying out of the demands and orders of the commander as well as the maintenance of regulations. They must unreservedly support the commander in further strengthening discipline and internal order.[101]

Little change appears to have occurred in the level of this indicator over the preceding period, except perhaps the opening of a military court of appeals. Although the party does play a role by helping the commander ensure discipline, it exerts no perceptible influence on the commander's decision regarding the application of disciplinary measures. For this reason, this indicator once again is classified as signifying a low level of political control.

The thirteenth indicator of political control present in this period deals with the handling of criminal offenses. This period is of particular importance for the development of this indicator. Previously no method existed other than ordinary disciplinary procedures to handle serious crimes against military discipline. As one East German legal expert noted:

Until the expanded criminal law (Strafrechtsergän-
zungsgesetzes) came into force on February 1, 1958, there
was no special military criminal code (Militärstrafbestände) in the Criminal Code of the GDR which protected
combat readiness and military discipline so that punishable acts against basic military behavior could only be
handled in a disciplinary manner.102

This law specified six actions as criminal and punishable in a
court of law: desertion, unauthorized absence, refusal to obey an
order, attack on a superior, misuse of duty or service authority
(Missbrauch der Dienstbefugnisse), and violation of state secrets.103
More important for this study than the establishment of the code was
the provision that these offenses were to be tried in civilian courts.
A "special military court system did not exist in the GDR" at this
time.104 To overcome problems that might arise as a result of the
court's unfamiliarity with special military conditions, it was recom-
mended that the court call on military specialists to explain the
situation.105

Placement of military crimes under the jurisdiction of civilian
courts strongly modified the influence of regular officers on such
proceedings.* A major change in the level of political control followed.
In Period I military authorities exercised complete control over criminal offenses, justifying a classification of low political control.
Removal of responsibility for prosecution of criminal offenses in this
period to civilian courts represented a drastic shift to a high level of
political control as military arguments fell on ears unaccustomed to
the problems of military life.

The last indicator of political control for this period deals with
the time spent on civilian projects. In reading East German publications, one gets the impression that the military devoted a considerable
amount of time to this end. Information appeared for two years during
this period.

In 1958 the NVA consisted of approximately 128,000 men.106
East German sources claim the military devoted a total of 1,050,000
hours to civilian projects that year.107 If one calculates that one man

---

*By criminal offenses, I mean militarily oriented criminal
offenses. Although I found no mention of the treatment of individuals
who commited capital crimes, such as murder, while in the military,
it appears such cases were handled by the civilian courts. This, I submit, is unimportant for the purposes of this study because military
offenses—even capital ones—are far more important to the regular
officer than are ordinary capital crimes.

TABLE 4.2

Level of Political Control in Periods I and II, 1949-59

Indicator	Period I	Period II
1. Political officer level	2	2
2. Secret police level	1	1
3. Training length	2	3
4. Prior service	2	2
5. Politorgane	1	2
6. Military party organization	1	2
7. Party membership	1	2
8. Political reliability	1	3
9. Indoctrination	1	2
10. Massenarbeit	1	2
11. Part-time training	3	—
12. Self-criticism	1	1
13. Discipline	1	1
14. Criminal offenses	1	3
15. Civilian projects	—	1
Total	19	27
Average	1.4	1.9

Note: 1 = low; 2 = medium; 3 = high; — = no information.

puts in approximately 2,000 working hours per year (50 weeks, 40 hours per week), then an army of 128,000 would have a potential of 256,000,000 work hours per year for whatever projects might be assigned them. Dividing the hours devoted to civilian work (1,050,000) by this total (256,000,000), one obtains the percentage of total work time devoted to civilian work for the year. In this case, it equals 0.4 percent—about eight hours per soldier per year, or two-thirds of an hour every month.

Using the same NVA figures for 1959,[108] the following situation emerges: The military devoted 639,214 hours to harvest work and 722,765 to industry, totaling 1,361,979 hours for the year.[109] Again, proceeding from the same premises used for 1958, we divide 256,000,000 (the number of hours available for the military for the year) into 1,361,979 (the number of hours actually devoted to civilian work) and come up with approximately 0.6 percent or twelve hours per soldier per year, or one hour per soldier per month.

In my opinion, there is little question that an average of two-thirds or even one hour per month can be managed with only minor influence on military attitudes. For that reason, it is classified as indicating a low level of political control.

As in the case of military technology, the indicators of political control will be combined to determine the average level for the period under study. This is done by entering the figures assigned to each indicator in Table 4.2. The overall average of political control is 1.9. A discussion of the meaning of this figure as well as that derived for technology follows.

OBSERVATIONS

The levels of technology and political control obtained in this period together with those for Period I are now entered on Figure 4.1.

Despite the fact that the East German authorities greatly expanded their efforts to build a modern military force during this period, the level of technology rose by only 0.1. Much of this can be explained, I think by two factors. First, the nature of the projects undertaken was such that the results would only appear in later periods. This is particularly true of work done in the educational area. New schools were established; the quality of the existing ones improved. Assuming the East Germans continue to emphasize educational factors—and there is no reason to suggest they will not—we should see an increase during the next period in such indicators as the percentage of officers possessing the mittlere Reife, Abitur, Fachschulausbildung, and academic degrees as well as engineers and technicians.

FIGURE 4.1

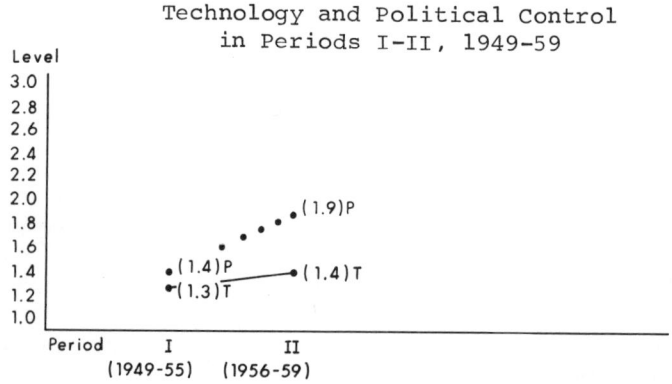

Note: P = political control; T = technology.

The PS level in the NVA also increased during this period. Anticipating the presence of better qualified officers, the Russians and East Germans felt the time was appropriate to begin upgrading their equipment. Thus, although the technical expertise of the military dual executive was far from a reality, the basis for its future development had been laid.

The second factor that slowed technical development was the decision to concentrate on political reliability. This meant that a number of technically qualified, but politically questionable, former members of the Wehrmacht were eliminated. In addition, much of the party's energy was devoted to producing "red" rather than "expert" officers.

The emphasis on political reliability is indicated by the sharp increase in political control while technology remained about the same during this period. Jolted by the Hungarian uprising, the SED leadership acted as though it had decided that technical competence would be forfeited for the sake of political reliability. As a result, an incompetent but politically reliable military would appear preferable to one that is technically competent but politically unreliable. Growing emphasis on political reliability was particularly evident in the increased importance attached to political qualifications and reliability for promotion or retention in the service. "Neutral" officers, although acceptable during Period I, were no longer welcome. The increasing influence of political factors also was evident in such indicators as the activities of the Politorgane and the influence of civilian organs in the handling of criminal offenses. Political control also rose in regard to responsibility for ideological indoctrination and work with the masses as the party began to move in the direction of overcoming the tendency of many regular officers to avoid contact with political work as far as possible.

Although the party appeared to be coming out in favor of the political half of the military dual executive, the final outcome remained uncertain. Despite the Hungarian uprising, the party continued to believe it possible to develop officers who were both politically reliable and technically competent, as Erich Honecker suggested in a 1959 speech:

> Consequently, the task of introducing measures which will place the political and military qualifications of all members of the military on a higher level is now before the Delegate's Conference.[110]

Developments during this period indicate that political control can be increased without sacrificing the maintenance of the prevailing level of technology. This is important insofar as this study is concerned.

It suggests—if substantiated by subsequent periods—that there is not a zero sum relationship between increases in political control and decreases in technology. It is possible to emphasize the political half of the military dual executive while maintaining a particular level of technical competence. Whether this can be done as the technical characteristics of the military increase, and whether it is possible to increase both halves at the same time are questions that only an analysis of subsequent periods can answer.

NOTES

1. One could of course argue that Khrushchev's speech of July 26, 1955, in East Berlin marked the decision by the Soviets to accept the two-state theory. See Hermann Weber, Von der SBZ zur DDR, 1945-1968 (Hanover: Verlag für Literatur und Zeitgeschehen, 1968), p. 101. While the speech laid the groundwork for the establishment of the NVA, the symbolic date of January 18, 1956, is used here for the purposes of this study.

2. Walter Ulbricht, "Der Kampf um den Frieden für den Sieg des Sozialismus, für die nationale Wiedergeburt Deutschlands als friedliebender, demokratischer Staat," Protokoll der Verhandlungen des V. Parteitages der Sozialistischen Einheitspartei Deutschlands (Berlin-Ost: Dietz, 1959), Vol I., p. 149.

3. Changes aimed at increasing political consciousness occurred throughout the country. See Weber, Von der SBZ zur DDR, p. 42; Ernst Richert, Sozialistische Universität (Berlin: Colloquium Verlag, 1967), p. 127.

4. Willi Stoph, "Remarks," Protokoll der Verhandlungen des V, Vol I., p. 446. Two comments are in order with regard to this quote. The first concerns the word Fachmann, which I translate as specialist. In the context in which the East Germans employ this term, it refers primarily to competence in a specialized area of technology, i.e., engineering. A nur-Fachmann is an expert in his own area of specialty but knows nothing about political factors. Second, care must be taken in translating the term Erziehung, or education. What is meant here goes beyond classes and involves political influence in all aspects of life.

5. Instruktion für die Arbeit der Parteiorganisation in der NVA von 5 Mai 1957 und Beschluss des Politbüro über die Rolle der Partei in der Nationalen Volksarmee von 14 January 1958. Despite extensive efforts, both overt and covert, to locate copies of this and subsequent instructions, I was unsuccessful. Nevertheless, as the reader will note, much secondary information that discusses their content is available and is utilized in this study.

6. Kapitän zur See D. Teuber, "Das Offizierkorps der Volksmarine am 10. Jahrestag des Nationalen Volksarmee," Marinewesen, March 1966, p. 369.

7. Karl Greese and Alfred Voerster, "Probleme der Auswahl und Förderung der Offizierskader in der NVA 1958-1963," Zeitschrift für Militärgeschichte, No. 5 (January 1966), p. 39. Indirect citation of "Zweite Durchführungsbestimmung zur Dienstlaufbahnordnung."

8. Generalmajor O. Pech, "Über die Entwicklung und Perspektive des Offizierskorps der Nationalen Volksarmee," Militärwesen, February 1966, p. 200. See also Greese and Voerster, "Probleme der Auswahl und Förderung," p. 38n.

9. Autorenkollektiv des Deutschen Instituts für Militärgeschichte, Zeittafel zur Militärgeschichte der Deutschen Demokratischen Republik, 1949 bis 1968 (Berlin-Ost: Deutscher Militärverlag, 1969), p. 76.

10. Helmut Bohn, et al., Die Aufrüstung in der Sowjetischen Besatzungszone Deutschlands (Bonn: Bundesministerium für Gesamtdeutsche Fragen, 1958), p. 119.

11. Schmidt, "Drei junge Offiziere," Die Volksarmee, No. 146 (December 15, 1959), p. 3.

12. Armeegeneral Heinz Hoffmann, "Die stolze Bilanz unserer Landesverteidigung und einige künftige Aufgaben," Militärwesen, September 1969, p. 1181; Generalmajor O. Pech, "Die ständige Sorge der Partei—und Staatsführung um die Entwicklung sozialistischen Militärkader," Militärwesen, September 1969, p. 1239. Pech also lists the figures for those having one and two years of education as follows: 2 years, 16.3 percent; 1 year, 27.4 percent. This means that over half of the NVA officer corps had less than one year of training at an officer training school.

13. Günther Schulz, "Erziehungs—und Ausbildungsprobleme an den Offiziersschulen der Landstreitkräfte nach der Schaffung der NVA," Zeitschrift für Militärgeschichte, April 1970, p. 447.

14. Armeegeneral Heinz Hoffmann, "Lenins militärisches Erbe und die Landesverteidigung der DDR," in Heinz Hoffman, Sozialistische Landes Verteidigung, Aus Reden und Aufsatzen 1963 bis Februar 1970 (Berlin-Ost: Deutscher Militärverlag, 1971), Vol. II, p. 864.

15. Schulz, "Erziehungs—und Ausbildungsprobleme an den Offiziersschulen der Landstreitkräfte nach der Schaffung der NVA," p. 447.

16. Pi/NVA, "Der Weg zum Offizier," Tribüne, XVIII, 178 (August 4, 1962), 8.

17. Ibid.

18. Heinz Hoffmann, Zur Militärpolitik der SED. Rede Anlässl. eines militärpolitischen Forums von Angehörigen der Universität am 6. April 1966 (Halle-Wittenberg: Martin Luther University, 1966),

p. 15; Heinz Hoffmann, "Zehn Jahre Nationale Volksarmee—Zehn Jahre Schutz des Volkes und Seines Sozialistischen Vaterlands," in Hoffmann, Sozialistische Landes Verteidigung, Vol. I, p. 296; Oberstleutnant Dr. Phil. K. Ilter, "Die Sozialistische Offizierspersönlichkeit: Probleme und Gedanken zum Bild des sozialistischen Offiziers," Militärwesen, November 1967, p. 1546; "Kurz und Knapp," Volksarmee, No. 9 (1969), p. 7.

19. Greese and Voerster, "Probleme der Auswahl und Förderung," p. 43.

20. Ilter, "Die Sozialistische Offizierspersönlichkeit: Probleme und Gedanken zum Bild des sozialistischen Offiziers," p. 1546; Hoffmann, "Zehn Jahre Nationale Volksarmee," p. 296; Hoffmann, Zur Militärpolitik der SED, p. 15.

21. "Kurz und Knapp," Volksarmee, No. 9 (1971), p. 7.

22. Pech, "Die ständige Sorge der Partei- und Staatsführung," p. 1239.

23. Greese und Voerster, "Probleme der Auswahl und Förderung," p. 43.

24. Ilter, "Die Sozialistische Officerspersönlichkeit," p. 1546.

25. Hoffmann, "Zehn Jahre Nationale Volksarmee," p. 297; Konstantin Pritzel, "SED und Nationale Volksarmee," Deutsche Fragen, No. 12 (1966), p. 144, citing Berliner Zeitung, March 1, 1966; "Ein würdiger Auftakt," Volksarmee, No. 29 (1965), p. 2.

26. Handbuch der Deutschen Demokratischen Republik (Berlin-Ost: Staatsverlag, 1963), p. 300.

27. Hoffmann, "Die stolze Bilanz unserer Landesverteidigung," p. 1181; "Kurz und Knapp," Volksarmee, No. 9 (1971), p. 7. In addition, Ilter lists the number as 3 percent, which may simply be a rounding off of 2.6 percent. Ilter, "Die sozialistische Offizierspersönlichkeit," p. 1546. It is also interesting to note that, according to Pech, less than 1 percent (0.2 percent) of all officers had graduated from a university-level military school. Pech, "Über die Entwicklung und Perspektive des Offizierskorps," p. 200.

28. Armeegeneral Heinz Hoffmann, "Zu den Grundfragen der Militärpolitik der Sozialistischen Einheitspartei Deutschlands," Militärwesen, June 1964, p. 782.

29. Konteradmiral W. Nordin, "Einige Erfahrungen aus der Zusammenarbeit zwischen der Fakultät für Seestreitkräfte der Militärakademie 'Friedrich Engels' und dem Kommando sowie dem Verbänden der Volksmarine," Marinewesen, April 1967, p. 397.

30. Walter Ulbricht, "Zur Eröffungen der ersten sozialistischen Militärakademie in der Geschichte Deutschlands," Militärwesen, Sonderheft, February 1959, pp. 45-46.

31. "Richtline über die Arbeit mit den Kadern der Nationale Volksarmee. Anlage Nr. 3; Zur 2. Durchführungsbestimmung zu

den Bestimmungen für die Dienstlaufbahn der Soldaten, Unteroffiziere, und Offiziere der NVA der DDR von 1 Dezember 1959," in Anordnungs— und Mitteilungsblatt des Min. f. N.V., Sonderdruck No. 8 (February 1, 1960), p. 3. As cited in Greese and Voerster, "Probleme der Auswahl und Förderung," p. 41.

32. Pech, "Über die Entwicklung und Perspektive des Offizierskorps," p. 199.

33. Ibid.

34. Ulrich Rühmland, ed., Nationale Volksarmee der SBZ in Stichworten (Bonn: Bonner Druck—und Verlagsgesellschaft, 1969), p. 5.

35. Taschenbuch für Wehrpflichtige (Berlin-Ost: Deutscher Militärverlag, 1965), p. 291.

36. Autorenkollektiv, Zeittafel . . . 1949 bis 1968, p. 187.

37. Generalmajor H. Wiesner, "Zehn Jahre Militärakademie Friedrich Engels—Zehn Jahre erfolgreiche Heranbildung sozialistischer militärischer Hochschulkader," Militärwesen, January 1969, p. 15.

38. Generalleutnant Siegfried Weiss, "Die Bedeutung der Militärakademie Friedrich Engels für die Heranbildung höher und mittlerer Offizierskader der Nationalen Volksarmee," in Militärakademie Friedrich Engels der Nationalen Volksarmee, 1959-1969 (Dresden: Militärakademie Friedrich Engels, 1969), p. 44.

39. "Meldung des M.f.N.V. Armeegeneral Heinz Hoffmann an den Ersten Sekretär des Zentralkomitees der Sozialistischen Einheitspartei Deutschlands und Vorsitzender des Staatsrates der Deutschen Demokratischen Republik, Genosse Walter Ulbricht, anlässlich des Empfangs der Absolventen der Militärakademie am 14. Oktober 1966," Volksarmee (Dok.), No. 40 (1966), p. 16.

40. Wiesner, "Zehn Jahre Militärakademie Friedrich Engels," p. 15.

41. Unsere Nationale Volksarmee (Berlin-Ost: Deutscher Militärverlag, 1964), p. 30. There also were some officers who served for shorter periods. I was unable, however, to find any information on them. Since the vast majority of officers obligated themselves for the full ten years, this problem was not thought serious.

42. Heinz Hoffmann, "Die Arbeit mit den Kadern—ein Hauptanliegen der Führungstätigkeit," in Hoffman, Sozialistische Landes Verteidigung, p. 33.

43. Hauptmann Franke, "Dienstlaufbahnabzeichnen," Die Volksarmee, No. 149 (December 17, 1957), p. 3.

44. Sources for these listings are Die Volksarmee, No. 151 (1957), p. 3, No. 8 (1958), p. 3, No. 33 (1958), p. 13.

45. All translations were made with the assistance of Langenscheidt's Fachwörterbuch Wehrwesen: English-Deutsch, Deutsch-

English (Berlin: Langenscheidts, 1957). Where no direct translation was available, an approximation was made.

46. In 1956, 14; in 1957, 19; in 1959, 28.

47. E. Erhart, "15 Jahre Nationale Volksarmee: Wachsame und Bereit," Volksarmee, No. 9 (1971), p. 8.

48. Oberstleutnant W. Liebert and Major Petzold, "Dem Gegner Keine Chance," Deutscher Motorkalender, 1971 (Berlin-Ost: Deutscher Militärverlag, 1970), pp. 11-12.

49. Ibid.

50. Autorenkollektiv, Zeittafel . . . 1949 bis 1968, p. 193.

51. Major Lins, "Aufgaben der Agitatoren bei taktischen Übungen," Die Volksarmee, No. 4 (1956), p. 4.

52. Heinrich v. zur Mühlen, "Die Überwachung der 'Nationalen Volksarmee' der DDR," SBZ-Archiv, VII, 16 (1965), p. 248, Heinz Godau, Verführter, Verführer, Ich war Politoffizier der NVA, (Cologne: Markus Verlag, 1965) p. 112.

53. Autorenkollektiv, Zeittafel . . . 1949 bis 1968, p. 70.

54. Ibid.

55. Offizier Zimmermann, "Zur Vorbereitung des Exams," Die Volksarmee, No. 112 (1957), p. 3.

56. Autorenkollektiv, Zeittafel . . . 1949 bis 1968, p. 90.

57. Ibid., p. 63.

58. Major Wuttke, "Aus den Erfahrungen einer Inspektion," Die Volksarmee, No. 18 (1956) p. 2.

59. "Bestimmungen für die Arbeit der Politorgane der Nationalen Volksarmee von 17 Juni 1958," printed in Bohn, Die Aufrüstung in der Sowjetischen Besatzungszone Deutschlands, p. 24.

60. For a detailed listing of the functions of the Politorgane with respect to the 1958 instructions, see ibid., pp. 25-26.

61. Generalmajor Dölling, "Die SED—Kraftquelle aller Erfolge," Die Volksarmee, No. 38 (1959), p. 5.

62. See Bohn, Die Aufrüstung in der Sowjetischen Besatzungszone Deutschlands, pp. 25-26 for a list that covers other areas as well.

63. Britsche, "Die Instruktionen unserer Partei mit politischen Leben erfüllen," Die Volksarmee, No. 82 (1957), p. 2.

64. M.B., "Es ist noch viel aufzuholen," Die Volksarmee, No. 37 (1957), p. 2.

65. "Wo stehen wir?" Die Volksarmee, No. 4 (1956), p. 1.

66. Oberstleutnant Mücke, "Die Parteiarbeit in Kompanien hat entscheidende Bedeutung," Die Volksarmee, No. 29 (1958), p. 2; Autorenkollektiv, Zeittafel . . . 1949 bis 1968, p. 89.

67. Oberst Helbig, "Die Arbeit der Parteigruppen ist noch nicht überall klar," Die Volksarmee, No. 15 (1957), p. 2.

68. According to East German sources, this secretary was to be elected by his fellow party members. Karl Greese and Günter

Schulz, "Zur Entwicklung der Gefechtsbereitschaft der Verbände der Landstreitkräfte im Jahre 1957," in Für den zuverlässigen Schutz der DDR (Berlin-Ost: Deutscher Militärverlag, 1969), p. 80. Although nothing was mentioned with regard to the operation of a nomenklatura principle in the selection of the secretary, it was operative in every other similar area. Hence, it would seem safe to suggest that it was operative here. As a result, one might suggest that only individuals ready to carry out party directions to the party's satisfaction would be elected.

69. Werner Schneidereit, "Zur militärischen Erfolgen nur unter Führung der Partei," Die Volksarmee, No. 87 (1957), p. 2 (emphasis added).

70. Zettler, "Einheitliche politische und militärische Führung setzt hohes Klassenbewusstsein voraus," Die Volksarmee, No. 80 (1957), p. 2.

71. "Voran die Mitglieder der Partei," Die Volksarmee, No. 80 (1957), p. 3. See also Admiral Waldemar Verner, "Zur führenden Rolle der SED beim Aufbau und bei der Entwicklung der Nationalen Volksarmee," Zeitschrift für Militärgeschichte, April 1969, p. 400.

72. Walter Borning, "Unter Führung der Partei erringen wir Erfolge," Die Volksarmee, No. 73 (1958), p. 2.

73. Helmut Mücke, "Den richtigen Genossen an den richtigen Platz," Die Volksarmee, No. 44 (1958), p. 2. See also Verner, "Zur führenden Rolle der SED," p. 400.

74. Hauptmann Vinz, "Standhefte und mutige Kämpfer für den Sozialismus erziehen," Die Volksarmee, No. 32 (1958), p. 2.; Verner, "Zur führenden Rolle der SED," p. 400.

75. Zettler, "Einheitliche politische und militärische Führung" p. 2.

76. Pech, "Über die Entwicklung und Perspektive des Offizierskorps," p. 197.

77. Hoffmann, "Zehn Jahre Nationale Volksarmee," p. 295.

78. Günther Glaser, "Die Initiative der Zentralen Komitee der SED in Mai und Juni 1957 zur Festigung der Einzelleitung in der NVA," Zeitschrift für Militärgeschichte, March 1968, p. 303. See also Greese and Voerster, "Probleme der Auswahl und Förderung," p. 34.

79. Ünter Führung der Partei zu neuen Erfolgen," Die Volksarmee, No. 131 (1957), p. 2. (emphasis added). See also "Sieben Fragen—Sieben Antworten," Die Volksarmee, No. 79 (1957), p. 2, for an even stronger statement about the need for the party to increase its influence over technical areas.

80. Borning, "Ünter Führung der Partei," p. 1. See also Hermann Matern, "Die Führung der Nationalen Volksarmee durch die SED—die Quelle ihrer Kraft und Stärke," Militarwesen, February 1958, p. 202; Autorenkollektiv, Zeittafel ... 1949 bis 1968, p. 102;

Generalmajor Dölling, "Die SED—Kraftquell aller Erfolge," Die Volksarmee, No. 38 (1959), p. 3; Oberst E. Helbig, "Zur Arbeit der Parteiorganisationen bei der sozialistischen Erziehung in der Nationalen Volksarmee," Militärwesen, January 1959, pp. 25, 31; Toni Nelles, "Der Aufbau und die Entwicklung der NVA—Schöpferische Anwendung des Leninischen Militärprograms durch die SED (I)," Zeitschrift für Militärgeschichte, No. 9 (January 1970), p. 31.

 81. Generalmajor E. Munschke, "Sozialistische Klassenbeziehungen—Quelle der Kampfkraft der Nationalen Volksarmee," Militärwesen, April 1959, p. 484. The increased role of political factors in promotion was discussed under indicator six, the role of the party organization.

 82. Autorenkollektiv, Zeittafel . . . 1949 bis 1968, p. 113. See also Ulbricht, "Zur Eröffnung der ersten sozialistischen Militärakademie," p. 41, Dölling, "Die SED—Kraftquell aller Erfolge," p. 6. This practice differs from that included under indicator fifteen in that it was a special policy designed for a certain group of officers and presumably would not be repeated after they had served their time.

 83. Autorenkollektiv, Zeittafel . . . 1949 bis 1968, p. 113. This policy of forcing individuals to work in the productive process was not limited to the military. Richert notes, for example, that according to a regulation issued in 1957, all individuals who sought Habilitation (a professorship) had to have at least one year of practical experience. See Ernst Richert, Sozialistische Universität (Berlin: Colloquium Verlag, 1967), p. 184.

 84. See for example, Die Volksarmee, No. 21 (1957), p. 2, and No. 22 (1957), p. 1.

 85. One question that remains unanswered is how long this process was utilized. Mention of officers who were participating in it was made as late as 1960. See Oberleutnant Göpner, "Drei Monate in der Produktion," Die Volksarmee, No. 63 (1960), p. 3. Personally, I do not think it continued beyond this point. All new officers who entered the service through the officer training schools would have spent a year in the productive process as part of their polytechnic education. Thus, once those in the service who lacked such a background were sent to factories and farms, there would be no reason to send others.

 86. Walter Ulbricht, "Zur Eröffnung der ersten sozialistischen Militärakademie in der Geschichte Deutschlands," Militärwesen, Sonderheft, February 1959, p. 42.

 87. "Produktionsarbeit für Funktionäre; Mannschaftsdienst für Offiziere," Neues Deutschland, January 20, 1959. See also "Marschrichtung; Basis," Die Volksarmee, No. 11 (1959), p. 2.; Dölling, "Die SED—Kraftquell aller Erfolge," p. 6.

 88. Bahnik und Bachmeier, "Der Genosse ist Klassenbewusst," Die Volksarmee, No. 144 (1958), p. 2.

89. Dressel, "Die ideologische Erziehung verstärken," Die Volksarmee, No. 3 (1956), p. 2. See also "Wo stehen Wir?" Die Volksarmee, No. 1 (1956), p. 1.

90. Zettler, "Einheitliche politische und militärische Führung," p. 2. See also W.S., "Parteiorganization—führende Kraft im Politunterricht," Die Volksarmee, No. 105 (1957), p. 4.

91. Oberst Poppe, "Es gibt bei uns viele Erziehungsmöglichkeiten," Die Volksarmee, No. 83 (1957), p. 2.

92. Major Schleicher, "Hohere Niveau, erziererisch wirksam," Die Volksarmee, No. 141 (1959), p. 5.

93. Generaloberst Willi Stoph, "Der Offizier—ein überzeugten Sozialist und ausgezeichneter Militärspecialist," Die Volksarmee, No. 90 (1959), p. 4.

94. Autorenkollektiv, Zeittafel . . . 1949 bis 1968, p. 75. See also Autorenkollektiv, "Zur Fragen der militärpolitischen Propaganda," Militärwesen, June 1959, p. 831.

95. Hauptmann Vollmering, "Kommanduer und Kulturarbeit," Die Volksarmee, No. 55 (1959), p. 6. Kulturarbeit or cultural work is used synonymously with Massenarbeit.

96. Beschluss des Politbüro "Über die Rolle der Partei in der NVA," as quoted in "Kritik und Selbstkritik erhöht die Kampffähigkeit unserer Volksarmee," Die Volksarmee, No. 33 (1958), p. 1.

97. Generalmajor W. Borning, "Die Nationale Volksarmee erfüllt ihre geschichtliche Aufgabe, weil sie von der Partei der Arbeiterklasse geführt wird," Militärwesen, December 1965, p. 1640. For other complaints in this area see, "Das neue fördern—Aufgabe der Parteiorganisation," Die Volksarmee, No. 107 (1958), p. 4; Borning, "Ünter Führung der Partei erringen wir Erfolge," p. 2. "Kritik und Selbstkritik—eine bewährte und wirksame Waffen," Die Volksarmee, No. 65 (1958), p. 2; Erich Honecker, "Remarks," Protokoll des V. Parteitages, p. 729.

98. "Diziplinar—und Beschwerdeordnung stärkt die Kampfkraft," Die Volksarmee, No. 119 (1957), p. 2, Autorenkollektiv, Zeittafel . . . 1949 bis 1968, p. 92.

99. Leutnant Sterz, "Junge Offiziere brauchen Unterstützung," Die Volksarmee, No. 126 (1957), p. 2.

100. Oberleutnant Hochsam, "Zur neuen Disziplinar—und Beschwerderordnung, Die Volksarmee, No. 129 (1957), p. 2.

101. "Nach der Vorschrift Leben und Handeln," Die Volksarmee, No. 43 (1958), p. 3.

102. Alfred Hartmann, Die Abgabe von Straftaten an den Kommandeur (Berlin-Ost: Deutscher Militärverlag, 1968), pp. 22-23.

103. Copies of this law are available in Gesetzblatt der Deutschen Demokratischen Republik (Berlin-Ost: VEB-Deutscher Zentralverlag, 1957) I, No. 78 (December 1957), pp. 643-47.

104. A. Schille, "Die Bedeutung der Strafrechtsnormen über die Verbrechen gegen militärische Disziplin," Neue Justiz (1958), p. 154.

105. R. Spank and B. Hillmann, "Einige Probleme der Verbrechen gegen die militärische Disziplin," Neue Justiz (1959), p. 581.

106. Thomas A. Forster, NVA—Armee der Sowjetzone (Cologne: Markus Verlag, 1966-67), p. 36. This figure is from 1957.

107. Jahrbuch der Deutschen Demokratischen Republik, 1959 (Berlin-Ost: Verlag die Wirtschaft, 1959), p. 88.

108. Forster, NVA—Armee der Sowjetzone, p. 36. This figure is from 1957.

109. Die Nationale Volksarmee der Deutschen Demokratischen Republik (Dokumentation) (Berlin-Ost: Deutscher Militärverlag, 1961), p. 14.

110. Erich Honecker, "Wende in der sozialistischen Erziehungsarbeit herbeiführen," in Erich Honecker, ed., Zuverlässiger Schutz des Sozialismus (Berlin-Ost: Deutscher Militärverlag, 1972), p. 12.

CHAPTER

5

THE PERIOD OF THE TECHNICIAN: 1960-63

Laying a foundation is one thing; building a modern highly technical military force on it is another. Fully aware of this problem, the East German leadership set to work constructing a viable military force. Success in this endeavor would require major advances in areas associated with technology.

But awareness of the need to increase the technological level of both civilian and military sectors was tempered by the realization that such changes involved considerable planning—planning that, in the eyes of East German authorities, would work only if they had a stable population base. Such was not the case, and would not be the case, as long as individuals could leave the GDR via West Berlin. Soldiers and civilians alike—particularly those with technical skills—often defected for more lucrative positions in the West.

The building of the Berlin Wall in 1961 virtually eliminated this problem. Serious work on raising the country's technological level could now begin.[1]

The drive to increase the technological level of the East German political system reached its peak in 1963 at the Sixth Party Conference with the introduction of the "New Economic System." The idea of scientific management served as the system's heart.[2] But scientific management requires individuals competent to deal with problems scientifically. So strong emphasis was placed on developing highly educated cadres throughout society. Walter Ulbricht stated; "I think that today one can say that the hour of the young specialists (Facharbeiter) and engineers has already found an important place."[3]

The same situation existed in the military. Although considerable effort had been expended during the preceding period to lay the foundation of a modern military, much remained to be done. Above all, the technical competence of NVA officers would have to be raised.

Erich Honecker took note of this need in a 1961 speech to party activists:

> As the course of our discussion shows, there appears to be general agreement at the meeting of party activists that the present level of scientific-technical qualifications is completely unsatisfactory. For that reason, with the aid of the party organization, it is time to direct all efforts toward overcoming the present loss of tempo (Tempoverlust) in this area in the shortest amount of time possible.[4]

During the preceding period, the political half of the military dual executive played a predominant role. Honecker's statement suggests that technical qualifications were to receive primary emphasis during this period.

Officially, however, the party maintained that both aspects of the military dual executive deserved equal attention. Walter Ulbricht stated at the Sixth Party Conference:

> It is the task of our party and its organization in the army to strengthen educational work (Erziehungsarbeit). It should provide:
> 1. That every combatant of the armed forces is filled with loyalty to his worker and peasant state, to the German Democratic Republic. . . . The most important thing is to maintain the close tie between members of the armed forces and the people (Volk) as well as the understanding by soldiers and officers for the problems of raising the all-encompassing socialist construction. This requires at the same time a struggle against dogmatism and revisionism.
> 2. It should provide that each soldier masters modern technology. Good knowledge of mathematics and the technical sciences make it possible for him to master modern technology and tactics.[5]

Viewed from the perspective of the basic proposition advanced in the introduction to this study, it would appear that such a marriage between technology and political control is highly unlikely. Emphasis on technology, it was suggested, can only be achieved if political control is sacrificed. Thus, if this proposition is correct, in the course of this period we should expect to see political control decrease as technology is emphasized.

MILITARY TECHNOLOGY

Of the 17 indicators of technology developed for this study, 16 were present during this period. The first indicator involves the educational level required for entrance into officer training schools.

One of the best ways to raise the intellectual level of the officer corps is to raise the standards required of those entering officer training schools. The East German authorities accomplished this in 1962 with the issuance of a new set of service instructions (Dienstlaufbahnordnung). According to these instructions, an individual who wishes to attend an officer training school must possess at least the mittlere Reife, or tenth-class certificate.[6] Thus, the requirements for entry into officer training schools were raised. In accord with the schema devised earlier, this represents a medium level of technology.

The second indicator of technology deals with the length of officer training schools. No change in length occurred during this period. But there was one alteration that, although only of peripheral interest for this indicator, affected overall development of the officer schools: In 1963 the officer training schools were consolidated into four schools. Previously, each branch of the service had its own officer training schools. In the navy, for example, there were three officer training schools: deck, intelligence, and engineering.[7] In 1963 all were combined into one officer training school for naval cadets, the Karl Liebknecht Officer School. (The other schools established were the Ernst Thälmann officer school for the army, the Franz Mehring officer school for the air force, and the Rosa Luxemburg officer training school for border troops.) But there was no change over the previous periods in the time required for commissioning, which continued to be three to four years.[8]

The third indicator of technology present in Period III treats the percentage of officers who had attended a three-year officer training school. The changes made during Period II in lengthening training for all officer cadets to at least three years failed to effect significant change in this indicator. Of all officers, 23.5 percent had attended three-year officer training schools during Period II, and the figure had increased only to 26.8 percent by 1961, the only figure available for Period III.[9] As a result, the level of technology is once again categorized as low.

The fourth indicator of technology, the value of an officer's education when compared with that provided by civilian institutions, also remained the same. But the status of the officer training schools as technical schools did receive further clarification during Period III. For example, the 1962 service order (Dienstlaufbahnordnung) mentioned earlier, stated, "the officer schools of the National People's

Army are military technical schools (Fachschulen) of the German Democratic Republic."[10] Thus, officer schools remained technical schools on a par with other technical schools in the GDR.

But important changes did occur. In 1963, for example, a plan was introduced whereby each officer cadet, in addition to his military training, was trained for a civilian occupation while attending officer training school. Upon graduation, he received not only his commission and certificate of technical competence in military science but also a certificate attesting to his qualifications in a civilian occupational category: "For example, all infantry, tank, and a part of the artillery officers receive the qualification certificate of a senior teacher (Oberstufelehrer) for technical subjects." In this way, the authorities hoped to facilitate the movement of military officers into civilian occupations upon completion of their service. According to the conditions outlined above for this indicator, however, there was no change during this period, so it will again be classified as indicating a medium level of technology.

The fifth indicator of technology concerns the percentage of military officers possessing the mittlere Reife as their highest level of education. The increased emphasis placed on educational qualifications in the NVA officer corps began to bear fruit in this period. In 1958, the last Period II figure available, the percentage of officers possessing the mittlere Reife was listed as 12 percent. By 1962, the only date for which a figure is available during Period III, the figure had risen to 36 percent.[11] Since the number indicates a medium level of technology, the classification of this indicator rises one step.

The sixth indicator of technology treats the percentage of officers possessing the Abitur. Progress in this area also occurred during Period III, although the percentage increase was not as great as for the mittlere Reife.* From 13 percent in 1958, the Abitur figure rose to 19.5 percent in 1962,[12] indicating a medium level of technology.

The seventh indicator involves the percentage of officers who were engineers or technicians (there was no information available on the percentage of officers who had attended a technical school for this period). Since any advanced military unit needs trained engineers and technicians, it is not surprising that effort was exerted in this area. It quickly produced results as the percentage of officers who were engineers or technicians doubled—from 5 percent in Period II to 10 percent in Period III.[13] Since 10 percent indicates a medium level

---

*One must not forget that the Abitur requires two more years of school than the mittlere Reife. In addition, those possessing the Abitur are eligible to attend college or university and the military must compete for them with civilian universities.

of technology, this indicator also rose one level over the preceding period.

The percentage of officers possessing a university-level education serves as the eighth indicator in this period. Although the military made great efforts in this area as well, the task was formidable and the percentage of officers possessing an advanced education increased by only 3.4 percent, for a total of 6 percent.[14] Although 3.4 percent may not seem to be much of an increase, one must remember that, in order for an officer to attain an academic degree, he must be released from active duty for three or four years to attend a special school. The cost in manpower and resources is considerable. Still, the increase in this indicator was not sufficient to warrant reclassification over the preceding period, remaining at a low level.

The ninth indicator present during this period records the percentage of army regimental commanders with an academic education. Of all the indicators for this period, few showed more dramatic change. In 1958 the Friedrich Engels Military Academy opened in Dresden, as mentioned in Chapter 4. Its impact can be illustrated as follows: In 1960, before the first class graduated from the academy, only 8 percent of all regimental commanders had an academic degree.[15] On September 28, 1962, the first class graduated, and by the following year, the percentage of army regimental commanders who had graduated from an academic institution had increased to 80 percent.[16] The seeds sown in Period II had borne fruit in a relatively short time. Educational problems might continue to exist in many segments of the military, but at least the regimental commanders now had a well educated leadership on which the party could rely in building the NVA into a modern force.

The significant change in this indicator in comparison with Period II raises it from a classification of low to high.

The tenth indicator of technology deals with the length of time officers are obligated to serve. This indicator remained unchanged. In the 1962 service instructions (Dienstlaufbahnordnung), for example, the following statement appears:

> (1) Officers remain in active military service until reaching the age limit of this position (Dienststellung) while serving with troops or the fleet, or alternatively until reaching the age limit in a position not involving service with troops or the fleet, in the main, however, at least ten years.[17]

It should be noted that the time served by an officer cadet—three or four years—does not count toward this ten-year service period.[18]

Since the obligated period of service did not change, the classification for the indicator remains high, as during Period II.

The eleventh indicator involves the importance of technical qualifications. As mentioned, apprehension mounted over the technical competence of NVA officers during this period. One NVA officer, a technical specialist, wrote in 1960:

> In relation to political and military knowledge, knowledge in the area of military technology on the part of a large number of officers, who do not perform special technical tasks in the army, is not sufficient in light of constantly increasing demands.[19]

This concern for an increase in the technical competence of officers continued through the next year and did not stop with those officers who dealt primarily with technical equipment. Indeed, it is for this reason that the following quotation is important. The author, a formal political officer and minister of the Interior, awarded competence in military technology a higher priority than political consciousness when he remarked:

> The best technology and the highest consciousness are however practically useless if the soldiers and officers do not understand how to operate the weapons and equipment, to skillfully and properly use them, to regularly and carefully attend to them and to take care of them, and show respect for them. Weapons and equipment can only be effective on the combat field if their use or operational possibilities are broadly known and one is able to make use of technology from all sides.[20]

Tension continued to build up until in 1963 Heinz Hoffmann, head of the NVA, launched the movement toward change with a rather strong attack on the promotion of officers on the basis of time in service rather than technical qualifications.* Such a practice, he said, was a thing of the past[21] and those who failed to qualify would not be promoted: "It is seen as basic that an officer, regardless of how long he holds a particular rank, can only be promoted to the next higher

---

*Hoffmann was appointed minister of National Defense on July 14, 1960, succeeding Willi Stoph, who left the military. He was promoted to general of the army (Armeegeneral), the highest rank in the NVA, on February 1, 1961.

rank when he has shown the necessary competence and theoretical qualifications."22

Those who did not qualify would not be promoted and, if that did not inspire them to meet the appropriate standards, they would remain on active duty in their present rank, and upon reaching the mandatory retirement age for that rank, be placed in the reserves. To determine whether or not an officer qualified for a position, Hoffmann called for a testing system whereby all officers, "must pass an intermediate examination (Zwischeprüfung) at least twice a year."23

As mentioned earlier, the drive for better qualified officers was not limited to those performing highly technical work. All officers had to become technically qualified if the goal of a modern military was to be realized. Again, according to Hoffmann:

> Military-technical qualification (Militärtechnische Qualifizierung) in my view does not mean only the further training of military technical cadres. It is concerned with systematically raising the military-technical knowledge of all commanders and officers, because combat (Gefechtshandlungen) is today above all the employment of men and modern technology for the achievement of victory on the field of combat. For that reason, the practical officer (Truppenpratiker) lacking all-around military-technical training no longer suffices today. Modern war demands well trained military-technical line officers.24

Toward the end of this period, on December 1, 1963, the military announced the adoption of a long-range policy aimed at improving the "scientific-technical qualifications" of officers.25 The details of this plan are discussed in Chapter 6.

Thus, in the short period of four years, the importance of technical competence for a military officer had changed from one among many factors to an absolute requirement for retention or promotion. This does not mean that political factors ceased to play a role. Indeed, as Hoffmann himself pointed out and as will be discussed later in this chapter, the party still sought to develop a military dual executive, both technically and politically qualified.26 Nevertheless, since technical competence did become a prerequisite for promotion or retention, this indicator rises to a level of high.

The twelfth indicator, the existence of technical awards, also increased. In addition to the insignia discussed in Chapter 4, a classification badge (Klassifizierungsabzeichen) was introduced.27 It identified three levels of expertise or classes. The higher the class—I, II, or III—the more difficult the examination and the higher the competence represented by the award. Five categories of this award existed: one for officers in the navy with seaman-technical qualifications, one for pilots, one for engineer-technical personnel, one for tank drivers, and one for all other individuals with special qualifications (Einheitliches Klassifizierungsabzeichen). Individuals possessing these medals (which must to be re-earned each year) receive extra privileges. Thus, the East German leadership again recognized the importance of technical incentives in its drive to develop a modern military force. Since the award of medals corresponds to a medium level of technology, this indicator is raised one level from Period II.

The next indicator of technology deals with the number of occupational categories recognized by the military. Although no mention was made of this indicator at all during Period III, I believe it is possible to evaluate it. It is highly unlikely that enough new categories would have been introduced during this time to raise this indicator another level (eight would be necessary), without some mention in the press to inform NVA members of the change. In light of the increase in recognized occupational groups in the next period, it is also unlikely that a decrease occurred. Accordingly, this indicator is classified the same as during the last period—medium.

The fifteenth indicator designed for this study treats the number of specialized journals. In keeping with the increased importance of technical qualifications, this indicator changed significantly.

In the first year of the period, two new journals appeared, Gefechtsausbildung (Combat training) and Militärtechnik (Military technology). Two more journals began publication the next year, Zeitschrift fur Militärgeschichte (Journal for military history) and Rückwärtige Dienst (Supply service). The last addition during this period occurred in 1962 with the introduction of Marinewesen (Naval science). Thus the number of periodicals jumped from three in Period II to eight in Period III, indicating a change from a rating of low to high.

The number of books published on military subjects, the sixteenth indicator, also evidenced an increase in the level of technology. The number of books printed on military topics went from 65 in Period II to 89 in Period III. In accord with the schema constructed above, this signifies a medium level of technology.

The final indicator of technology present during this period deals with the PS level. Although no citation specifying the PS level appeared during this period, classification still is possible. The degree to which technically complex equipment was utilized in the NVA continued to rise, leading in 1961 to the establishment of a committee under the Ministry of National Defense that concerned itself with possible military uses for the latest developments in the civilian world. The committee also concentrated on suggestions for scientific-technical research to be undertaken.[28]

Because a special commission had to be set up to deal with technical questions, and since there was no suggestion that the PS level decreased, it seems safe to assume that it continued to rise. The PS level was 15 in Period I and 25.4 in Period II. Assuming that the PS level continued to rise slowly, it might be assumed to have reached about 27 in Period III. Thus, it would still be indicative of a medium level of technology.

To obtain an average level of technology for this period, the scores were entered in Table 5.1. The level of military technology during Period III thus made a dramatic jump to 2.2. The corresponding response of political control should be particularly interesting.

POLITICAL CONTROL

Data for all of the 15 indicators of political control designed for this study were present during Period III. The first indicator concerns the organizational level down to which the political officer is present. Unlike most indicators, this one remained unchanged. According to the East German duty regulations (Innendienstvorschrift) of 1963, a political officer (deputy for political work) existed at the company level and was responsible to the commander for all political activities.[29] Whether or not the political officer occupied this position at the beginning of Period III is difficult to say. According to one normally authoritative East German writer:

> The company chiefs have a special responsibility, since they directly lead and organize the political education of the soldiers and NCOs and do not have a deputy for political work at their side.[30]

Although it is not clear what conditions prompted this statement, it does seem safe to suggest that by the end of the period the political officer was present down to the company level, as the regulations cited above state. This indicator is therefore listed as indicating a medium level of political control.

The second indicator of political control focuses on the organizational level down to which the SSD liaison officer is assigned. Two sources, both Western, agreed on the allocation of these officers. As one remarked:

> The liaison staffs at the division level are composed of three to five and in the corps by five to seven officers of the Ministry of State Security, while two liaison officers are, as a rule, allotted to the regiments. One liaison officer is attached to independent units of battalion strength.[31]

TABLE 5.1

Level of Technology in Periods I-III, 1949-63

Indicator	Period I	Period II	Period III
1. Entry education	—	1	2
2. School length	2	3	3
3. Three-year course	—	1	1
4. Educational value	1	2	2
5. Mittlere Reife	1	1	2
6. Abitur	1	1	2
7. Fachschulausbildung	—	1	—
8. Engineers or technicians	—	1	2
9. Total academic education	—	1	1
10. Regimental academic education	—	1	3
11. Length of service	2	3	3
12. Technical qualifications	—	1	3
13. Technical awards	—	1	2
14. Occupational categories	—	2	2
15. Journals	1	1	3
16. Books	—	1	2
17. PS Level	1	2	2
Total	9	24	35
Average	1.3	1.4	2.2

Note: 1 = low; 2 = medium; 3 = high; — = no information.

Since this indicator did not change with regard to the preceding period, it receives the same low classification.

The third indicator of political control concerns the length of time devoted to training a political officer. Major changes did occur in this indicator. At the beginning of Period III the political officer school lasted three years, as in the preceding period.[32] Although it devoted part of its curriculum to familiarizing students with military procedures, the political officer school was unable to impart the necessary military expertise to its cadets during this three-year period. Faced with the overriding need to increase the technical expertise of its officer corps, and in response to numerous complaints from regular officers who resented interference by political officers who knew little or nothing about the operation of a military unit, the SED decided to close down the school.[33] This was accomplished in 1961. As a result, individuals wishing to become political officers had two options. They could attend the regular officer school, but emphasize political studies. Or, once they were commissioned as regular officers, they could be selected for special political courses or take correspondence and short-term courses and then serve as political officers.[34] Regardless of the course selected, the goal remained the same: to produce a political officer who not only understood party dogma but also possessed a basic understanding of the technical environment in which he was to operate.

The closing of this school greatly shortened the political officers' specialized training in political subjects. It also produced individuals who could be expected to have greater empathy with the problems faced by regular officers. It is not possible to say with certainty how much purely political instruction they received, but it would appear logical to suggest that it would total a year at most under the former system. Although the individual might specialize in political subjects at an officer school, he was still required to pass the same military subjects as other students. These conditions correspond to a classification of low in the schema developed above.

The fourth indicator of political control deals with the prior military service of political officers. The change in the training of political officers discussed above affected this indicator as well. Now, instead of individuals fresh from civilian life or soldiers who had served no more than a year, political officers were selected from graduates of the officer training schools or commissioned officers with several years of experience.[35]

As a result, the classification of this indicator rose to high. Regardless of which route the individual followed, he would have been a member of the military for more than 18 months before becoming a political officer. An officer candidate studying at an officer training school would have three years in a military environment behind him before becoming a political officer, and the officer who decided to become a political officer would have spent even more time in a military environment.

The fifth indicator of political control deals with the degree of activism on the part of the Politorgane. One of the first changes affecting the Politorgane during this period was structural. In 1961 the Political Administration (Politische Verwaltung) became the Main Political Administration (Politische Hauptverwaltung or PHV).[36] In addition, the political sections on the command (Kommand) and district (Militärbezirk) levels were upgraded to political administrations. This change, according to East German sources, made it possible for the Politorgane to "guarantee a more complex, effective means of political leadership."[37]

These political administrations not only were superior to their predecessors in prestige but also were larger and had more authority (their size subsequently remained about the same).[38]

The party acted to strengthen the role of the Politorgane by building upon the above-mentioned structural changes in the 1963 "Instructions for the Work of the Party Organization of the SED in the National Peoples' Army and for the Politorgane of the National Peoples' Army."

As one East German political officer explained:

> What is new in this instruction? It fixes exactly the responsibility of the Politorgane for the work of the party organization which is on a higher level. This corresponds to the party structure, whereby the Politorgane, which as is known, organizes the work of the party organization in its area so that all political and military tasks will be fulfilled with the highest efficiency.[39]

The Politorgane was to concentrate its efforts primarily on the basic organization, a unit that was to play an increased role in the lives of party members in the military. The party organization was to be responsible for the effectiveness of the program.[40] All of this was to be accomplished primarily by increasing the control functions of the Politorgane. This increase in control functions was closely associated with an improvement of the effectiveness of the monthly meetings.[41] Controlling these meetings meant more than just seeing that they were held and all members attended.* The Politorgane bore responsibility for helping to prepare the meeting, for participating in it, and for evaluating it.[42] The Politorgane also coordinated political activities by the military unit with other party and party-related organizations like the local party units, the mass organizations, pre-military training (Wehrerziehung), work with reservists, the Society for Sport and Technology, and comradely cooperation with other socialist armed forces.[43]

A final important change that occurred during this period preceded the issuance of the above-mentioned instructions by seven months and involved the creation of ideological commissions (Ideologische Kommissionen).[44] These units were established at the

---

*The word control (Kontrollieren) means more than superior authority. As the East Germans use it, it means carefully analyzing the action of a unit and then comparing it and its members' performance with an agreed standard.

following levels: in the Main Political Administration, the political administrations of the military districts, the major military units (Teilstreitkräfte), the City Command of Berlin, and the political sections of the major units (Verbände). They were responsible in particular for seeing to it that the effectiveness of ideological work was maintained at a high level.

Both the creation of the Main Political Administration and the establishment of the ideological commissions strengthened the structure of the Politorgane. In addition, the Politorgane relied increasingly on preventive maintenance, going out to the military units and attempting to locate areas that would present problems before problems actually developed. Still, it would be difficult to justify reclassification of this indicator to a high level. Although the structure is tighter than in Period III, room for improvement remained, as developments in subsequent periods will demonstrate. In addition, based on later statements by East German sources, there were a number of cases in which the Politorgane responded rather than acting in advance to prevent difficulties. Although the foundation was laid for a much stronger form of control, the reality of this period warranted a continued classification of medium.

The sixth indicator of political control concerns the activities of the military party organization. The most important change here was the increased importance attached to the basic organization. The decision to place increased reliance on the basic organization appears to have been reached at the Fourteenth Meeting (Tagung) of the Central Committee in 1962.[45] According to this meeting the basic organization was the "main cell of the party." In addition, the membership meeting of the basic organization was considered the most important forum of the basic organization.[46]

The importance of the basic organization in the military was reemphasized at the Sixth Party Conference in Berlin at the beginning of 1963. As Admiral Verner put it, "in preparation for the party conference, the knowledge that the role and responsibility of the basic organization of the party should be increased became even clearer."[47]

The instructions issued in November 1963 also took cognizance of the increased importance of this organization. As one writer put it, "in order to make the leading role of the party and the example of its members a reality, party work must be activated first of all in the basic organization."[48]

One structural change during this period occurred in March 1962 and reflected the increased importance attached to the basic organization. This change, introduced by the Secretariat of the SED Central Committee, called for basic organizations to be established down to the level of battalions and independent companies.[49]

Although details are lacking on the specific areas in which the basic organization exerted increased influence, it does not appear that any major changes occurred, at least in terms of its influence over military-political decision-making. If anything, one gets the impression that the basic organization concerned itself more with ideological indoctrination and the evaluation of party members than with questions of a more technical nature. As a result of the increased importance placed on the membership meeting, the individual party member came under increased surveillance by the party organization during this period. But I do not believe these changes are significant enough to warrant reclassification of this indicator. The party member needed only to be particularly on his guard at party meetings, and since they occurred only at the regimental level—except in the special case of the independent companies—it may well have been possible for him to avoid expressing an opinion or to carefully prepare what he said. In addition, these party meetings occurred only once a month, not an unbearable frequency for subjecting attitudes to public criticism. For this reason, this indicator is again classified as indicating a medium level of political control.

The seventh indicator treats the percentage of officers who are party members. This period marks an important change as the percentage of officers belonging to the party increased significantly. During Period II, 86 percent of all officers belonged to the SED; by 1963 the percentage had increased to 96.3 percent.[50] As a result, the level of political control rose to high.

The eighth indicator of political control deals with the importance assigned to officers' political reliability. Concern with an officer's political reliability in determining whether or not to promote or retain him continued to play an important role during this period. No officer considered politically unqualified—or technically unqualified—could be promoted or retained. This emphasis on political qualifications manifested itself, for example, in the introduction of special courses complete with examinations that all officers were required to take. Prior to this time, such courses were voluntary.[51] Primary emphasis during this period may have shifted to increasing the technological level of the NVA but, at least in the case of this indicator, this was not to be accomplished at the cost of political control. As a result of the continued importance placed on political qualifications, this indicator is once again listed as high.

The ninth indicator of political control concerns responsibility for political indoctrination. This indicator remained at the same level as at the close of Period III. Although the regular officer continued to bear responsibility for the effects of political indoctrination, he shared this responsibility with the political officer, who actually carried out political indoctrination.[52] But this does not mean that only the political officer and the military commander were involved in the indoctrination process. The collective or other selected party members also played an important role, as Heinz Hoffmann pointed out:

> They (the regulations) give the commander new means to make the single leadership principle (Einzelleitung) even more effective. This is above all true in the measures of collective education which were laid down. Education with the help of the collective does not stand in contradiction to the principle of single leadership. On the contrary, they serve in the first place to educate all subordinates to the consequent fulfillment of the orders of the commander.[53]

For this indicator, the situation is very similar to that in the preceding period. The military officer participated in the indoctrination process but, due to the loose organizational structure of the Politorgane in its relations with the party organization, a lack of enthusiasm on the part of the regular officer might never be reported. One might suggest that, with the basic organization present all the way down to the battalion level, more actions would be observed. This is certainly true, but as will become evident in Chapter 6, the coordination between these two groups left much to be desired.

Under these conditions, the military officer was able to participate in political indoctrination sessions without fearing that a lack of total commitment would be reported. On the other hand, the political officer worked closely with him to ensure that political factors occupied an important place. Responsibility and participation in the political indoctrination process still was shared. The indicator is classified as indicating a medium level of political control.

With regard to the tenth indicator of political control, responsibility for work with the masses, the East German leadership decided to attempt to overcome the lethargy that characterized Massenarbeit at this time. It placed increased emphasis on shared responsibility for the program. Thus failure to improve would result in adverse reports for both the regular and political officers involved.[54]

Nevertheless, regular officers continued to resist involvement in activities, such as work with the masses, that they felt had little to do with the functioning of a modern military. Work with the masses was unnecessary, according to some officers, not only because it took time away from more important "military" tasks but also because they felt relations between superiors and subordinates were decided by the hierarchical command structure, not on the basis of comradeship. Men perform well on the field of battle, they believed, not so much because they are convinced of the justice of their cause but primarily because they are ordered into battle by a superior.[55] An example is provided by a political officer's complaint about the failure of military officers to recognize the need for work with the masses as a defense against Western propaganda:

> The opinion is often expressed that this problem could be solved with general political information or even by an order. In this way, however, the dangerous and refined influence of the enemy is not overcome. It is necessary to mobilize the entire power of the collective and of consciously thinking and acting comrades, to develop the revolutionary watchfulness in order to make all immune to the ideological poison.[56]

Therefore, despite party efforts, very little appears to have changed from the preceding period. Both the political and military officers continued to share responsibility. The fact that the military officer tended to ignore the program, or at least did not use it as much as the party desired, suggests that, although his participation was important, it remained limited. Individual involvement in work with the masses varied. Consequently, this indicator is again classified as indicating a medium level of political control.

The eleventh indicator deals with part-time ideological indoctrination. As mentioned above in discussing the eighth indicator, increased pressure for military specialists to improve their political qualifications accompanied requirements that they qualify technically, and in 1963 a course of study with examinations was made a requirement for all officers. It was called "Additional Education in the Social Sciences" (Gesellschaftswissenschaftliche Weiterbildung). This program lasted four years and was devoted to a study of the basics of Marxism-Leninism. Those passing the test at the end of the course received a certificate corresponding to that awarded by a district (Bezirk) party school.[57] Although it is not possible to state with accuracy what happened during Period III to officers who did not pass the examinations given every six months, it is important to note that every officer was required to take these tests and the results were promptly recorded in his service record.

The introduction of this system of political education meant an increase in the time devoted to part-time ideological subjects. Officers not only were required to spend two hours a week in classes but also had to devote time outside class to studying and preparing for them.[58] Because of the increased demands on the officer's time, demands that easily exceeded three hours per week, the level of political control signified by this indicator is again classified as high.

The twelfth indicator involves the effectiveness of self-criticism. Although the enforcement of this policy remained a problem, it was less a problem than in Period II. Military officers at least stopped suppressing criticism. Instead, they more often ignored it:

> For example, the criticism was made at a Border Company meeting that signal equipment was not always combat ready, although this had been known for some time . . . that shows that some suggestions and ideas presented by young comrades in the company are not always taken seriously nor put into action.[59]

Thus, although resistance continued, it was no longer active resistance. This meant that individual soldiers would not be afraid of retaliation from their commanders, and that regular officers were forced to go along with the process, at least formally. In accord with the schema designed for this study, this indicator is classified as medium.

The handling of disciplinary questions is the thirteenth indicator of political control. The East Germans issued a new disciplinary code (DV 10/6) during this period. These regulations made two basic points: First, they authorized the commander to decide personally how to handle disciplinary offenses, and second, they called on him to rely increasingly on the party collective. The idea behind these new regulations was to replace summary punishment by the commander with reeducation by the collective. As one source remarked:

> A superior can, when he sees these educational measures as purposeful and effective, now decide in accordance with paragraph 36, dealing with military collectives, to let it be handled by the military collective.[60]

But although these regulations put increased reliance on the military collective, and despite the fact that the individual soldier had the right to appeal disciplinary actions by his superior,[61] the regular officer remained in charge. He alone decided whether to discipline an individual. He also decided whether to make use of the collective. According to later complaints, mentioned in the discussion of period IV (see Chapter 6), most regular officers chose to ignore the "assistance" of the collectives. For this reason, the indicator will again be classified as low. In the areas where it counted—the decision of what measures to use—nothing had changed.

Period III marked an important alteration in the fourteenth indicator—the handling of criminal offenses. This occurred under the authority of a new military court system set up in 1963

(Militärgerichtsordnung).62 This 1963 law set up two levels of military courts placed under the Supreme Court of the GDR—the military supreme court (Militärobergericht) and, under it, the military courts (Militärgerichte). Thus military courts were established leading all the way up to the highest East German court, the Supreme Court of the GDR.

The military supreme court handles serious crimes and all offenses committed by individuals with the rank of major or above (paragraph 23). The military courts deal with less serious crimes and offenses committed by individuals of lesser rank (paragraph 27). In addition, the 1963 law provided for the establishment of a special section in the Ministry of Justice with responsibility for "political, professional and military qualifications of the judges of the two types of military courts" (paragraph 5).

Members of these courts were of two types, military judges (Militärrichter) and military jurors (Militärschöffen). All individuals appointed to either of these positions were to be members of the NVA (paragraph 6). Military judges, from all appearances, are officers of the NVA Legal Service (Justizdienst) especially trained for this duty, which they carry out for a period of four years. In addition, they are elected or appointed by various state organs, depending on the court on which they serve (paragraph 10).

The military jurors are elected by the soldiers themselves. But this does not mean that all members of the military are eligible for election as military jurors. A list is drawn up by the commander, in agreement with party organizations (gesellschaftliche Organisationen), from which the required number of jurors are elected for a period of two years.63 In the selection of individuals to serve as jurors, careful consideration is given to political reliability. One writer remarked:

> The military juror must offer the guarantee that he is
> unconditionally committed to the victory of socialism
> in the German Democratic Republic, that he is faithful
> to the workers' and peasants' state, that he lives
> according to the laws of socialist morals and ethics,
> and fulfills his military tasks in a superior manner.64

Court decisions are arrived at by majority. Judges or jurors not in agreement with the court's decision are authorized to write a dissenting opinion.65

Insofar as this indicator is concerned, the new regulations mark a change in the level of political control from the preceding period. Although offenses were handled completely by civilian authorities in the preceding period and restored to the hands of the military during this period, this does not mean that the political authorities were

TABLE 5.2

Level of Political Control in Periods I-III, 1949-63

Indicator	Period I	Period II	Period III
1. Political officer level	2	2	2
2. Secret police level	1	1	1
3. Training length	2	3	1
4. Prior service	2	2	3
5. Politorgane	1	2	2
6. Military party organization	1	2	2
7. Party membership	1	2	3
8. Political reliability	1	3	3
9. Indoctrination	1	2	2
10. Massenarbeit	1	2	2
11. Part-time training	3	—	3
12. Self-criticism	1	1	2
13. Discipline	1	1	1
14. Criminal offenses	1	3	3
15. Civilian projects	—	1	1
Total	19	27	31
Average	1.4	1.9	2.0

Note: 1 = low; 2 = medium; 3 = high; — = no information.

without influence. As should be obvious from the discussion above, political authorities determine who is eligible to serve on the courts. Furthermore, those elected can be recalled if they do not serve in accord with the highest ideals of socialism (paragraphs 13, 17).

The degree of military participation certainly increased when compared with Period II. Military officers are able to express their opinions with regard to the guilt or innocence of individuals brought before the court. But party presence curtails freedom of expression in this regard. Any attempt to present opinions at variance with those of the party might well result in the individual's removal from the court and, in some cases, disciplinary action.

Thus, military participation in criminal proceedings increased. Nevertheless, an individual hoping to avoid party influence in the disciplinary process would be disappointed since his behavior in this area is carefully monitored by the appropriate party organs. As a consequence, this indicator is again classified as indicating a high level of political control.

FIGURE 5.1

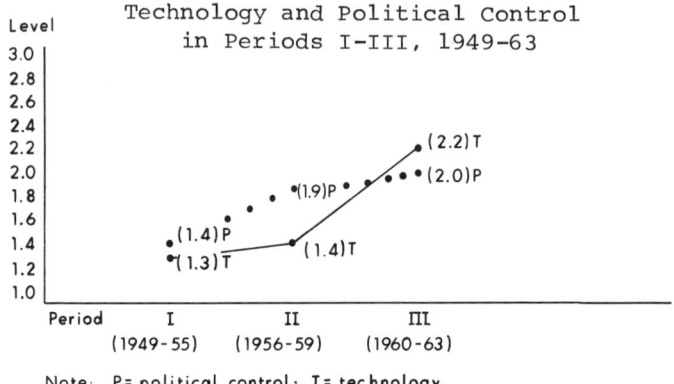

Note: P = political control; T = technology.

The last indicator considers part-time civilian work. Figures are available for only one year during this period—1960. At that time, the NVA totaled 190,000 men.[66] A total of 3,278,623 hours of civilian work was performed by members of the NVA.[67] Thus, assuming the availability of 380 million hours for duty during the year (190,000 multiplied by 2,000 hours per man) one obtains a figure of 1 percent for the percentage of total time devoted to civilian work projects. This translates into twenty hours per soldier per year, or one and two-thirds hours per month. This does not represent a particularly large amount of time, and is therefore classified as low.

In order to obtain the average level of political control for this period, the scores for each indicator are entered in Table 5.2. The average level of political control comes to 2.0. A discussion of the meaning of this figure as well as that derived from technology follows.

OBSERVATIONS

The findings for Period III are of major importance for the principal proposition advanced in this study. Period III is the first period in which technology increased significantly as shown in Figure 5.1.

According to Figure 5.1, political control leveled off in Period III, remaining roughly the same as in Period II, while technical development increased sharply. The technical orchard so carefully planted in Period II began to bear fruit. This is particularly true for those indicators dealing with overall educational level. Entrance requirements to the officer training schools, the percentage of officers with the mittlere Reife, Abitur, technical training, and engineering background all increased by one level, while the academic background of regimental level commanders jumped by two steps. The educational qualifications of the NVA officer corps had come a long way from the days of 1956. But it still had a long way to go before the NVA officers would be qualified to handle the most modern weapons.

The number of books and journals, particularly journals, also rose during Period III as the NVA sought to provide its burgeoning force of technicians with further avenues to increase their understanding of modern military technology.

In addition to expanding its instructional and printing facilities, the SED leadership also sought to motivate its officers to improve their qualifications by giving out technical awards on the one hand and raising the importance of technical qualifications for promotion or retention in the service on the other.

Interestingly, the PS level remained roughly the same during this period. Since modern equipment requires knowledgeable technicians to service it, the party leadership apparently decided that acquisition of the most modern weapons systems would have to wait a supply of properly trained personnel.

In view of the need to expand the technological basis of its armed forces, despite public statements to the contrary, the SED decided to forego any attempts to increase the level of politicization in the NVA at this time. Neutral but noncommited officers had been eliminated during Period II. As a consequence, the SED decided to maintain the same overall level of political control while expanding the technological base.

Despite the overall tendency for political control to remain the same, emphasis on technology did bring significant changes. One of the most important was the decision to close the political officer school. Faced with the need to establish a good relationship between regular military officers and the party, the SED leadership quickly recognized that continued use of nontechnical political officers was working against that goal. Thus, the level of political control decreased insofar as this indicator is concerned. Although one could expect that this decision would affect the party's influence in the short run—since political officers would not be as well grounded in Marxism-Leninism as in the past—it is interesting to speculate on the impact of this change on the party's long-run goal of developing dual executives. Instead of relying on graduates from political officer schools, the party decided to use individuals with prior military service. So it is possible that over time the regular officers will gain increased respect from their political colleagues who, unlike their predecessors, have an appreciation of military problems.

The SED leadership also planned for the future by following a strategy similar to that utilized in Period II to build the foundation for the significant increases in technology that occurred during Period III. In particular, they modified a number of policies to set the stage for future increases on the political side of the military dual executive. For example, new measures were introduced for the handling of disciplinary matters, part-time ideological training, activities by the military party organization, and the level down to which the Politorgane is present. These measures could be utilized as vehicles for significantly tightening up political control if the need should arise.

According to the proposition put forth at the beginning of this study, political control should have decreased during Period III. In fact, however, it remained the same. It is too early to tell whether the East Germans will be successful in their goal of creating a military dual executive. As pointed out earlier, the classification system devised for this study supplies only an approximation of either technology or political control. Consequently, one should not read too much into the change in the level of political control from 1.9 to 2.0. It is possible that political control has begun to decrease but the change has not yet been picked up on the classification system. In any case, despite the base the party has laid for a future increase in political control, the overall level of political control should drop during Period IV if the hypothesized relationship between technology and political control is accurate.

NOTES

1. Stefan Doernberg, Kurze Geschichte der DDR (Berlin-Ost: Dietz Verlag, 1969), pp. 465-71. This is the official East German history of the GDR.
2. Jean Edward Smith, Germany Beyond the Wall: People, Politics . . . and Prosperity (Boston: Little, Brown, 1969), p. 98.
3. Walter Ulbricht, "Das Programm des Sozialismus und die geschichtliche Aufgabe der Sozialistischen Einheitspartei Deutschlands," in Protokoll der Verhandlungen des VI. Parteitages der Sozialistischen Einheitspartei Deutschlands (Berlin-Ost: Dietz Verlag, 1963), Vol. I, p. 207. To understand the importance of the emphasis he placed on the need for highly trained individuals, it is interesting to note that in another part of his speech to the Sixth Party Conference, Ulbricht called for a high educational level on the part of party members: "The important thing is that the leading party workers are at the same time good specialists (Fachleute)." Ibid., p. 233.
4. Erich Honecker, "Für die allseitige Stärkung unserer Republik," in Erich Honecker, ed., Zuverlässiger Schutz des Sozialismus (Berlin-Ost: Deutscher Militärverlag, 1972), p. 56.
5. Ulbricht, "Das Programm des Sozialismus," p. 185. See also "Bericht des Zentralkomitees an den VI. Parteitag des Sozialistischen

Einheitspartei Deutschlands," in Protokoll der Verhandlungen des VI., Vol. IV, p. 82.

6. "Erlass des Staatsrates der Deutschen Demokratischen Republik über den Aktiven Wehrdienst in der Nationalen Volksarmee (Dienstlaufbahnordnung) vom 24. Januar 1962," in Gesetzblatt der Deutschen Demokratischen Republik (Berlin-Ost: VEB-Deutscher Zentralverlag, 1962), I, 1 (January 25, 1962), p. 10. See also Generalmajor O. Pech, "Über die Entwicklung und Perspektive des Offizierskorps der Nationalen Voksarmee," Militärwesen, February 1966, p. 200; Armeegeneral Heinz Hoffmann, "Remarks," in Protokoll der Verhandlungen des VI., Vol. II, p. 46.

7. Kapitän zur See F. Notroff, "Die Offiziersschule der Volksmarine 'Karl Liebknecht' ist die Kaderschmiede unserer Flotte," Marinewesen, March 1966, p. 336.

8. Neugebauer, Muller, and Häntzschel, Militärwesen, July 1963, p. 1062.

9. Karl Greese and Alfred Voerster, "Probleme der Auswahl und Förderung der Offizierskader in der NVA (1958-1963)," Zeitschrift für Militärgeschichte, January 1966, p. 39.

10. Gesetzblatt der DDR, I, 1 (January 25, 1962), p. 11.

11. The number 36 is a computation made by the author. According to one source, the percentage of those having the mittlere Reife tripled in the years 1958-62. By multiplying the figure for 1958 (12 percent) by 3, one would obtain 36 percent for 1962. See Greese and Voerster, "Probleme der Auswahl und Förderung," p. 43.

12. The same process of calculation was used for the figure of 19.5 percent as in the previous indicator. Percentage with Abitur increased 1.5 percent over 1958. Therefore 13 x 1.5 = 19.5. Ibid., p. 43.

13. Fregatten Kapitän H. Kubasch, "Zweite Kadertagung der Nationalen Volksarmee," Militärwesen, July 1966, p. 1037. Autorenkollektiv des Deutschen Instituts für Militärgeschichte, Zeittafel zur Militärgeschichte der Deutschen Demokratischen Republik, 1949 bis 1968 (Berlin-Ost: Deutscher Militärverlag, 1969), p. 46.

14. Armeegeneral Heinz Hoffmann, "Menschenführung als Grundproblem wissenschaftlicher Truppenführung," in Heinz Hoffmann, Sozialistische Landes Verteidigung: Aus Reden und Aufsätzen 1963 bis Februar 1970 (Berlin-Ost: Deutscher Militärverlag, 1971), Vol. I, p. 383.

15. Pech, "Über die Entwicklung und Perspektive des Offizierskorps," p. 200.

16. Hoffmann, "Die Arbeit mit den Kadern," p. 24; Armeegeneral Heinz Hoffmann, "Wir schützen zuverlässig Vaterland, Frieden, Sozialismus!", 1 Volksarmee, No. 4 (1963), p. 1.

17. Gesetzblatt der DDR, I, 1 (January 25, 1962), p. 11.

18. Ibid., p. 11, paragraph 38.
19. Oberstleutnant (Ing.) H. Raulein, "Zur Verbesserung der militärtechnischen Bildung in der Nationalen Volksarmee," Militärwesen, June 1960, p. 1049.
20. Generalmajor F. Dickel, "Die Notwendigkeit einer allseitigen, wissenschaftlich-technischen Qualifizierung des Offizierskorps der Nationalen Volksarmee," Militärwesen, July 1961, p. 868. See also p. 870.
21. Armeegeneral Heinz Hoffmann, "Antwort auf sechs Fragen," Volksarmee, No. 23 (1963), p. 9.
22. Hoffman, "Die Arbeit mit den Kadern," in Hoffmann Sozialistische Landes Verteidigung, Vol. I, p. 33. See also Hoffmann, "Antwort auf sechs Fragen," p. 5.
23. Ibid., p. 9. This also was mentioned in his speech: Hoffmann, "Die Arbeit mit den Kadern," in Hoffmann, Sozialistische Landes Verteidigung, Vol. I, p. 31.
24. Armeegeneral Heinz Hoffmann, "Wie erreichen wir in der Armee den wissenschaftlich-technischen Höchstand?" Militärwesen, February 1963, p. 173.
25. Autorenkollektiv, Zeittafel . . . 1949 bis 1968, p. 211.
26. Hoffmann, "Antwort auf sechs Fragen," p. 9.
27. Oberstleutnant Erich Vetter, "Warum wurden Klassifizierungsabzeichen in der NVA eingeführt," Junge Welt, XIX, 42 (February 18, 1965), 4.
28. Autorenkollektiv, Zeittafel . . . 1949 bis 1968, p. 173.
29. Innendienstvorschrift der Nationalen Volksarmee (DV 10/3) (Berlin-Ost: Deutscher Militärverlag, 1963), p. 118. For a detailed listing of his duties see pp. 118-121.
30. Oberst E. Helbig, "Die Einheit von politischer und militärischer Führung verwirklichen," Militärwesen, March 1962, p. 340.
31. Helmut Bohn, ed., Die Aufrüstung in der Sowjetischen Besatzungszone Deutschlands (Bonn: Bonner Berichte aus Mittel u. Ostdeutschland, 1960), p. 41. See also Der Staatssicherheitsdienst: Ein Instrument der Politischen Verfolgung in der Sowjetischen Besatzungszone Deutschlands (Bonn: Bundesministerium für Gesamtdeutsche Fragen, 1962), pp. 27-28.
32. Thomas A. Forster, NVA—Die Armee der Sowjetzone (Cologne: Markus Verlag, 1964), p. 194.
33. Thomas A. Forster, NVA—Die Armee der Sowjetzone (Cologne: Markus Verlag, 1966-67), p. 91.
34. Forster, NVA—Die Armee der Sowjetzone (1966-67), p. 91. See also Greese and Voerster, "Probleme der Auswahl und Förderung," p. 42.
35. E. Landgraf, "Vielseitige Offiziersausbildung," Tribüne, No. 266 (November 15, 1962), p. 4. See also Forster, NVA—Die Armee

der Sowjetzone (1966-67), p. 91; Greese and Voerster, "Probleme der Auswahl und Förderung," p. 42.

36. Autorenkollektiv, Zeittafel . . . 1949 bis 1962, p. 171.

37. Gerhard Lux and Toni Nelles, "Der Aufbau und die Entwicklung der NVA—schöpferische Anwendung des Leninischen Militärprograms durch die SED (II)," Zeitschrift für Militärgeschichte, June 1970, p. 665.

38. Lux and Nelles, "Der Aufbau and die Entwicklung der NVA," p. 665.

39. Oberst Helbig, "Zur neuen Instruktion," Volksarmee, No. 51 (1963), p. 2. See also Admiral W. Verner, "Für die weitere Stärkung der führenden Rolle der Partei in der Nationalen Volksarmee," Militärwesen, February 1964, p. 166.

40. Oberst Helbig, "Über die Aufgaben der neugewählten Parteileitungen der Grundorganisationen," Militärwesen, May 1962, pp. 656-57. This article preceded the introduction of these instructions, but since the author is a high-ranking political officer, and since the article discusses new measures to be taken, it would appear that the author had the instructions in mind when he wrote it.

41. Ibid., p. 657.

42. Helbig, "Über die Aufgaben der neugewählten Parteileitungen," p. 657. See also Autorenkollektiv, Zeittafel . . . 1949 bis 1968, p. 209.

43. By other armed forces of the GDR, the author refers primarily to the militia. Oberstleutnant H. Franke, "Über einige Aufgaben der Truppenteile bei der sozialistischen Wehrerziehung in der Öffentlichkeit," Militärwesen, September 1964, p. 1222n.

44. Autorenkollektiv, Zeittafel . . . 1949 bis 1972, p. 202.

45. Oberstleutnant Mehnert and Major Briess, "Grosseres Augenmerk den Parteiaktivisten," Volksarmee, No. 7 (1962), p. 3.

46. Ibid.

47. Admiral Verner, "Diskussionsbeitrag an den VI. Parteitag der SED," Protokoll der Verhandlungen des VI. Parteitages, Vol. III, pp. 545ff; Generalmajor Günter Teller, "In der Führungstätigkeit der Politorgane und Parteiorganisationen wirksamer werden," Der Parteiarbeiter, December 1967, p. 2.

48. Helbig, "Über die Aufgaben der neugewählten Parteileitungen," p. 656.

49. Autorenkollektiv, Zeittafel . . . 1949 bis 1968, p. 178.

50. Oberst E. Helbig, "Sozialistische Offiziere erziehen," Militärwesen, November 1963, p. 1603; Autorenkollektiv, Zeittafel . . . 1949 bis 1968, p. 193; Hoffmann, "Die Arbeit mit der Kädern," (Militärwesen) p. 965. Hoffmann lists the figure as 97 percent.

51. Forster, NVA—Die Armee der Sowjetzone, (1966-67), p. 162.

52. Major H. Jäkel, "Die neuen Grundsaztvorschriften," Militärwesen, June 1963, p. 846; Generaloberst Heinz Hoffmann, "Für die volle Durchsetzung der Einzelleitung in der Nationalen Volksarmee," Militärwesen, January 1961, p. 10.

53. Hoffmann, "Die Arbeit mit den Kadern," p. 26, Militärwesen, p. 26.

54. Innendienstvorschrift der Nationalen Volksarmee, p. 31. This document makes it very clear that responsibility is shared. For a statement of the problems present at this time see Honecker, "Für die allseitige Stärkung unserer Republik," p. 58.

55. Ibid., p. 64.

56. Kapitänleutnant G. Braune, "Die Wachsamkeit—eine wichtige Bedingung für die Erhöhung der Einsatz—und Gefechtsbereitschaft der Volksmarine," Marinewesen, June 1963, p. 646. See also Beck, "Erfahrungen, die gelesen werden sollten," Die Volksarmee, No. 69 (1960), p. 3; Konteradmiral H. Neukrichen, "Aufbauend auf den Erreichten zu neuen Erfolgen im Ausbildungsjahr 1962/1963," Marinewesen, January 1963, p. 7.

57. Oberstleutnant M. Mähler und Major H. Richter, "Methodische Hinweise für die Abschlussprüfung in der gessellschaftswissenschaftlichen Weiterbildung der Offiziere," Militärwesen, (June 1966), p. 861.

58. Major P. Sechaus and Hauptmann A. Bendrat, "Der Platz des gesellschaftswissenschaftlichen Selbststudium im Prozess der Ausbildung junger Offiziere," Militärwesen, September 1965, p. 1246.

59. Oberstleutnant D. Stöhr, "Jugendkommunique und unserer militärisches Auftrag," Militärwesen, December 1963, p. 1767.

60. H. Jäckel, "Die neuen Grundsatzvorschriften," Militärwesen, June 1963, p. 846. See also Oberstleutnant S. Schirrmann, "Zum Problem der kollektiven Erziehung," Militärwesen, December 1966, p. 1704.

61. Handbuch für Mot.-Schützen (Berlin-Ost: Deutscher Militärverlag, 1963), p. 61.

62. "Erlass des Staatsrates der Deutschen Demokratischen Republik über die Stellung und die Aufgaben der Gerichte für Militärstrafsachen, (Militärgerichtsordnugn) von 4 April 1963," in Gesetzblatt der Deutschen Demokratischen Republik (Berlin-Ost: VEB-Deutscher Zentralverlag, 1963), I, 4 (April 25, 1963), pp. 71-75.

63. G. Sarge, "Die sozialistische Militärgerichtsbarkeit in der DDR," Neue Justiz (1963), p. 365.

64. Dr. Hilde Benjamin, Minister der Justiz, "Zu den zweiten Militärschoffenwahlen," Militärwesen, March 1965, p. 309.

65. Leitfaden für Militärschöffen (Berlin-Ost: Ministerium der Justiz, 1967), p. 14.

66. Forster, NVA—Die Armee der Sowjetzone, (1966-67), p. 37. Figures from the London Institute of Strategic Studies are not broken down for this year. Hence, the larger West German figure was used. See Institute for Strategic Studies, The Communist Bloc and the Western Alliance (London: Institute for Strategic Studies, 1962), p. 7.

67. Jahrbuch der Deutschen Demokratischen Republik, 1961 (Berlin-Ost: Verlag die Wirtschaft, 1961), p. 88.

CHAPTER

6

THE PERIOD OF CONSOLIDATION: 1964-67

If Period III can be characterized as the period of the technician, Period IV deserves the title of the period of consolidation. Important strides had been made during the preceding period in the technical development of the GDR, particularly as a result of the introduction of the New Economic System. By 1964 the East German leadership had as a major goal securing these gains as well as furthering advancement through increased all-around use of technology. As Walter Ulbricht remarked at the Seventh Party Conference:

> We will only be able to create the material basis of production (Produktionsgrundlage) ourselves if we master the scientific technical revolution. That requires, above all, making the economic system of socialism effective as a whole, and especially bringing about an essentially higher quality of work, one more rational and socially effective than ever before in all areas of the economy and social life.[1]

Concern with the mounting role of technology was not limited to the civilian sector. Indeed, it increasingly occupied the time and energy of the NVA leadership. An article by a naval officer about the demands of increased technology in the officer training schools provides an example:

> It (the technical revolution) affected the outfitting of the Peoples' Navy with the most modern and complicated technology and in 1964 led to a qualitatively new profile in the training of younger officer cadres. The use of automated and electronic equipment and weapon-systems has continued in all combat units and is continuing at an

increasing rate. This makes it necessary to train officers, who on the one hand have a command over the existing technology and on the other have a sufficient amount of knowledge and ability to further develop and master the technology of future years.[2]

Technology, however, never stole the spotlight entirely. The advancing level of technology brought demands for equal attention to improving the effectiveness of political work. Authorities still worried about the danger that highly trained specialists could develop a technician mentality. Such a development could not be allowed, for it would produce an apolitical military whose basic loyalty was open to question. One article stated:

> As is known, an educated careerist is more dangerous for the society than a blockhead. For this reason not only must knowledge be imparted to officer cadets, they must also be educated. The purpose of this is to be sure that the knowledge which they receive is transformed into conviction, because a high level of political-moral character (Eigenschaften) and a firm conviction of the justice of our cause are the basic preconditions for victory.[3]

The demand for military dual executives was repeated at the Seventh Party Conference, which assigned the military the task of "further strengthening the armed forces as the core of the land forces and arranging its relations with the other components of society in an ever closer form."[4] In order to satisfy this demand, the party organs within the military introduced a new set of instructions entitled "Instructions for the Leading Party Organs (Politorgane) and for the Party Organization of the SED in the NVA." These instructions were aimed at consolidating the presence of the party and its effectiveness in a period of increased technology.

Thus, the task was to consolidate the gains, both political and technical, made during the previous periods. How well this goal was met will now be considered.

MILITARY TECHNOLOGY

Information on all 17 indicators of technology constructed for this study appeared during Period IV. The first indicator, the educational level required for entry into officer training schools, increased. During Period III an officer cadet was required to have completed the tenth class. Admission requirements were tightened during Period IV, however, as admittance was restricted to those who had completed "the expanded senior school or the general polytechnic senior school with a completed occupational education."[5]

The possession of an Abitur was not an absolute requirement for entrance into an officer school although education above the tenth-class level was necessary. But high-ranking East German officers stated at this time that over two-thirds of all officer candidates held the Abitur,[6] and there were complaints during the next period that the Abitur had become the most important consideration in selecting candidates.[7] These statements indicate that possession of the Abitur had become the norm rather than the exception for officer candidates. This situation would seem to justify a reclassification of this indicator to high.

The second indicator of technology, the length of officer training schools, remained the same during this period. According to the official 1965 NVA handbook, "Training to be an officer takes place at officer training schools of the National People's Army and, in accordance with requirements of the individual specialties (Fachrichtungen), lasts from three to four years."[8]

Although the length of officer training schools remained the same as in Period III, the technical complexity of the equipment with which these future officers were expected to deal continued to rise. Since the NVA leadership felt it could not afford to lengthen the course of study, attempts were made to rationalize the three-to-four-year training period to enable the individual cadet to gain more knowledge in the same period of time. An officer associated with the Karl Liebknecht naval officer training school, took note of this situation when he said:

> The newer and greater tasks confronting the National Peoples' Army as a result of the revolution in military science, and the relatively constant training period at the officer schools, bring about a constantly intensifying contradiction between training materials and training times. It is obvious that it will be impossible to bring the sharp increase in the new scientific mass of information into accord with the limited training time under the present form of training. For this reason, the effectiveness of the training in the available instruction time must be bettered.[9]

This indicator is again classified as indicating a high level of technology.

The third indicator deals with the percentage of the officer corps having attended at least a three-year officer school. The only available figure for this indicator during Period IV is for 1966.

According to this source, 60 percent of all officers had attended a three-year officer school by this time.[10] Sixty percent represents a considerable increase over Period III, when 26.8 percent had attended such schools. The improvement shows the impact of the 1956 decision to establish officer training schools that would turn out young officers capable of dealing with modern weapons systems. Sixty percent indicates a high level of technology according to the schema devised earlier.

The fourth indicator of technology concerns the value of an officer's education when compared to that provided by a civilian institution. The officer training institutions continued to occupy the same position as in Period III—military technical schools on a par with other technical schools in the GDR.[11] All officers received training not only in military-technical areas but in a civilian occupation as well. Upon graduation, they obtained a certificate recognizing them as graduates of a civilian technical school.[12] Since no change occurred in this indicator over the preceding period, it is again classified as indicating a medium level of technology.

The percentage of officers possessing the mittlere Reife as their highest level of education is the fifth indicator of technology. Two sets of figures are available for this period, one for 1965 and the other for 1966. In 1965 a total of 41 percent of all NVA officers possessed the mittlere Reife as their highest level of education.[13] By 1966 the figure rose to 47 percent.[14] This increase over the figure of 36 percent for Period III indicates the NVA leadership's continued concern with raising the educational level of its officer corps and requires a reclassification of the indicator as high.

The sixth indicator pertains to the percentage of officers possessing the Abitur. Two sets of figures are available for this indicator—from the same years (1965 and 1966) and the same sources as the previous indicator. By 1965 a total of 21 percent of NVA officers possessed the Abitur.[15] One year later, this figure had risen to 23 percent.[16] As in the case of the mittlere Reife this increase (from 19.5 percent in the preceding period) indicates the importance attached by NVA officials to a higher level of education. It is, however, not large enough to warrant reclassification. Consequently, it continues to be classified as medium.

The percentage of officers possessing a technical education serves as the seventh indicator of technology. Only one source gives a figure for this indicator during Period IV. According to this source, 73 percent of all NVA officers possessed a technical school certificate in 1966.[17] Although 73 percent represents a significant increase over the last available figures from Period II (31 percent in 1956), it is impossible to tell whether it represents a sudden increase in Period IV or is part of a gradual change that only became apparent during this period. From changes in other indicators associated with the educational background of NVA officers, it seems fair to suggest that the change probably occurred gradually over a ten-year time frame. It will be classified as high for this period.

Figures for the eighth indicator of technology, the percentage of NVA officers certified as engineers or technicians, are available for two of the four years in Period IV, 1965 and 1966. By 1965 the percentage of NVA officers certified as engineers had risen from 10 percent in Period III to 14 percent.[18] One year later, the figure stood at 16.6 percent.[19] This rise is sufficient to warrant a change in classification since, according to the schema constructed earlier, 16.6 percent indicates a high level of technology.

The ninth indicator of technology deals with the percentage of NVA officers with a degree at the university level. Figures for this period were available for two years, 1966 and 1967. According to the sources for 1966, 10 percent of the NVA officer corps possessed a university-level education.[20] By the following year, this figure reportedly increased by 18 percent.[21]

At this point confusion and inaccuracy begin to plague this indicator. Up to 1966 all percentages used were supplied in percentage form. But beginning with 1967 the following information was given: "The part (Bestand) of officers with university level education increased three times."[22] Taking the 1963 figure of 6 percent and multiplying it by three, we obtain 18 percent. But it is not clear whether the writer means that the percentage increased three times or the total number increased three times. This becomes an even greater problem in the next period. For Period IV, I have decided to use the figure of 10 percent. An increase from 10 percent to 18 percent within one year appears too great. For a change of that magnitude to occur, a special policy would be needed, which certainly would be reported in specialist journals. No such policy was ever mentioned. Still, the increase to 10 percent warrants reclassification of the indicator as medium.

The tenth indicator treats the percentage of army regimental commanders with an academic education. Three sets of figures are available for this period, for 1964, 1965, and 1966. According to the figures for 1964 and 1965, the percentage of army regimental commanders with an academic education remained at 80 percent, the same as in Period III.[23] The figure for the last year, 1966, drops to 77 percent.[24] What led to this apparent decrease is not indicated. Nevertheless, it does not seem serious since the number of academy graduates appears to have increased.[25]

The quality of teaching at the military academy also improved. Although only 8 percent of the teaching staff possessed a diploma in 1959, by 1966 the figure had risen to 76 percent.[26] In addition, the number of faculty members with professorial qualifications had increased over the same period from one to 21.[27] Recognizing the need for a more systematic approach to training methods, Heinz Hoffmann issued a directive establishing an Institute for Military Pedagogics and Military Psychology.[28]

Thus, not only did the percentage of officers with an academic education remain high but the quality of education increased as well. This indicator retains its classification of high.

The eleventh indicator involves the length of time officers are required to serve. This indicator remains the same as in Period III, with the term of obligated service remaining at 10 years.[29] The indicator again is classified as high.

The twelfth indicator of technology considers the importance of technical qualifications for promotion or retention in the service. Concern over the technical qualifications of military officers became acute during this period. It is interesting to note that this concern was not limited to technical officers—everyone was to be technically qualified. As one source put it:

> The fact that the revolution in military science has effects on all areas (Bereiche) of military life, and that today every member of the military comes into contact with technology, uses it, works on it, or attends it, means that the revolution in military science cannot be mastered if military technology remains the domain only of the specialist or the technician. Each officer and soldier must understand the problems of the technical revolution, recognize its connection with the revolution in military science, and master the tasks personally given to him in the truest sense of the word.[30]

One of the first programs introduced during this period, aimed at raising the technical competence of NVA officers, sought by 1970 to give all officers a natural science background equivalent to that mastered by a graduate of the expanded senior school. The courses were divided into two types, one for persons holding the mittlere Reife and the other for those less well educated. Among the courses offered were mathematics, physics, chemistry, pedagogics, and Russian.[31]

In addition to the part-time study, a system of efficiency reports (Attestation), including data on technical competence, was introduced. Through this process, the military hoped to determine which officers were best suited to remain and advance in the service. One high-ranking East German officer stated:

The attestations of 1964 were carried out very carefully and with a great deal of expertise. Now the commander is confronted with the task of evaluating the attestations with the same thoroughness. A series of other measures of the cadre program will be influenced by the evaluation of the attestations, for example, assignment to a military or civilian university or technical school; deployment to cadre-reserve; assignment to Nomenklatura positions, and reassignment of those officers who because of reasons of age or health are no longer able to perform the tasks of their positions. The evaluation contributes to a determination of the perspectives of all officers for a long period of time. This concerns the active duty period as well as the planned transfer into the reserve.32

Technical qualifications served as one of the most important aspects of this efficiency report system. Individuals who did not qualify technically could not be sent for training that might be required for promotion. As a result, they would not normally be promoted and could end up in the reserve.33 These efficiency reports were submitted every three years at this time.34 Technical competence became an absolute requirement for promotion.35 Thus, the situation was clear: Those who wished to be promoted or retained in the service had to improve their technical qualifications, in the main by participation in the technical evening study program. In addition to the evening study program, they were expected to devote a considerable part of their remaining free time to such study.36

In evaluating this indicator, it does not appear that much has changed since Period III. If anything, technical qualifications are more important. Those not technically qualified soon found themselves in civilian occupations. The weapons systems and equipment had become too complex to allow untrained individuals to continue to hold positions of authority. This indicator is once again classified as high.

The thirteenth indicator pertains to the existence of technical awards. There was no information on this indicator during Period IV. However, since it is very unlikely that a new award would have been introduced or withdrawn without any mention in the military press, I will proceed on the assumption that the awards discussed earlier were the only ones available during this period. The classification remains the same as during the last period—medium.

The number of occupational categories recognized by the military makes up the fourteenth indicator of technology. According to the Pocketbook for Military Policy Military Service, a total of

46 occupational categories existed in 1965, an increase of 20 over 1957.[37] The 46 occupational categories recognized in the NVA at this time were:

Air Force
1. Flugzeugmechaniker — air mechanic
2. Fallschirmdienst — parachute service
3. Kanoniere der Luftverteidigung — air force gunner
4. Flugzeugversorgversorgungs- technischer Dienst — air force technical service
5. Waffentechnische Dienst — technical weapon service
6. Pioniere und Flugplatzwartungs Dienst — engineering and airfield maintenance service
7. Meterologen — meteorologist
8. Navigation — navigator

Navy
9. Sperr — harbor defensive service
10. Torpedo — torpedo
11. Signal — signal
12. Ortung — position finding
13. E. Technik — electronics technician
14. Mot. Technik — motor technician
15. Taucher — diver
16. Funk — radio
17. Fernmelde — communication
18. Artillerie — gunner
19. Pionier — engineer
20. Kraftfahrer — driver

Army
21. Aufklärer — scout
22. Chemischer Dienst — chemical service
23. Nachrichten — communications
24. Fallschirmjäger — paratrooper
25. Panzer — tank
26. Artillerie — artillery
27. Funkortung — radio locator
28. Schirrmeister — motor sergeant
29. Kraftfahrttech. Dienst — technical transportation service
30. Pionier — engineer
31. Kommandantendienst — military police
32. Panzertechniker Dienst — tank technical service
33. Feuerwerker — ordnance technician
34. Nachrichtentechnischer Dienst — communications technical service

35.	Medizinischer Dienst	medical service
36.	Artillerie und Waffentechnischer Dienst	artillery and technical weapon service
37.	Militärtransportwesen	military transport service
38.	Musiker	musician

Border Troops

39.	Diensthundeführer	dog handler
40.	Bootsführer	boat commandant
41.	Bootsmachinist	boat machinist
42.	Deckmann	deck man
43.	Taucher	diver
44.	Pioniere	engineer
45.	Wiedergabe Mechaniker	broadcast mechanic
46.	Waffentechnischer Dienst	technical weapon service

One more occupational category was added in October 1966, legal service (Justiz Dienst),[38] bringing the total to 47 for this period. The importance of these additions can be seen by comparing this list to the one in Chapter 4. A large number of the categories are technical ratings, illustrating the increased need for specialization to handle the mounting complexity associated with a modern military. This indicator is indicative of a high degree of military technology.

The fifteenth indicator of technology deals with the number of specialized journals. Two more journals were added during the period, one in 1965 and one in 1966. The Parteiarbeiter (Party worker), apparently introduced in 1965, deals primarily with political questions. But problems associated with an increase in technology are discussed in it as well. In fact, in recent years, it has devoted considerable space to problems of political work in a highly technical military. The second journal added during Period IV is Luftverteidigung (Air defense), directed at members of the air force. A large proportion of its articles are of a technical nature. The addition of these journals makes a total of ten. According to the schema constructed earlier, this indicator remains at the high level.

The sixteenth indicator of technology involves the number of specialized books published. This period saw an increase from 84 specialized books published in Period III to 111 in Period IV. This figure indicates a high level of technology.

The last indicator of technology pertains to the PS level in the NVA. By the beginning of Period IV, the NVA authorities' continuing concern with increasing the technological level of the military manifested itself in an increase in PS level. The PS per soldier rose from 25.4 in 1958 to 29.1 in 1964.[39] Much of this rise in the PS level can be attributed to the fact that the T-34 tanks introduced earlier had become standard throughout the army. In addition, the T-54 was being introduced. MIG-15s, although not directly relevant to the PS level, also had been replaced by the newer and more complex MIG-19s, for all but training purposes. Although the PS level nearly attained the level necessary for a classification of high, it fell short, and as a consequence, is still classified as medium.

An average level of technology can be arrived at by entering the scores on Table 6.1. Thus, the level of technology continued to amount at a pace only slightly slower than in Period III as it reached a level of 2.7.

POLITICAL CONTROL

All of the 15 indicators of political control developed for this study were present during Period IV. The first indicator, which

TABLE 6.1

Level of Technology in Periods I-IV, 1949-67

Indicator	Period I	Period II	Period III	Period IV
1. Entry education	—	1	2	3
2. School length	2	3	3	3
3. Three-year course	—	1	1	3
4. Educational value	1	2	2	2
5. Mittlere Reife	1	1	2	3
6. Abitur	1	1	2	2
7. Fachschulausbildung	—	1	—	3
8. Engineers or technicians	—	1	2	3
9. Total academic education	—	1	1	2
10. Regimental academic education	—	1	3	3
11. Length of service	2	3	3	3
12. Technical qualifications	—	1	3	3
13. Technical awards	—	1	2	2
14. Occupational categories	—	2	2	3
15. Journals	1	1	3	3
16. Books	—	1	2	3
17. PS Level	1	2	2	2
Total	9	24	35	46
Average	1.3	1.4	2.2	2.7

Note: 1 = low; 2 = medium; 3 = high; — = no information.

treats the organizational level down to which political officers are present, once again remained unchanged.40 Although concerned about the effectiveness of these officers, the party appears to have felt that placing them lower down the hierarchical ladder would only complicate matters. It would call for a large number of additional officers at a time when the party was trying to hold the number of political officers constant while attempting to replace political officers who were "party hacks" with individuals who also understood something about military technology. This indicator continues to represent a medium level of political control.

The second indicator, the organizational level down to which secret police officers are present, also remained the same during this period.41 It is once again classified as low.

The third indicator concerns the length of training for political officers. Although this indicator changed in Period III and will change in Period V, it remained the same during Period IV. The party continued to seek to overcome the separation between political and military officers by selecting political officers from graduates of officer schools or from the ranks of experienced officers who underwent short periods of training to qualify for their new position.42 This indicator continues to be classified as indicating a low level of political control.

The fourth indicator deals with the previous military service of political officers. As mentioned, political officers continued to be selected from individuals with well over a year's service in the regular military. This indicator is again classified as high.

Changes in both the structure and activity of the fifth indicator of political control, the role of the Politorgane, took place during Period IV. Most of these innovations atemmed from the 1967 "Instructions for the Leading Party Organs (Politorgane) and the Party Organization of the SED in the NVA—Party Instructions."

The most important change at this time involved a structural modification of the Politorgane. This structural alteration appears to have followed the decision made during the previous period to extend the basic organization down to the battalion and independent company level. By introducing the basic organization down to this level, the party felt it would be able to force the military professional to become more involved in party activities. In addition, a way had to be found to ensure that political activities at the battalion level were carried out in accord with party desires. It was obvious that basic organizations in which there was little or no political activity would undermine the purpose of this change. Since there are many more battalions than regiments (the exact number of battalions in a regiment depends on the tasks assigned), increased supervisory activity became necessary.

Ordinarily, the Politorgane took care of the task of coordinating the activities of the basic organizations. In some cases, however, the Politorgane were not represented at lower organizational levels. This meant that a political control commission and party revision committee were missing. In addition, instead of a large political section, only a small number of political officers were present to deal with political activities at the regimental level and below. As a consequence, monitoring the actions of the increased number of basic organizations was difficult. Prior to extending the basic organization down to the battalion level, problems of coordination were handled at the division level. Now, however, this became increasingly difficult.

The SED leadership met this problem by establishing a unit at the regimental level known as the central party directory (Zentrale Parteileitung or ZPL). This body took over the coordinating task formally exercised by the political section at the division level. As one East German political officer remarked:

> With placement of the basic organization at a new level the necessity exists to create a central party directory (ZPL) in the staffs, regiments (Truppenteil), schools and other installations where a number of basic organizations exist and no Politorgane is available.[43]

The SED expected the ZPL to coordinate the activities of the basic organization so that "all parts of the military life would be impregnated with Marxist-Leninist ideology."[44] In carrying out this task of coordination, five general areas were singled out for particular attention. According to one East German political officer, they were:

> 1. To directly lead and coordinate the work of the basic organization as well as to carry out the scientific leadership of party work singlemindedly and creatively.
> 2. To lead the basic organization effectively by raising combat readiness, strengthening the "single leadership" (Einzeleitung), solving its problems in combat training as well as maintaining the Leninist norms of party life.
> 3. To effectively support political work with the masses by the basic organization with all army members.
> 4. To assure a rapid generalization of the progressive experiences of party work in all basic organizations.
> 5. To train a larger number of party members for active honorary party work and to qualify the party activists and functionaries.[45]

All five of these areas have considerable importance for the strengthening of party influence. By improving the quality of leadership, the party increases the probability that such policies will be implemented efficiently and in a way that the individual professional soldier may find more acceptable.[46] Paying increased attention to such factors as the "Leninist norms of life" decreases the ability of an individual to withdraw from active participation in party life. If he is not active, he may be cited and reported to higher authorities.

Similarly, greater Politorgane influence at this level in work with the masses means that the average military specialist will be increasingly forced to participate in this program. Taking increased cognizance of the possibility of constructing a set of generalized principles for party work increases the chances the party will be able to ensure that its policies are presented uniformly throughout the military. Finally, better qualified cadres might bring increased respect for the party, as a result of its better trained representatives. Raising the educational level of these individuals would improve the quality of their explanations, and perhaps increase the credibility of party doctrines.

In addition to this very important structural change, the Politorgane and, at the lower levels, the political section as it is known, became increasingly active, demonstrating heightened concern with such areas as civilian-military contacts. This is not to suggest that such contacts did not exist previously. In addition to the program of civilian work discussed in regard to indicator 17, other types of civilian-military contacts had long operated. One of the best known of these was the charter city (Patentstadt) program established in 1961. According to this program, ships received the names of various cities with which their crews then established close contact.[47] Although such programs had been only superficially examined by the Politorgane in the past,[48] they now became an important concern. An officer, usually the officer responsible for work with the masses, assumed responsibility for contacts with the civilian population.[49]

Although this increased stress on contact with the civilian population could operate as a political control mechanism, its importance should not be overemphasized. One of its primary purposes was to help recruit future members of the service.[50]

The intensified activity of the Politorgane also is reflected in the increased exposure of lower level units to the investigative functions of the Party Control Commission. Members of this commission carried out their control activities by visiting various units and reporting on the quality of political activities. In this way, they hoped to assure an increase in the quality of party educational undertakings.[51] In the past, their presence occasionally penetrated to the battalion level. Now investigations on the battalion level became official policy. Exactly how often or how many of these visits occurred, whether 20 or 80 percent of all units were visited, was not reported. Nevertheless, it appears that visits, although more frequent than in the past, still were limited and took place irregularly.[52]

By this period, the Politorgane had become very active. Through the central party directory, they could supervise and coordinate party affairs down to the battalion level. They extended party activities into the areas of work with the masses and increased control functions. Because of these conditions, this indicator is classified as high on the schema measuring political control.

The sixth indicator of political control deals with the activities of the military party organization. Along with the decision taken during Period III to make the basic organization active down to the battalion level, hope was expressed that this step would raise the level of political activity within the military party organization. Instead, the opposite had occurred. One East German officer said:

> Although it was possible to say a few years ago that the so-called general political propaganda had a place of preeminence, we must say today that ideological work is being pushed more and more in the background.[53]

In this period, the military party organization moved to reverse this image and vitalize political activity in the military. First, the 1967 instruction reaffirmed the primacy not only of the party but also of its highest form, the basic organization:

> The basic organizations are the main link (Hauptbindglied) between the party and all members of the NVA. They are the ones which discuss the policy of the party with the soldiers, noncommissioned officers and officers, and which mobilizes them for the active struggle for their realization. Members of the army have immediate contact with the party organization of their area.[54]

The military party organization encouraged individuals not only to improve political activity but also to meet the need for higher technical qualifications. It had the responsibility of aiding all members of the unit to become technically qualified.[55]

The party also assigned increased importance to the party groups.[56] Forced to interest himself in a party group, the regular officer would be unable to avoid taking part in party activities. The absence of a single individual from a meeting of five persons would easily be noticed.

This increased level of participation is evident, for example, in the party discussions preparing for the Seventh Party Conference. According to East German figures, 76 percent of all party members participated in activities at the party group level, while only 32 percent did so at the basic organization level.[57] A "party group leader" headed the party group and reported in turn to the company-level political officer.[58] Due to the activities of these small groups, it became possible not only to raise the level of political activitiy in the military but also to attain a better perspective on the attitudes and views of party members.

SED authorities also modified the relationship between the commanding officer and representatives of the party organization in his unit. Up to this time, the commanding officer and the party secretary of the basic organization occupied equal positions—both were charged with planning and carrying out political activities. Note, for example, the following explanation of the equal relationship that predominated up to this point:

> A correct socialist relationship between the commander (Einzelleiter) and the party secretary plays an important role. It is correct when the chiefs and commanders bring the party secretary into important discussions and decisions on important questions. The party secretary must be directly acquainted with the service problems which exist in the administration, staff, etc., and be able to correctly organize the activities of the party leadership and the party organization. He carries a great responsibility for seeing to it that the ideas, directives and order of the commander (Einzelleiter) become a concern for all party members.[59]

This relationship changed with the introduction of the 1967 instructions, under which the party organization became the direct concern of the Politorgane and not the commanding officer. Compare, for example, the following quotation referring to these instructions with the quotation cited above:

> The party organizations are led by their superior Politorgane. The party organizations are placed under their superior Politorgane and are responsible to them. For that reason, areas of main effort (Schwerpunkte) in the work of the party organization will neither be assigned nor confirmed by the commander.[60]

Instead of the previous relationship of mutual interaction, the party leadership now consulted the commander only on scheduling questions.

Insofar as the content of party activities is concerned, the commander had little or nothing to say. But this does not mean the commander ceased to bear responsibility for political work in his units. In fact, as I will show under indicators eight and nine, the opposite is true. The difference is that the commander had little to say about the way activities were conducted and had no alternative but to approve what the party organization, under the direction of the Politorgane, supported.

The freedom of action enjoyed by the commander in this area also was limited in another way. Instead of the titular head of the party organization in his unit, the commander was now perceived as no more than another member of the collective who had party responsibilities as did everyone else. As a consequence, the commander could be assigned party tasks (Parteiauftrage) for which he was completely accountable and responsible to the party organization.[61]

Changes in this indicator are closely tied to modifications in the previous one and also indicate a tightening of political control over the military. The level on which military officers were required to participate bore deep into the military organization. The party organization gained what appears to have been virtually complete autonomy with regard to the regular officer in matters of direct concern to the party. This situation indicates a high level of political control according to the schema outlined earlier.

The seventh indicator focuses on the percentage of NVA officers who are party members. The first figure available for this period is 96 percent for 1964.[62] The following year, membership had dropped by one percent, to 95 percent.[63] By 1966 it had risen to 99.8 percent, according to one source,[64] although another puts it at 96.1 percent.[65] Of the two figures for 1966, I am inclined to accept that of 96.1 percent since the source providing it has proved very reliable. In addition the figure of 99.8 percent may refer to the navy only, although this is not completely clear. By 1967 the figure had risen to 97 percent.[66] In any case, the level of this indicator remained high.

The eighth indicator of political control concerns the importance assigned to the political reliability of officers. The efficiency reports introduced in 1964 were not limited to discussion of technical matters. Ideological qualifications also played an important role. The many complaints lodged in the military papers against officers who tended to emphasize technical qualifications at the expense of political ones testified to the continued viability of the policy of evaluating political qualifications on a par with technical ones during this period. The following quotation is representative:

> We oppose . . . at the same time every tendency to limit ourselves onesidedly to the military and

military-technical education continuation and in that way to underestimate the political qualifications, the acquisition of knowledge and capabilities in the direction of political work with the masses, and to neglect the Marxist-Leninist education of the Party members.[67]

Commanders engaged in evaluating other officers were warned not to view the officers' qualifications solely from the military-technical standpoint but to consider their political consciousness as well.[68] This continued high regard for the political qualifications of the military officer suggests that little had changed from the preceding period. An individual who was not qualified would not be retained in the service, regardless of whether his deficiencies were technical or political. This indicator continues to suggest a high level of political control.

The ninth indicator of political control deals with responsibility for political indoctrination. The commander (Einzelleiter) remained responsible for both the military and political performance of his unit. Admiral Verner stated:

> Naturally, the commander is the single leader (Einzelleiter) who is completely responsible for all aspects of the education and training of members of the military, who has the responsibility to put the unity of political and military leadership into force in all of his activities.[69]

Much of this authority, as suggested in indicator six above, was more formal than actual and in many ways accompanied an attempt to remove the commander's influence from designing political activities while still making him responsible for their effectiveness. Political officers, for example, were in charge of setting up courses and lectures.[70] In addition, complaints made by a leading political officer suggest that the party organization tended to usurp the commander's authority in this area. He explained: "But how do they deal with it? In the main as if the party organization had taken over the commander's task and responsibility."[71]

Yet the military officer was more involved than this description suggests. He continued to determine how much time would be allocated to political indoctrination. He also was expected to familiarize himself with the program and run checks on it. As Heinz Hoffmann remarked:

> In the first place, he has more responsibility, above all to see that the training goal is reached. That will also be the criterion for evaluation by controls and inspections.

The commander has the task of determining how the entire time for training is to be divided among the types of training as well as the individual themes. The hourly schedule in the program merely serves as a basis. He must make certain that the longest amount of time will be used where there is the greatest need.72

Still, changes discussed under indicator six above suggest that there was little the commander could actually do if he opposed as excessive the amount of time the party organization said was needed for political indoctrination. To refuse such a request might invite trouble. Since the party organization reported directly to the Politorgane and received instructions from it, such an action might engage the commander in a contest of will with the Politorgane, a confrontation he certainly would not welcome, and in all probability would lose. Thus, the commander's authority in this area was strictly limited. With this limitation came an increase in the degree to which the military professional was required to be knowledgeable of and participate in political activities. As a consequence, the classification of this indicator will be changed to high.

The tenth indicator of political control involves responsibility for work with the masses. Military officers, burdened with their regular duties, tended to feel their responsibility for political work stopped with the conduct of political-ideological indoctrination.73 They found little time for work with the masses—they not only ignored this program but found it a burden. One writer stated:

> There are still commanders who are not aware of the advantageous influence of cultural work on combat readiness, who either pay little or no attention to cultural work or consider it to be a burden.74

East German authorities could not continue to allow this lack of attention to work with the masses to continue indefinitely. During this period, they determined to overcome this mental separation on the part of regular officers between the technical and political aspects of life in the NVA. After all, from the party's point of view, the building of a socialist consciousness required more than one approach to succeed. It called for utilizing all the tools of political work, including work with the masses.75

In the eyes of the SED, work with the masses picks up where political indoctrination leaves off. It is carried on during off-duty hours and assists the individual soldier to internalize lessons learned in class. As one writer stated:

> The cultural work . . . aids in the solution of political and
> military tasks and must lead to the creation of a new qual-
> ity in the thinking of our commanders and firmly convince
> them of the correctness and victory of the military policy
> of our party.[76]

One of the first party moves to correct this "mistake" by military commanders was to force them to play a part in this process.[77] New stress was laid on the commander's responsibility for the program's effectiveness.[78] It was the commander's responsibility to see that his men devoted more time to such endeavors. Failure to do so might well result in a complaint being filed by the party secretary with the appropriate component of the Politorgane. Since the party organization had supreme control of activities in this area and therefore closely watched the handling of such activities, this indicator of political control will be reclassified as high.

The eleventh indicator of political control concerns part-time ideological indoctrination. The part-time political courses on Marxism-Leninism required of all officers, which were begun during the last period, continued through this one. Aside from a lack of interest in these political indoctrination courses by officers attending them,[79] a primary problem revolved around the time involved. Only eight duty hours a month were available for class time.[80] This meant a great deal of the officers' free time must be devoted to the study of political material. A number of officers appear to have found it impossible to allocate sufficient hours to political studies.[81] Many failed because they were under pressure to increase their technical qualifications and decided to give technical competence first priority.[82] East German officers were in a truly precarious situation. Should they fail to devote enough time to technical subjects, they would not be promoted. But if technical endeavors absorbed so much time that they neglected political courses, they would face the same fate.

The examination in political areas required of all officers was quite elaborate.[83] In 1966 every officer had to take a final examination between September 1 and November 30. Provided his semester and final examination scores were high enough, by December 15 he would receive a certificate equivalent to one issued by a Bezirk or district party school. The test consisted of written and oral sections. The written section had to be completed by September 30. The test asked such questions as, "Why is the military security of socialism a deeply revolutionary and humanitarian task?" and "Discuss the relationship (Wechselwirkung) between political-ideological education and military order."[84]

While the written examination focused on subjects studied during the last two semesters, the oral was comprehensive and covered the entire four-year program. At the time of the oral examination, the testee received a question for which he had 30 minutes to prepare an answer. The questions were not concerned with details but they required "a thorough explanation of the relationships and an exact use of evidence."[85] One such question stated, "Establish the scientific and offensive character of the military policy of our party."[86]

When taking the oral examination, the officer appeared alone before the testing commission. The examination lasted at least half an hour during which time both his written and oral answers were evaluated. According to one report, about 50 percent of the officers had passed the examination by the end of the year.[87] Upon completion of the course on the basics of Marxism-Leninism (Grundlagen der Marxismus-Leninismus) in 1966, a new course on the history of the German worker's movement (Geschichte der Deutschen Arbeiterbewegung) was initiated:

> With the three-year study, begun on December 1, 1966, officers receive for the first time the opportunity to study coherently, systematically, and basically the history of the class which has been called since its appearance as an organized and politically independently acting class to take over the leadership of the nation in all of Germany.[88]

Insofar as the amount of time devoted to part-time ideological study is concerned, two hours per week were taken up with classes. In addition, the officer had to contribute many hours of his free time to study, particularly as the semester examinations approached. The final examination required even more preparation. Like it or not, the officer was forced to increase his knowledge of party ideology. As a result, this indicator is once again classified as high.

The twelfth indicator of political control, the effectiveness of self-criticism, continued as an important aspect of party policy during this period. Although no mention of actual suppression of self-criticism appeared, the practice does seem to have been ignored or at least not very actively used in a number of cases, as illustrated by complaints leveled at some officers in the military press. One complaint stated:

> There are, however, comrades among us who are no longer used to evaluating their thoughts and actions sufficiently and who must ask themselves earnestly whether they are doing justice to their duty as well as the expectations which our party and leadership have placed in them. The party organization should energetically work on such comrades, in that it confronts them with their false conceptions and behavior.[89]

Thus, although the party had been successful in overcoming the direct opposition to this practice prevalent up to Period II, apathy still appeared to plague its effectiveness. Accordingly, this indicator is classified as medium.

The handling of disciplinary questions serves as the thirteenth indicator of political control. The party continued to encourage the commander, who had formal authority over disciplinary questions, to make use of the military collective in disciplinary matters whenever possible. The military commander, it proposed, should first meet with members of his collective and decide whether the offense should be handled by the collective.[90] Once a matter was turned over to the collective, the following would occur:

> The disciplinary offense with its effects will be explained by the commander. The accused will then take a position with regard to his offense and give an account of it. The collective itself will determine what must be improved, i.e., how the collective can help the accused.[91]

Although the party went to great lengths to institute this system of handling disciplinary questions, it does not appear to have been very successful. This became apparent when General Hoffmann sent out his now famous letter of April 30, 1965, to all commanders demanding that more attention be given the use of the collective. According to Hoffmann, the collectives actually received only 10 percent of the cases they were eligible to handle.[92]

Despite these efforts by General Hoffmann, little apparently changed. A study at the end of this period gave the following breakdown for the treatment of disciplinary questions: "settled by the commander alone through disciplinary measures . . . 91.4 percent. . . . Handled by the military collective . . . 8.6 percent.[93]

Consequently, despite efforts by the party, power remained in the hands of the regular officer. He determined whether a matter would be handled by the collective, and as long as he continued to have that power, he would be able to apply special pressure to those manifesting nonmilitary attitudes. This indicator continued to indicate a low level of political control.

The fourteenth indicator deals with the handling of criminal offenses. The military court system mentioned in Chapter 5 remained in force.[94] Although military officers continued to serve on the courts, their influence was limited. About all they could hope to accomplish was to convince the court to be more lenient or harsher in certain cases. For example, they might point out that, although an individual had committed a political offense, he was a good soldier, had a good record, and should be given a light sentence. Consequently, this indicator is again classified as high.

Part-time civilian work serves as the last indicator of political control. The available figures were incomplete and covered only one year. The NVA, with 189,500 officers and men,[95] had a potential of 379 million work-hours for civilian or military projects (2,000 multiplied by 189,500). According to one East German source, 1,202,000 hours were spent on harvest work.[96] This figure is approximately double that for 1959 (639,214). If we consider the number of hours worked in industry to be approximately double those in 1959, we arrive at a figure of 1,335,530 hours (2 times 722,765). Added together, this provides a total of 2,647,530 hours of civilian work performed by the military. On a yearly basis, this means that soldiers served an average of approximately 14 hours per year, or a little over one hour per month in this capacity. This represents a decrease from the last period, and seems to indicate that the military found this type of work less practical in a modern military and industrial world, although more figures would be necessary to determine the existence of any such trend. The indicator is classified as low.

In order to compute the average level of political control for Period IV, the scores derived for the individual indicators are entered in Table 6.2. The average level of political control is 2.3. A discussion of the relationship of this figure to the increase in technology follows.

OBSERVATIONS

The changes that have occurred up to this point are depicted in Figure 6.1. Period IV shows a steady rise in the level of technology. This is particularly evident in the indicators associated with educational level. The requirements for admission to officer training

FIGURE 6.1

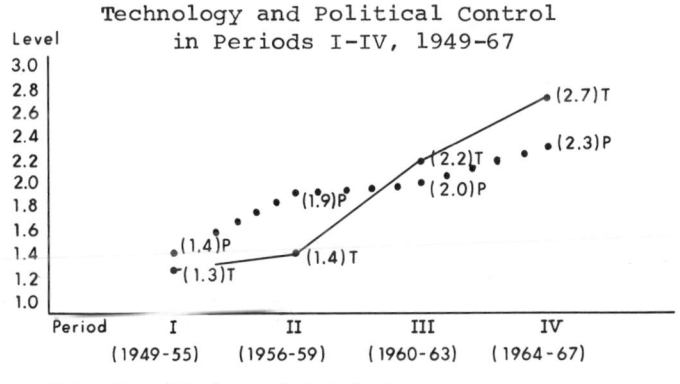

Technology and Political Control in Periods I-IV, 1949-67

Note: P = political control; T = technology.

TABLE 6.2

Level of Political Control in Periods I-IV, 1949-67

Indicator	Period I	Period II	Period III	Period IV
1. Political officer level	2	2	2	2
2. Secret police level	1	1	1	1
3. Training length	2	3	1	1
4. Prior service	2	2	3	3
5. Politorgane	1	2	2	3
6. Military party organization	1	2	2	3
7. Party membership	1	2	3	3
8. Political reliability	1	3	3	3
9. Indoctrination	1	2	2	3
10. Massenarbeit	1	2	2	3
11. Part-time training	3		3	3
12. Self-criticism	1	1	2	2
13. Discipline	1	1	1	1
14. Criminal offenses	1	3	3	3
15. Civilian projects		1	1	1
Total	19	27	31	34
Average	1.4	1.9	2.0	2.3

Note: 1 = low; 2 = medium; 3 = high; — = no information.

schools rose to almost equal those of universities in the GDR. The percentage of officers classified as engineers or technicians also increased. In addition, the percentage of officers possessing an academic education mounted. Sharp increases were registered on two of these indicators: the percentage of officers who had completed a three-year officer training school and the percentage with a Fachschulausbildung. A number of years were required before the older graduates of the six-month or one-year officer training schools could be replaced by younger graduates of the three-year course. By the end of Period IV, a large enough reservoir of young graduates of the three-year schools was available to permit retirement of a significant portion of older officers who lacked training, permitting the indicator to rise sharply. The increase in Fachschulausbildung probably is not as spectacular as it appears. It is possible that the increase would have been more gradual if information had been available for the preceding period. Other indicators that increased during this period are the number of occupational categories and the number of specialized books. In both cases, the military leadership was reacting to increased usage of highly technical equipment by developing highly educated specialists and then providing them with more specialized reading material.

All but four indicators of political control remained the same during Period IV. All four of these indicators rose. As a result, the overall level of political control continued to increase. The four indicators that rose were responsibility for political indoctrination, responsibility for work with the masses, activities of the Politorgane, and activities of the military party organization. All four of these indicators are important for the party's goal of developing a military dual executive.

By making the military officer bear full responsibility for the effectiveness of political indoctrination and work with the masses, the party made it very difficult, if not impossible, for a military officer to avoid active participation in party life. Not only is the officer responsible for its success or failure but, in order to assure success, he must know something about the ideological questions under discussion—that is, he must become not only politically active but aware as well.

Increasing the supervisory activities of such organs as the Politorgane and the military party organizations raises the probability that an officer's failure to take full cognizance of the role of ideology in military life will be reported. An unsatisfactory report would result in a reprimand, if not dismissal from the service.

Instead of decreasing as technology increases, political control continues to increase. At this point the party appears relatively successful in its goal of creating a military dual executive. The NVA officer corps is technically qualified, as evidenced by its overall educational level. Nevertheless, as a number of political indicators show—and not only the four that increased during this period—these "technical" experts are being forced to be "red" as well, assuming of course that they intend to make the military a career.

Still, it is too soon to determine whether the proposition presented in the introduction to this study will be rejected. A number of political indicators—such as the level down to which the secret police are active, the length of training political officers receive, responsibility for discipline, and work on civilian projects—remain at a low level. It is possible that the level of these indicators is indicative of some problems the party experienced—problems that have not yet surfaced in the indicators that registered as medium or high. In any case, Chapter 7 should provide a better indication of whether the trend, which now appears clear, will hold up over all five periods.

NOTES

1. Walter Ulbricht, "Die gesellschaftliche Entwicklung in der Deutschen Demokratischen Republik bis zur Vollendung des Sozialismus," Protokoll der Verhandlungen des VII. Parteitages der Sozialistischen Einheitspartei Deutschlands (Berlin-Ost: Dietz Verlag, 1967), Vol. I, pp. 136-37.
2. Kapitän zur See F. Notroff, "Die Offiziersschule der Volksmarine 'Karl Liebknecht' ist die Kaderschmiede unserer Flotte," Marinewesen, March 1966, p. 338; Generalmajor O. Pech, "Die richtige Arbeit mit den Kadern—Bestandteil sozialistischer, militärischer Führungstätigkeit," Militärwesen, December 1964, p. 1671.
3. Fregettenkapitän (Ing.) W. Reimer, Korvettenkapitän G. Raschpichler, Kapitänleutnant H. Dittrich, "Das neue System der Heranbildung von Offizieren der Volksmarine—Ein Erfordernis der wissenschaftlichtechnischen Entwicklung," Marinewesen, August 1965, p. 95. See also Admiral Waldemar Verner, "Die Ergebnisse und Aufgaben der 11. Tagung des Zentralkomitees der SED," Parteiarbeiter, January 1965, p. 21; Major Beck, "Offensiv mit den Lehroffizieren arbeiten!", Parteiarbeiter, January 1966, p. 42.
4. Gerhard Lux and Toni Nelles, "Der Aufbau und die Entwicklung der NVA—schöpferische Anwendung des Leninischen Militärprograms durch die SED (II)," Zeitschrift für Militärgeschichte, June 1970, p. 670.
5. Taschenbuch für Wehrpflichtige (Berlin-Ost: Deutscher Militärverlag, 1965), p. 240. See also "Erlass des Staatsrates der Deutschen Demokratischen Republik über den aktiven Wehrdienst in der Nationalen Volksarmee (Dienstlaufbahnordnung) in Fassung vom 14. Januar 1966," Gesetzblatt der Deutschen Demokratischen Republik (Berlin-Ost: VEB Deutscher Zentralverlag, 1966), I, 4 (February, 1966), 50.
6. Generalmajor O. Pech, "Über die Entwicklung und Perspektive des Offizierskorps der Nationalen Volksarmee," Militärwesen, February 1966, p. 200.
7. Generalleutnant O. Pech, "Wachsende Aufgaben in der Nachwuchsgewinnung für militärische Berufe," Militärwesen, February 1971, p. 204.
8. Taschenbuch für Wehrpflichtige, p. 241.
9. Korvettenkapitän R. Müller, "Anwendungsmöglichkeiten von Lehrmaschinen im Ausbidlungsprozess an der Offiziersschule 'Karl Liebknecht,'" Marinewesen, March 1967, pp. 298-99. It should be noted that, although the term army (National People's Army) is used, this does not mean the writer is referring only to the land forces. The navy and air force, although seperate units, are still part of the National People's Army. The term land forces

(Landstreitkräfte) is used if only they are being specifically referred to.

10. Karl Greese and Alfred Voerster, "Probleme der Auswahl und Förderung der Offizierskader in der NVA (1958-1963)," Zeitschrift für Militärgeschichte, January 1966, p. 35.

11. "Erlass des Staatsrates der Deutschen Demokratischen Republik," p. 51.

12. Taschenbuch für Wehrpflichtige, p. 286.

13. Armeegeneral Heinz Hoffmann, "Zehn Jahre Nationale Volksarmee—zehn Jahre Schutz des Volkes und seines sozialistischen Vaterlandes," in Heinz Hoffmann, Sozialistische Landes Verteidigung (Berlin-Ost: Deutscher Militärverlag, 1971), Vol. I, p. 296.

14. K. Ilter, "Die sozialistische Offizierspersönlichkeit: Probleme und Gedanken zum Bild des sozialistischen Offiziers," Militärwesen, November 1967, p. 1546.

15. Hoffmann, "Zehn Jahre Nationale Volksarmee," p. 296.

16. Ilter, "Die sozialistische Offizierspersönlichkeit," p. 1546.

17. Ibid.

18. Hoffmann, "Zehn Jahre Nationale Volksarmee," p. 297.

19. Autorenkollektive des Deutschen Instituts für Militärgeschichte, Zeittafel zur Militärgeschichte der Deutschen Demokratischen Republik 1949 bis 1968 (Berlin-Ost: Deutscher Militärverlag, 1969), p. 259; Fregattenkapitän H. Kubasch, "Zweite Kadertagung der Nationalen Volksarmee," Militärwesen, July 1966, p. 1037; Armeegeneral Heinz Hoffmann, "Menschenführung als Grundproblem wissenschaftlicher Truppenführung," in Hoffmann, Sozialistische Landes Verteidigung, Vol. I, p. 383.

20. Hoffmann, "Menschenführung als Grundproblem" p. 383; Autorenkollektiv, Zeittafel . . . 1949 bis 1968, p. 259; H. Kubasch, "Zweite Kadertagung der Nationalen Volksarmee," Militärwesen, July 1966, p. 1037.

21. Redaktion, "Für unsere sozialistische DDR—unter Führung der Partei—immer Gefechtsbereit," Militärwesen, May 1967, p. 620.

22. Ibid.

23. For 1964: Autorenkollektiv, Zeittafel . . . 1949 bis 1968, p. 219; Armeegeneral Heinz Hoffmann, "Zu den Grundfragen der Militärpolitik der Sozialistischen Einheitspartei Deutschlands," Militärwesen, June 1964, p. 782. For 1965: Hoffmann, "Zehn Jahr Nationale Volksarmee," p. 297.

24. Pech, "Uber die Entwicklung und Perspektive des Offizierskorps," p. 200.

25. The figures available for academy graduates are: For 1965, 200; see "Militärischer Schild sichert den friedlichen Aufbau," Volksarmee, No. 43 (1965), p. 4. For 1967, 225; see Armeegeneral Heinz Hoffmann, "Die Offiziere der Nationalen Volksarmee erfüllen

den Auftrag der Partei," Volksarmee (Dokumentation), No. 43 (1967), p. 10. For 1968, 330; see Volksarmee, No. 43 (1968), p. 3. For 1970, 345; see Volksarmee, No. 45 (1970), p. 3.

26. "Meldung des M.f.N.V., Armeegeneral Heinz Hoffmann an den Ersten Sekretär des Zentralkomitees der Sozialistische Einheitspartei Deutschlands and Vorsitzender des Staatsrates der Deutschen Demokratischen Republik, Genosse Walter Ulbricht, anlässlich des Empfangs der Absolventen der Militärakademien am 14. Oktober 1966," Volksarmee (Dokumentation), No. 43 (1966), p. 16. By 1968 almost all faculty members had an academic education. See Armeegeneral Heinz Hoffmann, "Fest und unerschütterlich bereit jeden Befehl der Arbeiter—und Bauern Regierung bedingungslos zu erfüllen," Volksarmee (Dokumentation), No. 43 (1968), p. 6. This information is included here because indicator ten is not present in the next period.

27. Ibid. Another sign of the qualitative increase in academy education is the decision to eliminate the previous special education courses for individuals about to attend the academy (five to ten months in duration). Henceforth, only short special courses were offered for this purpose. From all appearances, the quality of officers attending the academy had improved enough to dispense with this training. Armeegeneral Heinz Hoffmann, "Die Arbeit mit den Kadern . . . das Kern Problem der Führungstätigkeit," Militärwesen, (July, 1963), 975.

28. Autorenkollektiv, Zeittafel . . . 1949 bis 1968, p. 282.

29. "Erlass des Staatsrates der Deutschen Demokratischen Republik," p. 50.

30. Generalmajor (Ing.) W. Fliessner, "Die Revolution in Militärwesen und das militärtechnische Denken unserer Offiziers," Militärwesen, January 1966, p. 5. See also Korvettenkapitän K. Kettner, "Die neue Technik in der Flotte erfordert höhere pädagogisch-psychologische Fähigkeiten der Offiziere," Marinewesen, September 1966, p. 1080; Admiral Waldemar Verner, "Remarks," Protokoll der Verhandlungen des VII. Parteitages, Vol. III, p. 701.

31. Generalmajor S. Weiss, "Alle Voraussetzungen für eine wirksame Qualifizierung schaffen," Militärwesen, January 1964, p. 37.

32. Pech, "Über die Entwicklung und Perspektive des Offizierskorps," pp. 202-20.

33. Armeegeneral Heinz Hoffmann, "Die Militärpolitische Situation in Deutschland erfordert hohe Gefechtsbereitschaft der Nationalen Volksarmee," in Hoffmann, Sozialistische Landes Verteidigung, Vol. I, p. 195.

34. Fregattenkapitän W. Schottmann, "Mehr Aufmerksamkeit dem zweckmässigen Kadereinsatz," Militärwesen, July 1966, p. 977.

35. Armeegeneral Heinz Hoffmann, "Die sozialistische Militärdoktrin und die Aufgaben der Nationalen Volksarmee bei der Verwirklichung der Beschlüsse des VI. Parteitages," Hoffmann, Sozialistische Landes Verteidigung, Vol. I, p. 33.

36. Weiss, "Alle Voraussetzungen," p. 37.
37. Taschenbuch für Militärpolitik und Wehrdienst, (Berlin-Ost: Deutscher Militärverlag, 1968), pp. 155, 128-29, 185-86, 201.
38. "Forum des Soldaten," Volksarmee, No. 12 (1966), p. 7.
39. Hoffmann, "Zu den Grundfragen der Militärpolitik," p. 779.
40. Thomas A. Forster, NVA—Die Armee der Sowjetzone, (Cologne: Markus Verlag, 1966-67), p. 90.
41. Ibid., p. 160.
42. Ibid., p. 41.
43. Oberst G. Teller, "In der Führungstätigkeit der Politorgane und Parteiorganisationen wirksamer werden," Parteiarbeiter, December 1967, p. 7. Truppenteil normally is translated as unit or formation, but when used in regard to the NVA, it refers specifically to the regimental level.
44. Oberstleutnant Eckard and Oberstleutnant Fritz, "Einige Erfahrungen aus der Arbeit einer ZPL mit Arbeitsgruppen," Parteiarbeiter, March 1969, p. 8.
45. Oberst Teichmann, "Die Schulung der Sekretäre der ZPL mit hoher Qualität vorbereiten und durchführen," Parteiarbeiter, May 1969, p. 8. See also Admiral W. Verner, "Die führende Rolle der SED in der Nationalen Volksarmee allseitige festigen und verwirklichen," Militärwesen, February 1968, p. 178; Teller, "In der Führungstätitkeit," p. 7.
46. By making political work more acceptable to the professional soldier, I mean the institution of scientific methods or training that not only require less time but also function on a level the regular officer may find acceptable. See, for example, Arno Bendrat and Alfred Nikolaus, Methodik der Politischen Schulung (Berlin-Ost: Deutscher Militärverlag, 1968); Klaus-Dieter Uckel, Militärische Ausbildung: Für die militär-pädagogische Aus- und Weiterbildung der Offiziere der Nationalen Volksarmee (2nd ed.; Berlin-Ost: Deutscher Militärverlag, 1967).
47. See for example, Fregatten Kapitän D. Pevestorf, "Patentschaftsarbeit—ein Mittel zur Unterstützung der sozialistischen Bewusstseinentwicklung," Militärwesen, November 1966, pp. 1546-51. Similar programs existed in the other services.
48. Fregattenkapitän G. Vogelsang, "Volksmarine volksverbunden," Marinewesen, May 1965, p. 524.
49. Pevestorf, "Patentschafsarbeit," p. 1547.
50. Ibid., p. 1549; Vogelsang, "Volksmarine volksverbunden," p. 524; Kapitänleutnant (Ing.) D. Flohr, "Der Öffentlichkeitsarbeit der Volksmarine mehr Aufmerksamkeit," Marinewesen, September 1968, p. 1036.
51. Fregattenkapitän Glapa, "Parteierziehung—nicht nur vor der PKK," Parteiarbeiter, June 1967, pp. 9-10.

52. See Oberst Pretzsch, "Des Einfluss der PKK auf die Erziehung leitender Kader," Parteiarbeiter, June 1965, pp. 10-12.

53. Kapitän zur See Wegner, "Von der Wende in der Parteiarbeit," Parteiarbeiter, March 1965, p. 8.

54. Admiral Verner, "Ziel der Parteiarbeit—Sicherung einer hohen Kampfkraft und ständigen Gefechtsbereitschaft der Nationalen Volksarmee," Parteiarbeiter, September 1967, p. 11. See also Admiral W. Verner, "Die führende Rolle der SED in der Nationalen Volksarmee allseitig festigen und verwirklichen," Militärwesen, February 1968, p. 177; Admiral W. Verner, "Die Grundorganisation—Fundament der Partei," Volksarmee, No. 52 (1967), p. 4; Generalmajor G. Teller, "Einige Grundfragen der Führung des politisch-ideologischen Arbeit im Ausbildungsjahr 1966/67," Militärwesen, January 1967, p. 7.

55. Hauptmann Gleis, "Die Verantvortung des Gruppenorganisators," Parteiarbeiter, December 1966, p. 18.

56. Hoffmann, "Menschenführung als Grundproblem," p. 383.

57. Generalmajor G. Teller, "Die Parteiwahlen in Vorbereitung des VII. Parteitages der SED festigen die Kampfkraft der Parteiorganisationen der NVA," Militärwesen, March 1967, p. 293.

58. Fregattenkapitän H. Bergel, "Die politische Arbeit auf kleinen Kampfschiffen und booten bei der Entwicklung und Festigung militärischer Kampfkollektiv," Militärwesen, September 1970, p. 1044.

59. Oberst R. Raubach, "Einzelleitung, wissenschaftliche Führungstätigkeit und Parteiarbeit," Militärwesen, November 1964, p. 1510.

60. Oberst S. Falke, "Einige notwendige Bemerkungen zum Artikel 'Organisationspolitische Aspekte zur Tätigkeit einer Arbeitsgruppe für politische Arbeit,'" Luftverteidigung, August 1970, p. 11.

61. Oberstleutnant H. Tilgner, "Die Rolle des Kommandeurs in der Parteiorganisation," Militärwesen, April 1967, pp. 492-93.

62. Hoffmann: "Zu den Grundfragen der Militärpolitik," p. 782.

63. Armeegeneral Heinz Hoffmann, "Die Nationale Volksarmee auf Friedenswacht," in Hoffmann, Sozialistische Landes Verteidigung, Vol. I, p. 257.

64. Kapitän zur See R. Wegner, "Die führende Rolle der Sozialistischen Einheitspartei Deutschlands ist die Quelle unserer Erfolge," Marinewesen, March 1966, p. 304.

65. Pech, "Über die Entwicklung und Perspektive des Offizierskorps," p. 197.

66. Verner, "Remarks," Protokoll der Verhandlungen des VII. Parteitages, Vol. III, p. 701.

67. Verner, "Die Ergebnisse und Aufgaben der 11. Tagung," p. 23. See also Vizeadmiral W. Ehm, "Wissenschaftliche Führung und klassenmässige Erziehung—Grundlage für die Erfüllung des

Aufgaben des neuen Ausbildungsjahres," Marinewesen, January 1967, p. 7; Major H. Trinks, "Auf die Abschluss Prüfungen in der gesellschaftswissenschaftlichen Weiterbildung gewisshaft vorbereiten," Luftverteidigung, February 1966, p. 10; Tilgner, "Die Rolle des Kommandeurs," p. 488; Oberstleutnant J. Wolf, "Kontrolle— Bestandteil der Führungstätigkeit," Militärwesen, June 1968, p. 800; Hoffmann, "Zu den Grundfragen der Militärpolitik," p. 783.

    68. Pech, "Die richtige Arbeit mit den Kadern," pp. 1667, 1672. It should be noted that Pech is not a political officer. In general, he appears to be one of the NVA's most concerned officers insofar as technical qualifications are concerned. Consequently, an admonition from him is particularly important in this regard.

    69. Admiral Waldemar Verner, "Wissenschaftlich fundierte Führungstätigkeit in allen Bereichen unser politischen und militärischen Arbeit durchsetzen!", Militärwesen, May 1964, p. 614. See also Notroff, "Die Offiziersschule der Volksmarine," p. 339; Verner, "Die führenden Rolle der SED," pp. 168-69; Dr. Werner Butter, Die Autorität des Offiziers (Berlin-Ost: Deutscher Militärverlag, 1966).

    70. Verner, "Die führenden Rolle der SED," p. 168.

    71. Wegner, "Von der Wende," p. 9.

    72. Armeegeneral Heinz Hoffmann, "Mit neuen Erfolgen dem VII. Parteitag entgegen," Militärwesen, (December, 1966), 1666-1667. By types of training Hoffmann means both political and technical.

    73. Generalleutnant K. Wagner, "Anforderungen des Erziehungs- und Bildungsprozesses in der Nationalen Volksarmee an die Ausbilderspersönlichkeit," Militärwesen, February 1966, p. 190.

    74. Fregattenkapitän R. Schreiber, "Sozialistische Kulturarbeit in der Volksmarine," Marinewesen, March 1964, p. 287. This was a rather frequent complaint. See Hauptmann F. Schneider, "Kulturwettstreit 1967," Luftverteidigung, January 1967, p. 46; Fregattenkapitän R. Schreiber, "Der Einfluss der kulturellen Massenarbeit auf die Gefechtsausbildung," Marinewesen, April 1966, p. 394; Oberst G. Teller, "Einige Ergebnisse und Aufgaben der politischen Massenarbeit in der NVA," Militärwesen, August 1965, p. 1054.

    75. Vizeadmiral W. Ehm, "Worauf kommt es in den letzten Wochen des Ausbildungsjahres an?", Marinewesen, June 1965, p. 649; Wagner, "Anforderungen des Erziehungs- und Bildungsprozesses," p. 190; Oberstleutnant R. Leuschner, "Rundfunk und Fernsehen für die ideologische Erziehung der Soldaten nutzen," Militärwesen, January 1965, p. 51.

    76. Schreiber, "Sozialistische Kulturarbeit," p. 390. See also Verner, "Die Ergebnisse und Aufgaben der 11. Tagung," p. 18. For a very interesting discussion of the ways of investigating the most influential factors in this area see Oberst A. Vogel, "Die Analyse der Entwicklung des Bewusstseins der Angehörigen der Nationalen

Volksarmee—wichtiges Element der Führungstätigkeit," Militärwesen, June 1966, pp. 819-29.

77. Major Hans Göbel, "Die politische Schulung ist Parteischulung," Parteiarbeiter, March 1967, p. 16.

78. Tilgner, "Die Rolle des Kommandeurs," p. 493.

79. Oberstleutnant E. Nowak, "Das Niveau der gesellschaftswissenschaftlichen Weiterbildung verbessern," Militärwesen, March 1966, p. 353.

80. Oberstleutnant H. König, "Mit dem Selbststudium steht und fällt die gesellschaftswissenschaftliche Weiterbildung der Offiziere," Militärwesen, December 1965, p. 1718.

81. Vizeadmiral W. Ehm, "Das Erreichte ist die Grundlage für neue Erfolge im Ausbildungsjahr 1964/1965," Marinewesen, January 1965, p. 11.

82. Oberstleutnant H. Mehner, "Eine Wende in der politisch-ideologischen Arbeit herbeiführen," Militärwesen, February 1965, p. 149.

83. The discussion of the testing system is taken from Oberstleutnant M. Mähler and Major H. Richter, "Methodische Hinweise für die Abschlussprüfung in der gesellschaftswissenschaftlichen Weiterbildung der Offiziere," Militärwesen, June 1966, pp. 861-66. This article was written to help officers prepare for the examination.

84. The factors that are important for an evaluation are six in number and too lengthy to repeat here. They can be found in Ibid., pp. 862-65.

85. Ibid., p. 866.

86. Ibid.

87. Autorenkollektiv, Zeittafel . . . 1949 bis 1968, p. 269.

88. Korvettenkapitän F. Bieler, "Die Geschichte der deutschen Arbeiterbewegung und einige Maritime Berührungspunkte," Marinewesen, March 1967, p. 259. The goals of these classes are six in number and too long to list here. They can be found in Autorenkollektiv der Politischen Hauptverwaltung, "Grundliches Studium der Geschichte der deutschen Arbeiterbewegung—wichtiger Bestandteil unseres Kampfes um hohe ideologische Gefechtsbereitschaft," Militärwesen, October 1966, p. 1368.

89. Oberstleutnant Dr. W. Butter, Über den Einfluss der Parteiorganisation und des militärischen Kollektivs auf die Autorität des Offiziers," Militärwesen, April 1965, p. 470. See also Major H. Müller, "Der sozialistische Wettbewerbobjektive Notwendigkeit auch an der Offiziersschule," Luftverteidigung, January 1966, pp. 36-37; Alfred Hartmann, Die Abgabe von Straftaten an den Kommandeur zur Behandlung nach der Disziplinarvorschrift der Nationalen Volksarmee, DV 10/6 (Berlin-Ost: Deutscher Militärverlag, 1968), p. 47; Oberst Pretzsch, "Der Einfluss der PKK auf die Erziehung leitender Kader," Parteiarbeiter, June 1965, p. 10.

90. Major d. J. D. G. Schulze und Kapitänleutnant K. Kästner, "Die Aufgaben der militärisches Kollektiv bei der Festigung der Disziplin und Ordnung," Marinewesen, March 1965, p. 304; Major H. Schierz, "Fordernde und hemmende Faktoren der Bewusstseinsbildung," Luftverteidigung, January 1967, p. 15. In addition there are a number of offenses that are not handled by the collective. For a discussion of these, see Hartmann, Die Abgabe, pp. 52-53.

91. Schulze and Kästner, "Die Aufgaben der militärisches Kollektiv," p. 304; Oberstleutnant S. Schirrmann, "Zum Problem der kollektiven Erziehung," Militärwesen, December 1966, p. 1710.

92. Although a copy of this letter was not available, its contents are discussed in a number of articles. See Oberstleutnant Günter Münch, "Aus dem Protokoll der IV. Delegiertenkonferenz der FDJ—Organisation in der Nationalen Volksarmee Mai 65," Parteiarbeiter, Sonderheft 2, 1965, pp. 13-14; Hartmann, Die Abgabe, p. 15; and especially Korvettenkapitän W. Tülling and Oberleutnant zur See E. Schmolinsky, "Kollektive Erziehungsmassnahmen—Voraussetzung für eine bewusste Disziplin," Marinewesen, May 1966, p. 559.

93. Hartmann, Die Abgabe, pp. 61-62. For a listing of the reasons given by officers for not allowing the military collective to handle these matters see Schirrmann, "Zum Problem der kollektive, Erziehung," p. 1704.

94. Politische Hauptverwaltung der Nationalen Volksarmee, Argumentation, December 1967, p. 6; Oberstleutnant d. J. D. Zöller, "Vor den Schöffenwahlen," Parteiarbeiter, April 1965, p. 16; A. Leibner, G. Sarge, et al., "Nationale Volksarmee und Rechtspflege," Neue Justiz, XV, 5 (1966), p. 130.

95. Gerhard Baumann, "Die militärische Kapazität der SBZ," Wehrkunde, XV, 6 (1966), p. 303; Institute for Strategic Studies, Military Balance, 1966-1967 (London, 1966), p. 7.

96. Redaktion, "Für unsere sozialistische DDR," p. 613.

CHAPTER 7

THE NVA EMERGES
AS A MODERN
MILITARY FORCE
1968-72

By 1968 the East Germans possessed one of the most modern armed forces in Europe.[1] Within the Warsaw Pact, it occupied second place behind the Soviet Union. In addition to a modern air force, it possessed a small but modern navy and an army of 90,000 divided into six divisions, four of motorized infantry and two of armor. Due to high marks earned in past maneuvers and East Germany's strategic geographical location, the Soviets view the NVA as an important addition to the Soviet forces stationed in the GDR.[2]

Should Mutual and Balanced Force Reductions (MBFR) become a reality, and Russian rather than Eastern European troops bear the brunt of reductions, it is probable that the importance of the NVA within the Warsaw Pact will increase even more. The important position the GDR occupies in the Warsaw Pact, like its economic role in COMECON (Council of Mutual Economic Assistance), provides it with a useful bargaining tool in its relations with the Soviets. As long as the East Germans are able to convince the Russians that the NVA is both militarily prepared and politically reliable, they will be in a good position to bargain with the Soviets for favors in other areas.

From all appearances, the Soviets, at present at least, remain convinced that the NVA fulfills both these requirements. The Soviets have provided the East Germans with the most modern equipment of any of the Warsaw Pact countries, attesting to both its technical competence and political reliability. In view of Soviet suspicions that combat preparedness or ideological purity could be undermined by a relaxation of tensions, which in turn would undermine this beneficial relationship, it is not surprising that the SED has gone to great lengths to alleviate any effects that a gradual movement toward detente in Europe might have on its military in order to assure the Russians that the NVA continues to be worthy of their trust.

Concern over the effects on the NVA of movement toward detente is not prompted solely by foreign policy considerations. The internal political situation in the GDR also plays an important role. The party, as noted above, has had a tendency to utilize the level of politicization in the NVA as a barometer of party control throughout society. Having paid particular attention to assuring a high degree of political reliability in the NVA, the party has long felt that, if a deemphasis on ideological factors occurred there, the situation in the rest of society probably was even more serious.

Unfortunately, from the SED's standpoint, there are signs that the movement toward detente has adversely affected the NVA, both in terms of combat preparedness and ideological purity. There is an indication that some members of the NVA feel that, since war is becoming less of a danger, perhaps the West Germans and Americans are not as much a military threat as in the past. If this is so, some ask, then why all the concern over problems of military preparedness?

The party reacted to this situation by arguing—much like the American and Soviet military—that detente is only possible because of military strength. The West has not changed, the party says, and it is only because of the military strength and preparedness of the Soviet Union and other socialist countries, including the GDR, that the West has been forced to recognize the futility of military adventures in Europe. This situation will continue, the party argues, only as long as the socialist states remain militarily alert and ready to repel any Western acts of aggression. SED Party Secretary Erich Honecker emphasized this point in an unusually strong speech before members of the NVA at Prora on January 7, 1972. In referring to the "Western-Imperialist bloc," he stated:

> Nevertheless, it remains aggressive, malicious and dangerous. . . . As a result, we have no reason to let down in our military and political vigilance. Our picture of our enemy (Feindbild) is completely accurate. There is nothing in the picture to change, because our enemy has not changed.[3]

Closely associated with the tendency to downplay the military threat from the West is the tendency of some to equate peaceful coexistence with ideological convergence. After all, if one can peacefully coexist with the imperialists politically and economically, then why not ideologically? On this point, the party's reaction has been immediate and to the point. The two ideologies are basically incompatible the party argues, as exemplified by Honecker's 1972 interview with C. L. Sulzberger of the New York Times in which he stated, "Ideological convergence will not come about. We proceed from two different positions."[4]

Party ideology further underlined the incompatibility of military detente and ideological convergence by pointing out that the West, faced with a situation in which the balance of power has shifted to the side of the socialist countries, has merely substituted bourgeois ideology for military power in pursuit of its unchanging goal of undermining the socialist countries. The class struggle has not ceased; it has merely shifted to another area. Consequently, it has become necessary for the GDR and other socialist states to continue defending themselves against the subverting influence of Western ideas and thoughts.[5] As a result, the party introduced its policy of Abgrenzung or separation from the West. Contacts with the West, particularly for members of the NVA, are to be avoided at all costs. In addition, assuming that some aspects of bourgeois ideology do penetrate, the SED emphasizes such factors as party activities and ideological indoctrination to maintain its hold within the NVA.

Therefore, the party has taken steps to maintain a high level of combat readiness and political reliability within the NVA, for both internal and external reasons. Insofar as combat readiness is concerned, the party has placed heavy stress on maintaining a high degree of technology. The need for a high degree of political reliability has resulted in great efforts by the party to assure that political control remains high.

MILITARY TECHNOLOGY

Data on 15 of the 17 indicators constructed for this study appeared during this period. The first deals with the educational level required for entry into officer training schools. The increase in educational requirements that occurred in Period IV remained in force during Period V.[6] The only tendency noticeable during this period was the increasing predominance of those possessing the Abitur among entering cadets. If the trend continues, almost all officer cadets will soon possess the Abitur.[7]

Raising the requirement for individuals attending officer training schools to the same level as those entering a university shows not only the important technological progress that occurred in the NVA but also its ability to obtain individuals with this background. This is a far cry from 1949, when many individuals commissioned as officers has not completed even the basic school (Grundschule). The classification of this indicator remains high.

The length of officer training schools, the second indicator of technology, also remained the same. Individuals wishing to become officers had to attend an officer training school for three or four years.[8] The NVA apparently settled early—in 1959—on this length of time as appropriate for the education of officers. Despite the increasing demands of modern technology, the NVA has refused to lengthen this training period, perferring to "rationalize" the time available, as discussed in Chapter 6. The classification of this indicator remains high.

The third indicator, the percentage of officers having attended a three-year officer training school, continued to mount. By 1969 a total of 80 percent of all officers had completed a three-year officer training school.[9] The only other figure available for this period, from 1971, gives the same percentage.[10] This indicator is again classified as high.

The value of an officer's education when compared with civilian institutions serves as the fourth indicator of technology. Important changes occurred in this indicator during Period V, as the officer training schools gained the status of colleges or universities in the GDR. This occurred through a decree issued by the State Ministry (Staatsrat) on December 10, 1970. According to this decree:

> The facilities of the National Peoples' Army for training or further education (Weiterbildung) of officers on active duty carry the title (Charakter tragen) of colleges (Hochschulen) of the German Democratic Republic.[11]

This change, first mentioned by Walter Ulbricht in 1968,[12] meant that graduates of the NVA officer schools would receive degrees comparable to those awarded by civilian universities. The importance of this change should not be underestimated. It is the first time in German history that an officer training school attained this level. Although attempts are being made to raise West German officer training schools to this status, as of 1971 they remained technical schools.[13] As a result of this rise in the status of officer training schools, the level of technology represented by this indicator rose to high.

The fifth indicator, the percentage of officers who have the mittlere Reife as their highest level of education, again increased. By 1969 the percentage of officers who possessed at least the mittlere Reife rose to 52 percent.[14] Two years later, this figure rose to 53.9 percent,[15] which represents quite an accomplishment when one considers that only 0.1 percent of all KVP officers had this certificate. It is indicative of a high level of technology.

The percentage of officers who possess the Abitur, the sixth indicator of technology, also rose significantly over the preceding period. Whereas 23 percent of all officers possessed the Abitur in 1966, the figure mounted to 34 percent by 1969[16] and 37.1 percent by 1971.[17] As a result of this increase, the indicator is classified as signifying a high level of technology.

The seventh indicator of technology, the percentage of officers who possess a technical education, rose two percentage points at this time, to 75.2 percent.[18] This figure represents a significant accomplishment when one considers that the earliest figure was 31 percent. The 75.2 percent figure is indicative of a high level of technology.

The percentage of officers in the NVA officer corps who are engineers or technicians, the eighth indicator of technology, rose slightly over the preceding period, from 16.6 percent to 17 percent.[19] It continues to be indicative of a high level of technology.

The ninth indicator concerns the percentage of officers having an academic education. Four sources give percentage figures for this indicator. The first, for 1968, lists 13 percent; the next, from 1969, is 14 percent; and the third, from 1971, is 16 percent.[20] In a speech on March 1, 1973, on the occasion of the seventeenth anniversary of the founding of the NVA, Heinz Hoffmann put the figure at 25 percent.[21] The sharp rise in the 1973 figure is no doubt due in large part to the upgrading of the officer training schools to the status of colleges. By 1973 three classes of officers had graduated from these schools and received academic degrees. But since the 1973 figure pertains to a year beyond the confines of this study, it was omitted from the figures utilized in classifying this indicator. In any case, regardless of the figure used, the percentage of officers possessing an academic education is high and shows the results of the tremendous effort put forth in this area. By comparison, for example, the percentage of officers in the Bundeswehr (The Armed Forces of the Federal Republic of Germany) who possessed an academic education in 1971 was only 10 percent.[22] In this area at least, the educational qualifications of the NVA officer corps far outstrip those of its chief opponents. As more graduates of the officer training schools enter the ranks of the NVA officer corps, this percentage can be expected to rise even higher.

Since there was no information on the percentage of army regimental commanders with academic education in this period, the tenth indicator present treats the length of time officers are obligated to serve. Figures available at the beginning of the period indicate the requirement continued to 10 years' service. Some confusion appears during the latter part of the period in the wording of the "Service Career Regulation" (Dienstlaufbahnordnung) issued in 1970.[24] Paragraph 28 of this document states:

> (1) The minimum time of service for officers on active duty is, in the main, determined according to the rank considered attainable for the duty station or position and by the age of the officer.
> (2) The following age is set as a minimum period of service in accordance with the rank attainable in the duty station.

a) up to captain/naval lieutenant   38 years [of age]
b) major/naval lieutenant commander   43 years
c) lieutenant colonel/naval commander   50 years
d) colonel/naval captain   55 years.[25]

These figures imply that an individual starting the officer training school at the age of 20 and finishing as an army captain will be required to remain in the service until he is at least 38 years old, or for 13 years. No mention is made of the former 10-year minimum service time. This could be an oversight or a change, or it could indicate the maximum amount of time an officer may remain in the service at a particular grade. In any case, however, this indicator remains high.

The eleventh indicator of technology present during this period deals with the importance of technical qualifications for promotion and retention in the service. The demand for a technically well educated officer corps continued. Indeed, not only was knowledge of the natural sciences and Marxist ideology required, an acquaintance with social science was expected as well. As Admiral Ehm explained:

> A basic requirement for commanders and officers of the staff is a high political, ideological, military, and natural science education. The increasingly technical nature of the armed forces, and above all, the means of leadership, assumes knowledge in the area of mathematics, physics, chemistry, electronics and cybernetics. One who wants to lead a military collective successfully can no longer fail to acquire a knowledge of socialist psychology, pedagogics, and sociology.[26]

In order to determine which officers qualified educationally for assignment to higher positions, another efficiency report or attestation program like that of 1964 was undertaken in 1968.[27] All officers were once again rated according to their technical competence—as well as political reliability. Those receiving the highest scores would be sent to schools like the military academy in Dresden to prepare for regimental command. Since attendance at this or a similar school in the Soviet Union is a prerequisite for assignment at the regimental command level, a low score on an efficiency report might well mean the end of a career.

East German authorities were concerned by the apparent reluctance of commanders who filled out the reports to recommend that individuals who did qualify for advancement be placed in the reserve. Nevertheless, those up for promotion are carefully rated by the commander, who must justify his choices if challenged. Technical competence makes up a large part of his evaluation.[28] The importance of the reports for retention in the service varies, as mentioned above.[29] Since technical qualifications continue to play an important role in the decision on who is to be promoted and, at least in principle, who is to be retained in the service, the indicator deserves the same high classification given it in period IV.

The issuance of technical awards, the twelfth indicator of technology present during this period, registered a very important change. On January 4, 1969, Heinz Hoffmann issued a directive entitled "Regulations on the Classification and Awarding of Classification Medals to Members of the NVA."[30] Although this order concerned medals that had been issued since 1962, rather than a wholly new type of medal, individuals qualifying for such awards gained recognition as qualified for comparable civilian occupations.

These awards were intended to encourage improvement of NVA members' technical qualifications.[31] The three numerical classification levels introduced in 1963 received titles. An individual who passed the examination at the first level would be classified as a skilled worker (Facharbeiter). Those passing it at the second level received the title master (Meister). Those who passed it at the third level qualified for the title of technician or engineer (Techniker or Ingenieur).[32] This meant that, upon leaving the service, a person who had attained the title of engineer could qualify for a job in a civilian factory requiring that level of skill.

The examinations for these technical awards test knowledge encompassing both the practical operation of the equipment in question and the theory on which it is based. As one naval officer explained:

> An ammunition officer can not do without a basic knowledge of inorganic and organic chemistry, electro-technology, and other specialties. Such basic knowledge is unavoidable for a complete understanding of specialized problems. For that reason, these types of demands will be reflected in the tests for the classification medals.[33]

The intensive testing required for these awards and their substantial value to individuals receiving them qualifies this indicator for a classification of high on the schema established earlier.

The thirteenth indicator present during this period deals with the number of occupational categories recognized by the NVA. No changes were detected in this indicator over the previous period.[34] Its classification remains high.

The fourteenth indicator of technology present during this period treats the number of specialized journals in the NVA. Three journals, Militärwesen, Marinewesen, and Luftverteidigung, were combined into one—Militärwesen. But this journal continued to have three sections dealing with specific army, air force, and navy problems. In addition, it also had a large general section dealing with broad topics common to all services. One additional journal was introduced during this period, Der Ausbilder (The educator). It deals primarily with the problems associated with technical and political training in a modern military. Although technically the number of journals decreased by one during Period V, I do not feel that this change is important for purposes of this study, due to the expanded nature of Militärwesen. Instead of three smaller journals, one now had a single larger one. This indicator continues to be classified as high.

The fifteenth indicator of technology present during this period is the PS level (there was no information on the number of books published on specialized military subjects). Four sources reported figures for three different years. According to those for 1968, the PS level rose from 29.1 in 1965 to 30.5 in 1968.[35] Part of the reason for this rise in PS level may be the introduction of the T-62 tank during this period. In addition, the MIG-21 replaced the MIG-19 as the backbone of the East German air force. The PS level remained the same in 1969 and 1971.[36] Continuation of the PS level at 30.5 for four years suggests that the NVA has reached a point beyond which increases in the PS level come very slowly. Although one can certainly expect the PS level to increase in the future, the dramatic changes that occurred in earlier periods appear to be a thing of the past. This indicator is classified as high for Period V.

In order to obtain an average level of technology for Period V, the scores arrived at for each indicator are entered on Table 7.1.

Technology has reached the highest point possible in this study, 3.0. This does not mean that it is impossible for the level of technology to increase in absolute terms in the future. In fact, one would expect that it will. This scoring system was devised in order to make it possible to see the effect an increase in the level of technology would have on political control. In doing this it was assumed that the level of technology would be high or at least closely approximate high by the end of the study. Someone replicating this study five or ten years from now would set up a scoring system so that the final year in their time frame would be high. What is important in this study is not that technology has become high on any absolute scale but the effect the increase in technology has had on political control. The fact that the level of technology within the NVA may be viewed as high relative to other military units is not unimportant, but is insignificant for the scoring system adopted for this study. In order to discover the effect of this level of technology on political control, the focus now turns to the indicators of political control.

TABLE 7.1

Level of Technology in Periods I-V, 1949-72

Indicator	Period I	Period II	Period III	Period IV	Period V
1. Entry education	—	1	2	3	3
2. School length	2	3	3	3	3
3. Three-year course	—	1	1	3	3
4. Educational value	1	2	2	3	3
5. Mittlere Reife	1	1	2	2	3
6. Abitur	1	1	2	2	3
7. Fachschulausbildung	—	1	—	3	3
8. Engineers or Technicians	—	1	2	3	3
9. Total academic education	—	1	1	2	3
10. Regimental academic education	—	1	3	3	—
11. Length of service	2	3	3	3	3
12. Technical qualifications	—	1	3	3	3
13. Technical awards	—	1	2	2	3
14. Occupational categories	—	2	2	3	3
15. Journals	1	1	3	3	3
16. Books	—	1	2	3	—
17. PS Level	1	2	2	2	3
Total	9	24	35	46	45
Average	1.3	1.4	2.2	2.7	3.0

Note: 1 = low; 2 = medium; 3 = high; — = no information.

POLITICAL CONTROL

Thirteen of the 15 indicators of political control constructed for this study were mentioned during Period V. The first indicator deals with the organizational level down to which the political officer is present. Despite all of the political changes that occurred in the NVA and in its predecessor, the KVP, in their 24-year combined history, the organizational level down to which the political officer is present never changed. Once again, references placed him at the company level.[37] The indicator is classified as medium.

The second indicator, the organizational level down to which the SSD officer is present, has a position similar to the first. During the entire course of this study, no change occurred in this indicator as data for Period V once again said the SSD officer was assigned down to the regimental and, in the case of independent battalions, to the battalion level.[38]

The length of training for a political officer, the third indicator, increased. In period IV political officers received a year or less of training. In an effort to produce more competent political officers, this situation changed in 1970, when the school for individuals wishing to become political officers was accorded the status of a college (Hochschule). Two years later, by a resolution of the Secretariat of the Central Committee, the political officer school, like other officer schools in the GDR, was given a name that commemorated an important figure in the history of German communism. It was named the Wilhelm Pieck Military-Political College (Wilhelm Pieck militärpolitische Hochschule).[39]

The past practice of relying on young graduates of the various officer training schools as political officers after a four-or five-month course at the higher political officer school no longer sufficed. As Hoffmann noted upon the opening of the school:

> Old experiences and good will no longer suffice to lead the ideological work with the necessary quality. Only when our commanders and political officers possess advanced scientific knowledge as well as the necessary educational ability and skills will it be possible to do justice to the increasing demands of work with the masses.[40]

Although specific details concerning this school are not available, it apparently is aimed at training graduates of the officer training schools who have served in the field for a couple of years as political officers at the company and battalion level.[41] Presumably, individuals selected to serve as political officers would attend this school for at least a year and, from all appearances, probably longer. The opportunity also exists for selected individuals to continue beyond the one-year course and obtain the academic degree of a diploma in social science (Diplomgesellschaftswissenschaft).[42] In addition to training young officers for work as political officers, this college also offers short courses for higher-ranking officers.

Political officers, like their military counterparts, are still required to attend the Friedrich Engels Military Academy in Dresden if they hope to attain command positions at the regimental level. The increased weight assigned to the Wilhelm Pieck college assisted the party in overcoming a very serious weakness in its efforts to create military dual executives. Up to this point, company and battalion political officers—the most numerous and those with the most contact with the masses of soldiers and NCOs—usually were expected to carry out their tasks with only the ideological training they received at the officer training school supplemented by a short course at the higher political officer training school. This meant that, although they might be convinced communists, their knowledge of pedagogics as well as their familiarity with the more sophisticated arguments both for and against communism would be lacking. As a result, they often were ineffective in presenting the party line. But as a consequence of the qualitative increase in the training received by political officers at the new Wilhelm Pieck School, the future officer is not only familiar with military technology as a result of his education at the regular officer training school and time served in the field but has the advantage of a year or more of training in the latest techniques of presenting party dogma. This change results in a classification of medium.

The fourth indicator of political control concerns the military service of political officers. Period V presents a far different picture from earlier periods when individuals fresh out of the civilian world often were sent directly to political officer schools and commissioned after two or three years' training as political officers. As indicated above, students at the political officer college are graduates of an officer training school and have a few years of experience in the field as regular officers behind them.[43] The indicator is still classified as high.

The fifth indicator deals with the level of activity of the Politorgane. The Politorgane continued to bear full responsibility for the basic organization.[44] As in Period IV, it exerted its authority over the basic organizations through the central party directory. But problems with this arrangement did appear. Some central party directories failed to work collectively:[45] One individual might push one policy very hard while another argued for a diametrically opposed policy. This presented extensive difficulties for coordination of the activities of the basic organization.

But one must not overrate these problems. Although they might lower the efficiency of the Politorgane in some cases, the fact that these structures existed and functioned as well as they did suggests that the party was able to continue to exert tight control over the members of the basic organizations.

The Politorgane continued to intensify their activities by improving the qualifications of party functionaries.[46] Apparently, qualifications had continued to be a problem despite past efforts.

Little if any change was observed in the activities of the Politorgane in comparison with the preceding period. The structure, despite difficulties, remained tight, and the level of Politorgane activity high. Therefore, the indicator is again classified as indicative of a high level of political control.

The sixth indicator of political control concerns the activities of the military party organization. The military party organization or, more specifically, the basic organization, continued to be heralded as one of the most important components of political work. As one source explained:

> In order for the party organizations to be able to do justice to the increased responsibility for the carrying out of party resolutions in their area, the <u>further strengthening of the basic organization</u> has been placed in the center point of our work.[47]

Six areas received particular attention from the party in its effort to strengthen the basic organization. First, the party mounted a campaign to increase the degree of participation by party members in membership meetings (Mitgliederversammlungen) of the basic organization, which continued to be viewed as the heart of the basic organization.[48] Participation during the preceding period was only 32 percent. By 1969 it had risen to 45 percent.[49] But two years later Admiral Verner, disparaging the fact that participation was not 100 percent, reported it as 76 percent.[50] The fact that the percentage of those participating in membership meetings rose from one in three to three in four over four short years is impressive. But this achievement is tempered by the fact that, although a larger number of individuals participated in these meetings, most found them boring or irrelevant.[51] In any case, the chances that an individual could avoid participating in the basic organization membership meeting were drastically reduced.

Closely related to the increased emphasis on the membership meeting of the basic organization was the continued stress placed upon the party groups. These groups were divided in most cases according to function—for example, flying and ground technical personnel were divided into two groups, according to one source.[52] In the military as in the civilian world, they were to make certain that members knew and followed the party line.[53] Individuals who failed to give evidence of the requisite knowledge of the party line, or who were less than enthusiastic about carrying it out, would be reported and probably have their shortcomings entered in their service record.

Discipline and order also increasingly concerned the military party organization. Although the regular officers became completely responsible for the administration of discipline during Period V, the party organization was brought into play in the cases of those who violated military regulations with the justification that a high degree of combat readiness was only possible in a military force with strict order and discipline. Consequently, it was the party's task to talk with those who violated regulations and to explain to them the serious effects such violations could have on combat preparedness.[54]

The party also moved to improve the qualifications of party secretaries.[55] The scarcity of qualified individuals continued to plague party efforts since one could hardly expect military experts to accept the word of a party secretary whom they considered unqualified.

In addition, the party organization sought an even greater role in both the political indoctrination and military educational qualification processes. As one writer commented:

> The basic organization of the party in this connection should devote itself more to furthering educational programs in the social sciences and military qualifications of officers in the respective school groups, as well as evaluating them. The main interest is, among other things, to consequently carry out the political qualification order, full of ideas, by using the proven methods of political work with the masses.[56]

The party organization was not only to fill its traditional role of setting an example for other members of the military but also to participate in the presentation and development of courses.[57]

The party organization also focused attention on the relationship between itself and the commander. Regular officers once again came under fire for failing to pay sufficient attention to political factors. The main complaint centered around the commanders' failure to utilize the party organization adequately. One author noted the commander's reluctance to make proper use of the party groups;[58] another decried the lack of interest in the collective method of decision making.[59] In another case, the commander was chastised for not behaving properly in his relations with the party group leader. Only when the commander recognizes that the party group is very important and the party group leader is the representative, the writer argues, will the commander learn to accept the party group leader's advice and work with him properly toward the common goal of strengthening socialism.[60]

The regular officer's ability to perceive himself primarily as a military technician further decreased during Period V. He would find it very difficult to avoid participation in the basic organization or other party activities. In addition, the party groups were increasingly active and deviant behavior would be noted and reported. The influence of the party organization in the decision-making process also increased. Refusal on the part of a regular officer to consult with the party could mean the end of his career. As a result, this indicator is classified as high.

The seventh indicator of political control, the percentage of NVA officers who are SED party members, showed a slight increase over the preceding period. But the figures suggest that this indicator had begun to stabilize. At the end of Period IV, 97 percent of all NVA officers belonged to the SED. By 1970 the figure had risen to 98 percent,[61] the same figure reported a year later.[62]

The SED leadership perceived the importance of party membership by NVA officers from the beginning. Consequently, it carefully and deliberately instituted a policy aimed at increasing the percentage of officers who were party members, a policy that was very successful by the end of Period V. Due to this high membership ratio, it would be very difficult indeed for any NVA officer to be apolitical. With very few exceptions, all are SED members, which means they are required to attend political meetings and engage in other political activities. Consequently, this indicator remains high.

The eighth indicator of political control treats the importance assigned to the officers' political qualifications. Military and political qualifications continued to play equally important roles in the writing of officers' efficiency reports. This is particularly apparent in the following statement by an East German political officer listing the factors—both political and military—that would be considered in evaluating officers during 1972:

> 1. The results which the cadre, in the political and military activities of his post, as a member of the party of the workers' class, as a military educator, trainer, i.e., a military specialist, has accomplished taking into consideration the demands of the respective position.
> 2. The knowledge, activities, and abilities which were observed in the process of solving the political and military tasks in his respective posts as well as his development since his last efficiency report.
> 3. The behavior of subordinates in political-social life off-duty as well as in the collective with respect to superiors and/or equals.
> 4. The level of consciousness, the class-oriented and struggle-manifested (Kampfgezogene) thinking and behavior, the political and military attitudes, convictions, needs, interests, desires, and characteristics.[63]

If anything, perhaps in anticipation of the Abgrenzung policy introduced in 1972, slightly more emphasis was placed on political factors in these reports than in preceding periods. After all, as one source put it, "These reports are, in the first place, political undertakings."[64] Particular stress was placed on "the political activity and capability of cadres insofar as the creative realization of the resolutions of the party is concerned."[65]

As a result of this increased emphasis on the political half of the military dual executive, an individual could now hope to be promoted or retained in the service only if he paid proper attention to the political side of military life. Simply being a first-rate technician was no longer sufficient. There were enough technically competent officers available so that those who did not show the requisite interest in political life could be replaced by others equally qualified from a technical standpoint. Insofar as this indicator is concerned, the point has been reached where being "red" is as important as being "expert" insofar as promotion or retention in the service in concerned. This indicator is indicative of a high level of political control.

Responsibility for political indoctrination serves as the ninth indicator of political control. During Period IV the military party organization began to play an increasingly important role in the area of political indoctrination. It further expanded this role in Period V, as discussed above.

The aloofness of many military specialists from political indoctrination continued to concern the party during this period, particularly in light of its concern over ideological threats from the West. This resulted in further efforts to convince military officers to work closely not only with the political officer but with the party collective as well. As one writer explained:

> They, the commanding officer and the political officer, must regularly discuss the political-ideological content of their respective tasks in combat training and combat service in their party collective and present their ideas of how they want to solve these tasks.[66]

Pressure on the military specialist to engage in political indoctrination activities was not limited to such appeals for cooperation—he also was called on and often required to participate in delivering such lectures.[67]

Forcing the military specialist to become more closely involved in the indoctrination process might at first glance appear to open an avenue for the presentation of his own ideas, which of course could be at variance with those of the party. Although this was to some degree possible, it was largely negated by the strict control of the indoctrination program exercised by the party.

One must not forget that the party organization, which has a direct line to the Politorgane through the ZPL, also participates in the political indoctrination program. As a result, a regular officer's articulation of what the party considers unfriendly ideas would be reported to the Politorgane and result in disciplinary action against him. In addition, the commander has direct responsibility for political indoctrination.[68] Should one of his subordinates—regardless of whether a regular or political officer—fail to show the proper enthusiasm for the party line, he also will be reported. As a result, the commander can be expected to take a great deal of interest in seeing that political indoctrination is carried out in accord with party desires. If anything, the influence exercised by the party in this regard increased during Period V. But in any case this indicator remains the same as during the last period—indicative of a high level of political control.

The tenth indicator of political control pertains to responsibility for work with the masses. Regular military officers showed no greater inclination to become involved in work with the masses than to participate in ideological indoctrination. Military commanders are very busy men. They must deal with a myriad of problems, all of which call for close attention. Participation in political indoctrination took time enough in the eyes of many commanders, but spending spare time conducting work with the masses cut even deeper into time already limited by political and technical self-study requirements, not to mention personal activities. Therefore, many regular officers simply ignored the subject. This tendency did not go unnoticed by the party. As one article put it, "the opinion, we do not have time for cultural work after we have fulfilled our military and political obligations still exists."[69]

To the party, threatened by "ideological subversion" from the West at a time of increasing detente, this situation was unacceptable. The party reacted once again by stressing the individual commander's responsibility for work with the masses by his unit.[70] Because of this responsibility, failure to insure a high degree of participation by all members of the unit, including himself, could result in a bad efficiency report for the unit commander, hurting his opportunity for promotion.

The dominant role of the party military organization again negated any chance for the regular officer to utilize his responsibility in this area as a forum for propagation of his own ideas. The party organization, in close cooperation with the political officer, directs the work. When a regular officer participates, he does so under the supervision of the party organization.[71] Failure by the regular officer to send his troops to the right museum, to show the appropriate number of propaganda films, or to explain the exhibits visited in the correct manner might well excite party dissatisfaction. Since the party has a direct line to the Politorgane, such actions can very easily be reported and dealt with. As a result, this indicator is classified as indicating a high level of political control.

The eleventh indicator of political control deals with part-time ideological training. This period saw the end of the second program of political schooling for officers and the beginning of the third. Interestingly, there was no comment in the press on how NVA officers did in the second course of political training, which was devoted to a history of the German workers' movement. On one occasion, Admiral Verner, head of the Main Political Administration, simply noted that it was drawing to a close in 1969 and would be suceeded by a new course.[72] General Hoffmann remarked that an "important niveau of Marxist-Leninist education has been achieved."[73]

The new part-time study course required officers to deal with the basic policies of the SED. As Admiral Verner put it, "the highest niveau in political-ideological work—demanded by the Seventh Party Conference—requires the leading cadres and propagandists to dictate particular attention to their further education in Marxism-Leninism."[74] Some of the main points of the new course were outlined by one East German officer as follows:

> 1. Problems of socialist theory, in particular questions of the form of the developed social system of socialism, the military policy of the SED, and the role of the service leadership by the solution of the class-oriented task of the NVA.
> 2. Problems of the development of socialism on a world scale, in particular questions of the strengthening and development of the socialist state commonwealth, (Sozialistischen Staatsgemeinschaft), the socialist military policy in the present stage of the class struggle and of the development of the all-sided cooperation of the GDR and the Soviet Union as well as the comradeship in arms (Waffenbrudderschaft) between the NVA and the Soviet army.
> 3. Problems of the class struggle between socialism and imperialism, in particular questions of the development of the state monopolistic capitalism, the increasing aggressiveness of West German imperialism in the realm of global strategy, and its course in NATO.[75]

This new course presumably will have semester and final examinations, providing those who pass it with the equivalent of a district party school certificate, as in earlier periods.

All indications suggest that, despite the increased importance the party placed on this indicator, the time regular officers devoted to part-time political study remained fairly constant. Although there is no way to be certain that this is the case, it seems very unlikely that the amount of time devoted to such studies would decrease at the same time that the importance of political qualifications for an officer's promotion or retention in the service increased.

The amount of formal class time devoted to political indoctrination could have remained constant for a number of reasons. First, the officers' understanding of the basic tenets was high enough that valuable class time did not have to be devoted to basic questions. Instead, utilizing better trained instructors with modern pedagogic methods and devices, this valuable time could be devoted to more complex questions. Second, the majority of the officer corps appears to have internalized the party's Weltanschauung, or at least long since ceased to exhibit open opposition, so it no longer was necessary to devote this time to overcoming hostile attitudes. Third, the commander was made responsible for the performance of his subordinates.[76] As a result, it can be assumed that he would emphasize to his charges the necessity of spending off-duty hours on the study of party ideology. Failure to do so would be noted not only by the party organization but by his superior officer as well, and his efficiency reports would no doubt reflect this fact. Because the time devoted to political indoctrination remained constant, this indicator continues to be classified as indicating a high level of political control.

The twelfth indicator of political control present during this period concerns the handling of disciplinary questions (there was no information on the effectiveness of self-criticism for this period). The problem of how to create a strong disciplinary system received considerable attention during Period V.

One means of handling disciplinary questions mentioned in the preceding period was responsibility by the commander in close consultation with the collective. This approach continued to be stressed during the early part of Period V. As one writer put it:

> We are aware that only in a collective well-grounded in Marxism-Leninism, a collective which thinks and acts together, will it be possible to produce socialist fighters with ability, with conscious military discipline, and the virtue associated with excellent soldiers.[77]

Whether or not the regular officer made use of the collective during the early part of this period is difficult to determine. From all apearances in other areas, he continued to decide the majority of cases himself. The regular officer also continued to decide whether to make use of the collective: "The commander, in accordance with the disciplinary regulations, has the option of either allowing the case to be handled by the collective, or issuing nonjudicial punishment."[78]

But by 1971 the party began to recognize that this approach was unsatisfactory. Discipline apparently was becoming a serious problem.[79] The party took two steps to deal with this situation. First, it increased the time devoted to disciplinary questions at party meetings and schooling sessions. Proper discipline, the party argued, is primarily an ideological question. Who was better equipped to handle such a problem than the party organization itself, through the party groups?[80]

The second step taken by the party was the decision to deemphasize the importance of the collectives. Recognizing that the collectives were ignored or the source of friction with commanders, the party apparently felt either that sufficient other controls on the commander's behavior already existed or that the commander had internalized the party line enough to permit relaxation in this area. As a result, new service regulations (DV 010/0/003) were issued. According to Kessler, these regulations were created:

> ... to make it possible for the commander to make responsible decisions in a broader area. In this way, differences according to area, special technical, structural and other conditions can be better handled and the responsibility of the commander for the carrying out of order and discipline raised.[81]

As a result, the commander now bore full responsibility for disciplinary questions. It was no longer necessary for him to consult with the collective. He could, if he wished, call on the collective, but the decision of whether they would be utilized was his alone. The only difference between this period and the preceding one is the party's decision to stop trying to force regular officers to use the collective. The reality of how these matters were handled, however, remained the same. This indicator remains indicative of a low level of political control.

The thirteenth indicator of political control present in this period involves the handling of criminal offenses. A new military code of offenses was issued during Period V as part of an overall change in the GDR criminal code.[82] Among the alternations this code introduced over the 1962 code was the addition of a number of offenses to the criminal category. These included mutiny (paragraph 259), failure to follow operating instructions at sea (paragraph 265), violation by the commander of his supervisory tasks (paragraph 269), collaboration with the enemy while a prisoner of war (paragraph 276), use of forbidden means of war (paragraph 279), and violation of the rights of parliamentarians (paragraph 282).

As another innovation, the code included a clear statement fixing the authority of the commander to determine whether an offense would be considered disciplinary or criminal.[83] But this does not empower a commander to avoid bringing an individual to trial if he committed a serious crime, such as murder. In such a case, he is bound to turn the case over to the military justice organs. But in less serious cases, the commander may decide to handle the case himself.

The role of the military collective in the handling of criminal cases became clearer during Period V. Its importance when a case is tried by a military court makes a more detailed discussion necessary.

When a criminal case arises, the military collective selects representatives to assist in the investigation. This means they not only aid the investigators in ascertaining the actual facts of the case but also go into the circumstances that may have influenced an individual to commit the crime. When the matter is taken to court, the collective's representatives testify on both the facts of the case and the individual's personality, e.g., he is a loyal son of the GDR who inadvertently commited a crime, or he was driven to it by his commander who failed to observe proper forms of socialist relationships between himself and his subordinates. These representatives remain present throughout the trial. If the individual is found guilty, the collective, with the permission of the commander, may take responsibility (Bürgschaft) for the guilty party. The responsibility for his reeducation then passes to the collective.[84]

Slight changes in the military court system also appeared in the criminal code referred to above. In the main, these changes are not important for the purposes of this study as they involve the types of offenses to be tried by the military supreme court (Militärobergericht)[85] and procedural changes in the investigative methods employed.[86]

The role of the regular officer in handling criminal offenses centers on two areas. First, the commander has authority to decide whether a case is to be tried by a court, as mentioned above. As a result of the 1969 criminal code, a commander's failure to report a violation that higher authorities consider damaging to the proper functioning of the military might result in his conviction of a criminal offense, with imprisonment of up to five years.[87] If the commander was subject to a regulation of this type prior to the introduction of the 1960 code, it was not mentioned. Facing five years' imprisonment for hiding an offense surely would encourage commanders to err in the direction of referring too many offenses to the courts rather than too few. Thus, the commander's freedom to act autonomously is limited.

Military officers also play a role in the criminal trial procedure as members of the military courts. Here, too, their authority is limited. A military officer who is a member of the court is selected, after all, by the party organization and serves at its pleasure. Failure to show the proper enthusiasm for political factors could very well result in his removal. If the failure was serious enough, he could be disciplined. In addition, members of the military also continue to serve as jurors. Still, like officers who are members of the court, they are approved by the party and subject to recall if they fail to act in accord with party wishes.[88] In this indicator, as in so many others during this period, the regular officer's authority seems more formal than real. The authority is present but is limited by a countermeasure. The indicator is classified as indicating a high level of political control.

The final indicator of political control, time devoted to civilian projects, was not mentioned during this period. In order to derive an average level of political control, the indicators discussed during this period are entered in Table 7.2. The average level of political control increased to 2.3. The relationship of this increase in the level of political control to technology is the subject of the final section of this chapter.

TABLE 7.2

Level of Political Control in Periods I-V, 1949-72

Indicator	Period I	Period II	Period III	Period IV	Period V
1. Political officer level	2	2	2	2	2
2. Secret police level	1	1	1	1	1
3. Training length	2	3	1	1	2
4. Prior service	2	2	3	3	3
5. Politorgane	1	2	2	3	3
6. Military party organization	1	2	2	3	3
7. Party membership	1	2	3	3	3
8. Political reliability	1	3	3	3	3
9. Indoctrination	1	2	2	3	3
10. Massenarbeit	1	2	2	3	3
11. Part-time training	3	—	3	3	3
12. Self-criticism	1	1	2	2	—
13. Discipline	1	1	1	1	1
14. Criminal offenses	1	3	3	3	3
15. Civilian projects	—	1	1	1	—
Total	19	27	31	34	33
Average	1.4	1.9	2.0	2.3	2.5

Note: 1 = low; 2 = medium; 3 = high; — = no information.

OBSERVATIONS

With the addition of figures for Period V, the changes that occurred in both technology and political control for the entire period of the study can be viewed on Figure 7.1.

Combat preparedness, at least as viewed from the vantage point of the indicators of technology discussed in this study, has been a continuing concern for the party leadership. Having attained second position behind the Russians in the Warsaw Pact after 12 years of hard work and sacrifice, there was little question the East Germans would do everything necessary to maintain this position, despite the gradual movement toward detente in Europe. Since this could be accomplished only by placing continued emphasis on maintenance of a modern highly technical armed force, this is what they did. The NVA apparently was too important as a bargaining tool in relations with the Soviets to permit a relaxation of combat preparedness.

The situation with regard to political reliability is similar. The SED party leadership remained firm in its conviction that there would not be a "relaxation of tensions" in the NVA. Externally, such a relaxation could lead to a loss of trust by the Russians and thus damage the utility of the NVA as a bargaining tool in bilateral relations. Internally, since the party has often used the NVA as a barometer of societal politicization, a decrease in the level of political control would have been construed as indicating a general drop in political control throughout society. Consequently, in the face of a relaxation of tensions in Europe, the East Germans not only maintained the prevailing level of political control but expanded it.

Methodologically, the results for Period V serve to confirm the tendencies observed earlier. Technology, as was preordained by the

FIGURE 7.1

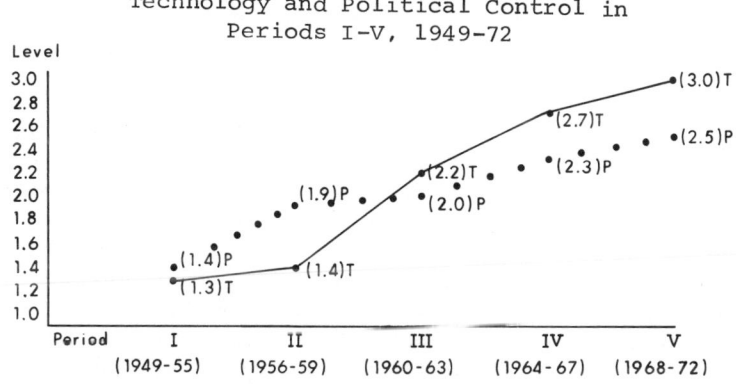

Note: P = political control; T = technology.

methodology employed, reached its highest possible level in this study during Period V. Five indicators showed an increase during Period V. In all five cases the indicators required a long period of careful planning and the devotion of considerable time and resources to reach this level. The three educational indicators—the percentage of officers possessing the mittlere Reife, the Abitur, and an academic education—demanded considerable effort from many officers who achieved these certificates through part-time study. In addition, they involved considerable investment in officer training schools and academies by the party so that the military could attract individuals with better backgrounds.

The PS level is closely associated with the educational level. It was only after the NVA had a body of individuals with an acceptable educational level that it was possible to introduce the latest and technically most modern equipment. The raising of technical awards to the point where individuals who passed examinations associated with their military jobs could be certified as technicians or engineers in the civilian world probably is the best compliment that could be paid the technical level of the NVA. The GDR is a highly advanced society in which there is little room for unqualified technicians. It therefore, seems unlikely that the state would grant such recognition to military skills if they did not closely approximate those in the civilian world.

Although the level of political control apparently rose during Period V, this increase may be unduly influenced by the absence of two indicators present during the preceding period. In fact, only one indicator, the one associated with the length of training political officers receive, increased. As a result, although the numerical score for political control is higher, the level is roughly the same as in the preceding period. This does not mean, of course, that slight changes did not occur. Indeed, political control did increase somewhat on some indicators such as the role of the military party organization, the importance of political reliability for retention or promotion, responsibility for indoctrination, work with the masses, and part-time ideological training. Unfortunately, however, the scaling system utilized in this study was not sensitive enough to pick up these slight changes.

By this point it is obvious that the proposition presented at the beginning of this study does not accurately depict the relationship between technology and political control in the NVA. The East Germans have succeeded in developing individuals, and a military force, that are technically quite advanced. At the same time, they have created conditions under which it is extremely difficult, if not impossible, for the highly skilled technical officers to avoid learning political skills or participating in party activities. To be an officer in the NVA, one must at least approximate the military dual executive.

NOTES

1. This is particularly true of the air force. Of its 19 interceptor squadrons, 17 are made up of MIG-21s. International Institute of Strategic Studies, The Military Balance, 1972-1973 (London, 1972), p. 12.

2. Thomas A Forster, NVA—Die Armee der Sowjetzone (Cologne: Markus Verlag, 1966-67), p. 69.

3. Erich Honecker, "Der Sozialismus gewann an Stärke—der Frieden ist sicher geworden," Volksarmee, No. 3 (1972), p. 4. An indication of the importance attached to the NVA is the fact that Honecker chose it as his audience for this very important speech. See Heinz Hoffmann, "Friedenssicherung und sozialistische Militärmacht," Militärwesen, January 1972, p. 9.

4. "Antwort auf zusätzliche Fragen von Herrn C. L. Sulzberger," Neues Deutschland, November 25, 1972, p. 3.

5. See Peter C. Ludz, "Continuity and Change since Ulbricht," Problems of Communism, March-April 1972, p. 61.

6. Taschenbuch Militärpolitik und Wehrpflicht (Berlin-Ost: Deutscher Militärverlag, 1968), p. 34.

7. This is predicted by Teubner in Kapitän zur See D. Teubner, "Die Offizierskorps der Volksmarine am 10. Jahrestag der Nationalen Volksarmee," Marinewesen, March 1966, p. 369.

8. Taschenbuch (1968), pp. 345-46. The following list provides a breakdown of the length of training required for the various occupational groups: infantry, 3 years; tank, 3 years; intelligence, 3 years; air force (pilot and engineer), 4 years; border troops, 3 years; navy, 4 years.

9. Generalmajor O. Pech, "Die ständige Sorge der Partei- und Staatsführung um die Entwicklung sozialistischer Militärkader," Militärwesen, September 1969, p. 1240. Armeegeneral Heinz Hoffmann, "Die stolze Bilanz unserer Landesverteidigung und einige künftige Aufgaben," Militärwesen, September 1969, p. 1181. In another article, Hoffmann cites the figure as 72 percent, perhaps a mistake by his speech writer. See Heinz Hoffmann, "Lenins militärisches Erbe und die Landesverteidigung der DDR," in Heinz Hoffmann, Sozialistische Landes Verteidigung; Aus Reden und Aufsätzen: 1963-1970 (Berlin-Ost: Deutscher Militärverlag, 1971), p. 872.

10. Günter Glaser, Gerhard Lux, and Toni Nelles, "Die Entwicklung der Landesverteidigung zu Beginn der sechziger Jahre," in Institut für Gesellschaftswissenschaften beim Zentralkomitee der Sozialistischen Einheitspartei Deutschlands, Wissenschaftliche Entscheidungen—historische Veränderungen—Fundamente der Zukunft: Studien zur Geschichte der DDR in den sechziger Jahren (Berlin-Ost: Staatsverlag der DDR, 1971), p. 339.

11. Erlass des Staatsrates der Deutschen Demokratischen Republik über den aktiven Wehrdienst in the Nationalen Volksarmee (Dienstlaufbahnordnung) vom 24 Januar 1961," Gesetzblatt der Deutschen Demokratischen Republik (Berlin-Ost: VEB-Deutscher Zentralverlag, 1970), I, 25 (December 24, 1970), p. 387.

12. Walter Ulbricht, "Unsere vereinte Verteidigungskraft zügelt jeden Aggressor," Volksarmee (Dokumentation, No. 11), No. 38 (1970), p. 5.

13. Helmut Berndt, "Bundeswehr plant drei Hochschulen," Der Tagesspiegel (Berlin), July 18, 1971, p. 15.

14. Hoffmann, "Lenins militärisches Erbe," in Hoffmann, Sozialistische Landes Verteidigung, p. 872.

15. "Kurz und Knapp," Volksarmee, No. 34 (1972), p. 7.

16. Hoffmann, "Lenins militärisches Erbe," p. 872.

17. "Kurz und Knapp," Volksarmee, No. 34 (1972), p. 7.

18. This figure was derived by subtracting the percentage of university graduates (16 percent) in Wissenschaftliche Entscheidungen, p. 339, from the percentage of officers who possessed either a university or technical education (91.2 percent) in "Kurz und Knapp," Volksarmee, No. 34 (1972), p. 7. Thus: 91.2% - 16.0% = 75.2%.

19. Ibid.

20. For 1968, 13 percent; Armeegeneral Heinz Hoffmann, "Von Freund geschätzt, vom Feind gefürchtet," Volksarmee, No. 43 (1968). For 1969, 14 percent; Hoffmann, "Lenins militärisches Erbe," p. 872. For 1971, 16 percent; Hoffmann, "Die stolze Bilanz," p. 1181; Wissenschaftliche Entscheidungen, p. 339.

21. Armeegeneral Heinz Hoffmann, "Wir sind Soldaten des Friedens und Kämpfer für den Sozialismus," Neues Deutschland, March 1, 1973, p. 3.

22. Letter from Major Winfred Vogel of Leitungsstab 2 of the Bundeswehr, October 7, 1971.

23. Taschenbuch, (1968), p. 349.

24. Gesetzblatt der Deutschen Demokratischen Republik, I, 25 (December 24, 1970), 382-88.

25. Ibid., p. 386.

26. Vizeadmiral W. Ehm, "Wissenschaftliche Führung und klassenmässige Erziehung—Grundlage für die Erfüllung der Aufgaben des neuen Ausbildungsjahres," Marinewesen, January 1967, p. 8. See also Gesetzblatt der Deutschen Demokratischen Republik, I, 25, p. 387.

27. Armeegeneral Heinz Hoffmann, "Worauf es in neuen Ausbildungsjahr ankommt," in Hoffmann, Sozialistische Landes Verteidigung, Vol. I, p. 635.

28. Admiral W. Verner, "Für die Erhöhung der Kampfkraft der Partei und ständig hohe Gefechtsbereitschaft der Nationalen Volksarmee," Parteiarbeiter, special issue, 1971, p. 48.

29. See Generalleutnant O. Pech, "Die Attestierung des Offiziersbestandes vorbereiten," Militärwesen, November 1970, pp. 1555-61. A new attestation is planned for 1971-72. Ibid, p. 1555.

30. Autorenkollektiv des Deutschen Instituts für Militärgeschichte. Zeittafel zur Militärgeschichte der Deutschen Demokratischen Republik 1949 bis 1968, (Berlin-Ost: Deutscher Militärverlag, 1969), p. 294.

31. Fregattenkapitän P. Schubert, "Der Erwerb der klassifizierungsabzeichen—ein Mittel zur Erhöhung der Einsatzbereitschaft der Bewaffnung der Volksmarine," Marinewesen, July 1969, p. 818.

32. Ibid., p. 822.

33. Ibid.

34. "Waffengattung nach Wunsch," Volksarmee, No. 38 (1970), pp. 53-54.

35. Taschenbuch (1968), p. 176; Die Nationale Volksarmee der Deutschen Demokratischen Republik (Dresden: Verlag Zeit im Bild, 1968), p. 36.

36. For 1969, "Kurz und Knapp," Volksarmee, No. 9 (1969), p. 7. For 1971, Oberstleutnant R. Schleicher, "Die NVA ist eine moderne und schlajkräftige Armee," Volksarmee, No. 14 (1971), p. 3; interview with Armeegeneral Heinz Hoffmann, "Kampfauftrag erfüllt—vor neuen Bewährungsproblem," Militarwesen, February 1971, p. 167.

37. Ulrich Rühmland, NVA in Stichworten, (Bonn: Bonner Druck- und Verlagsgesellschaft, 1969), p. 67.

38. Georg Waidhausen, Nationale Volksarmee als Parteischule (Pfaffenhofen-Ilm: Ilmgau Verlag, 1965), p. 60.

39. "NVA Hochschule 'Wilhelm Pieck,'" Neues Deutschland, October 12, 1972, p. 1.

40. Armeegeneral Heinz Hoffmann, "Siebziger Jahre setzen hohe Massstäbe für die marxistisch-leninistiche Bildung, für die Erziehung, Lehre und Forschung," Parteiarbeiter, special issue 1, 1970, p. 12.

41. Admiral W. Verner, "Für die Erhöhung der Kampfkraft der Partei," p. 48; Armeegeneral Heinz Hoffmann, "Siebziger Jahre setzen hohe Massstabe, p. 12.

42. Oberst Hans Beckmann, "Lernen und lehren im Geiste unserses Vorbilders," Neues Deutschland, October 14, 1972, p. 15.

43. R.N. "Gut vorbereitet auf neuen Aufgaben," Volksarmee, No. 32 (1972), p. 2. Oberstleutnant E. Hasemann and Oberstleutnant K. Morbitzer, "Erfahrungen und Gedanken zum wissenschaftlichproduktiven Studien des Marxismus-Leninismus," Militärwesen, November 1970, p. 1587. The term Offizierhörer is normally used in East German military literature for individuals who already are officers and are attending some type of advanced training course. See W.G. "Der militärpolitischcn Hochschule der NVA wurde der Name 'Wilhelm Pieck' verliehen," Volksarmee, No. 43 (1972), p. 9.

44. Generalmajor W. Rothe, "Die Wirksamkeit der Parteiarbeit in der NVA allseitig erhöhen," Militärwesen, April 1971, pp. 524-25.

45. Admiral Waldemar Verner, "Die Parteiarbiet zur Entwicklung militärischer Kampfkollektive," Parteiarbeiter, special issue, 1971, p. 8.

46. Oberst W. Hammer, "Einige Ergebnisse und Schlussfolgerungen aus den Parteiwahlen 1969 in der Nationalen Volksarmee," Militärwesen, July 1969, p. 897.

47. Oberst Pahnke, "Zur führenden Rolle der SED in der NVA," Parteiarbeiter, special issue 2, 1968, p. 12 (emphasis in the original).

48. Generalmajor Alfred Vogel, "Schule der Parteierziehung," Volksarmee, No. 22 (1972), p. 3.

49. Hammer, "Einige Ergebnisse und Schlussfolgerungen," pp. 893-94.

50. Verner, "Für die Erhöhung der Kampfkraft der Partei," p. 52.

51. Admiral W. Verner, "Die Parteiarbeit zur Entwicklung militärischer Kampfkollektive," Parteiarbeiter, special issue, 1971, p. 7.

52. Oberstleutnant Göldner, "Zwischen Landung und Start," Volksarmee, No. 16 (1972), p. 1.

53. Vogel, "Schule der Parteierziehung," p. 3. For the view from the civilian world, see Rudolf Wettengel, "Vielfältig wie das Leben," Neuer Weg, No. 20 (1972), pp. 921-25.

54. "Entschliessung der VIII. Delegiertenkonferenz der Parteiorganisationen der Sozialistischen Einheitspartei Deutschlands in der Nationalen Volksarmee am 22. und 23. Mai 1971," Parteiarbeiter, special issue, 1971, pp. 6-10.

55. Oberstleutnant H. Lolischkies and Major W. Schmökel, "Die kollektivität der Parteileitungen und die Funktionsverteilung," Luftverteidigung, February 1968, p. 18.

56. Rothe, "Die Wirksamkeit der Parteiarbeit," p. 524.

57. See, for example, the article by Fregattenkapitän M. Zawichowski and Fregattenkapitän G. Fink, "Die Rolle des militärischen Kampfkollektivs bei der Erziehung sozialistischer Soldatenpersönlichkeiten in der Volksmarine," Marinewesen, December 1970, p. 1423.

58. Generalmajor W. Rothe, "In unserer Parteiarbeit den Massstäben der siebziger Jahre Rechnung targen," Parteiarbeiter, March 1970, pp. 6-7.

59. Oberleutnant G. Pohle, "Wie wir den sozialistischen Wettbewerb zur Entwicklung unserer Kampfkollektiv nutzen," Militärwesen, January 1970, p. 117.

60. Fregattenkapitän H. Bergel, "Die politische Arbeit auf kleinen Kampfschiffen und-booten bei der Entwicklung und Festigung militärischer Kampfkollektiv, Marinewesen, September 1970, p. 1043.

61. Generalleutnant O. Pech, "Leninische Prinzipien sozialistischer Kaderpolitik und ihre Anwendung in der Nationalen Volksarmee," Militärwesen, April 1970, p. 524.

62. Admiral W. Verner, "Die Kampfkraft der Partei in der NVA stärken—unser Beitrag zum VIII. Parteitag der SED," Militärwesen, April 1971, p. 473; Wissenschaftliche Entscheidungen, p. 339.

63. Oberstleutnant E. Köppe, "Einige Hinweise zur Einschätzung und Beurteilung der Kader," Militärwesen, May/June 1971, pp. 690-91 (emphasis in the original). See also Generalleutnant O. Pech, "Die Attestierung des Offiziersbestandes vorbereiten," Militärwesen, November 1970, p. 1556.

64. Köppe, "Einige Hinweise zur Einschätzung," p. 698. Political factors also were important in the 1968 attestation. See, for example, Hoffmann's statement expressing his displeasure with the secondary role he felt political qualifications played in the past: Armeegeneral Heinz Hoffmann, "Worauf es im neuen Ausbildungsjahr ankommt," Militärwesen, January 1968, p. 15. See also Pech, "Die Attestierung des Offiziersbestandes," pp. 1556-57. He also stresses the need to pay more attention to political qualifications.

65. Köppe, "Einige Hinweise zur Einschäntzung," p. 698.

66. Schmökel and Jung, "Die Tätigkeit der Grundorganisationen bei der Erziehung," p. 7. See also Bergel, "Die politische Arbeit auf kleinen Kampfschiffen," p. 1044; Major Zierold, "Sozialistische Soldatenkameradschaft zwischen Vorgesetzten und Unterstellten in den Einheiten der NVA," Militärwesen, May 1969, p. 609.

67. Jörg Lolland, Zu Befehl Genosse Unterleutnant (Stuttgart: Seewald Verlag, 1971), p. 179.

68. Verner, "Für die Erhöhung der Kampfkraft der Partei," p. 34.

69. Fregattenkapitän G. Vogelsang and Kapitänleutnant R. P. Rath, "Kultur und Kunst erhöhen Gefechtsbereitschaft und Kampfkraft," Marinewesen, October 1970, p. 1157.

70. Autorenkollektiv, "Die Potenzen des geistig-kulturellen Lebens noch wirksamer für die Erhöhung der Kampfkraft und Gefechtsbereitschaft nutzen," Militärwesen, January 1971, pp. 48-49; Armeegeneral Heinz Hoffmann, "Kluge Menschen—moderne Waffen—treue Verbündete," in Hoffmann, Sozialistische Landes Verteidigung, Vol. I, p. 826; Kapitänleutnant H. Häuser, "Die kulturelle Massenarbeit—wichtiger Bestandteil des sozialistischen Erziehungstätigkeit," Marinewesen, June 1969, p. 649.

71. For one of the best discussions of this process during this period, see ibid., pp. 643-58.

72. Admiral W. Verner, "Die marxistisch-leninistischen Gesellschaftswissenschaften und die Aus- und Weiterbildung der Offiziere," Parteiarbeiter, January 1969, p. 6.

73. Armeegeneral Heinz Hoffmann, "Das Ausbildungsjahr im Zeichen der fortgesetzien Offensiv des Sozialismus," Militärwesen, January 1971, p. 11.

74. Admiral W. Verner, "Den Marxismus-leninismus wirksamer für die Erhöhung der militärischen Kampfkraft und Gefechtsbereitschaft nutzen," May 1971, p. 1018. See also Verner, "Für die Erhöhung der Kampfkraft der Partei," Militärwesen, p. 34; Oberstleutnant G. Fritz, "Das aktuelle Gespräch wirksam gestahlten!" Militärwesen, July 1972, p. 28.

75. Oberstleutnant H. Knäfel, "Probleme des gesellschaftswissenschaftlichen Weiterbildung der Offiziere in den Ausbildungsjahren 1970/71 und 1971/72," Militärwesen, September 1970, p. 1275.

76. Verner, "Für die Erhöhung der Kampfkraft der Partei," p. 48.

77. Korvettenkapitän K. Dethloff, "Probleme der Erziehungsarbeit bei der Maaten- und Matrosenausbildung," Marinewesen, February 1969, p. 167.

78. Handbuch Militärisches Grundwissen (2nd ed.; Berlin-Ost: Deutscher Militärverlag, 1969), p. 55.

79. Verner, "Für die Erhöhung der Kampfkraft der Partei," pp. 34-35.

80. Oberst H. Grosse and Oberstleutnant M. Neitsch, "Politischpädagogische und psyclogische Probleme der Festigung der militärischen Disziplin in der NVA," Militärwesen, January 1972, pp. 29-30.

81. Generaloberst Heinz Kessler, "Die neuen Dienstvorschriften," Militärwesen, July 1972, p. 5.

82. See Strafgesetzbuch der DDR- StGB- und angrenzende Geseteze (Berlin-Ost: Staatsverlag der DDR, 1969), pp. 117-26.

83. Ibid., p. 117, paragraph 253, particularly section 2.

84. Handbuch Militärisches Grundwissen, pp. 65-69.

85. Strafgesetzbuch der DDR, p. 133.

86. Ibid., p. 130.

87. Ibid., paragraph 269.

88. Oberst G. Kalwert, "Als Mitglied der Partei erfüllt der Militärschoffe einen wichtigen Parteiauftrag," Parteiarbeiter, January 1972, pp. 22-25.

PART III
CONCLUSION

CHAPTER

8

POLITICAL CONTROL AND TECHNOLOGY IN A COMMUNIST POLITICAL SYSTEM

Contrary to the proposition presented in the introduction to this study, the results suggest it is possible to develop individuals closely approximating the military dual executive. Although they do not represent a perfect combination of "expertness" and "redness," East German officers do combine both of these characteristics to a considerable degree. They are not only highly trained military officers but also politically aware participants in party activities.

Roman Kolkowicz argues, in analyzing the Soviet military that its increased autonomy in relations with the party has been aided by the fact that "the officer corps is become transformed from a group of relatively expendable commanders with minimal skills into a body of younger, more sophisticated and self-assured technocrats, who are becoming increasingly indispensable, individually and collectively to the defense and political interests of the party."[1]

Although this may be an accurate description of events in the Soviet Union, it does not describe what has happened in the GDR. The NVA officer corps has been transformed into a group of technocrats, but these officers give little indication of being overly self-assured and are not treated as though they were indispensible. In fact, the party appears to have made an officer's career attractive enough to easily find applicants for officer training schools.* In addition, the NVA has a large enough reserve of highly skilled officers

---

*This is particularly true in light of the fact that there are more individuals in the GDR who hold the Abitur than there are openings in the universities. Consequently, rather than spend the rest of their lives as workers, many of these young people turn to the officer training schools from which they will receive diplomas.

to be able to afford to eliminate those who are judged unsatisfactory. Since those who are eliminated for political reasons may not be well received in the civilian community, the pressures to conform politically are considerable.

One might object that the Soviet and NVA officer corps are not comparable. The Soviet military has worldwide commitments; the NVA does not. The Soviet military also is much larger and has in its inventory many more weapons systems than does the NVA. For these and other reasons, it might be better to compare the East German military with that of a more similar military force—another member of the Warsaw Pact might offer a better comparison. Unfortunately, there are no comparable studies of other Warsaw Pact members. Nevertheless, certain observations are possible. First, it is probable that in at least two of the Warsaw Pact countries, Hungary and Czechoslovakia, the level of political control, which can be expected to be high, results not from a reaction to increased technology but from anti-Soviet nationalistic tendencies. Conditions in two other countries, Bulgaria and Romania, would not be applicable due to the low level of technical development in their armed forces. This leaves Poland as a possible comparison.

The Polish armed forces are larger and, on the whole, somewhat less developed technically than the NVA.[2] Nevertheless, they probably are the most comparable of the East European armed forces since the two military units work closely together, are assigned similar military tasks, and in general have exhibited a similar degree of loyalty to the party. A study of the Polish military might make it possible to determine whether the German case is unique. It is possible that the Russians and East Germans, remembering the casualties of German militarism in the past, as well as the twenty-odd Soviet divisions located in the GDR, have handled the NVA differently than other Eastern European armed forces. Whatever the results of such a comparison, it would provide important insights. It would show either that the better known East German case is not representative and hence should not be generalized for all of Eastern Europe or that the East German case is similar to the Polish and perhaps indicative of a pattern.

This brings us to the East German case itself. Peter Christian Ludz, as discussed in the Introduction, suggests in his study of the SED party bureaucracy that the party rarely requires more than party membership for technocrats in the economic sphere. But this study indicates that, although such a development may be occurring in the party bureaucracy, it is not taking place in the military. By extrapolation, this writer also would be suprised if such a development were occurring in other security organs, such as the secret police, the People's Police, or the special police.

This raises the obvious question of why the SED would permit a low degree of politicization in one technical skill group such as the party bureaucracy, while at the same time demanding a high level of politicization in another such as the NVA. Although a number of variables no doubt are operative in this situation, one that might have particular importance is the group's concern with questions of national security. The party may well feel that it can afford a low level of political control in technical skill groups not directly concerned with national security. But the potential threat to the system from the NVA and other security organs may be too great in the eyes of the party to permit anything less than politicization that is as complete as possible.*

Further study of other skill groups in the GDR encompassing both those involved with security and nonsecurity affairs would help resolve this question. One possibly revealing group concerned with national security affairs is the East German diplomatic corps. Although it does not represent the same type of threat to the party as the military, this group does have access to information potentially damaging to the GDR's national interests. Consequently, politicization probably would be high.

On the other hand, factory managers might serve as a useful group not oriented to security affairs. They do not, in the main, have access to classified information. As a result, they may be left alone by the party as long as they produce the appropriate industrial commodities. Both skill groups have seen their means of carrying out their daily tasks affected by technology, but because of security concerns the party might choose to react differently to the development of technical prerogative and expertise in each group.

In addition to questioning the accuracy of the relationship of technical expertise and political involvement in the NVA hypothesized in the Introduction, this study also revealed a number of other interesting findings. The low level of technology in the East German military in 1956 demonstrates a lack of concern by the Soviets with the creation of a modern military force at that time. In fact, there is some question whether the East Germans could have satisfactorily operated their antiquated equipment during peacetime, let alone under conditions of combat. As long as the Russians felt there was hope for a reunified, although neutral Germany, and as long as failure

---

*Other skill groups, such as writers and artists, also may be highly politicized. They are not included in this discussion because the performance of their skill is not significantly affected by modern technology. The party does not need to rely on their technical expertise in order to operate a modern industrial society.

to provide the East Germans with their own modern army might persuade the West to deny such a force to the West Germans, the Russians opposed creating a modern military force in the GDR. But once the decision was made to establish a modern military force, the East Germans constructed one with typical Prussian thoroughness. A firm technological basis was established, and in less than 15 years, the East Germans had a highly modern military force, second only to the Russian army among members of the Warsaw Pact.

Remembering their past experience with a modern "German" military, the East German party leadership—and one assumes the Russians as well—always placed political considerations ahead of technical ones. This is illustrated, for example, by the party's reaction to the Hungarian revolution. Although there was concern with building the foundation of a modern military, politicization of the NVA officer corps nevertheless took precedence. Despite the importance of the technical skills of former members of the Wehrmacht, the party quickly decided to dismiss any of them judged less than completely reliable politically. It would be better to sacrifice skill and start from the beginning to build a dependable force, rather than take the chance that the gun might one day control the party rather than the other way around. At no time did the level of political control decrease throughout the course of this study.

Although the findings of this study are not conclusive, they do suggest that, at least in the case of the East German military, a zero-sum relationship between the political and technical halves of the military dual executive is absent. Nevertheless, a relationship does appear to exist between the degree to which one is emphasized and the other deemphasized. In those periods when strong emphasis was placed on one side, the other increased very little. During Period II, for example, political control increased by 0.6, technology by only 0.1. During Period III, on the other hand, technology jumped by 0.8 while political control increased by only 0.1. During the remaining two periods, both factors increased at a somewhat closer rate (in Period IV, political control by 0.3 and technology by 0.6; in Period V, political control by 0.2 and technology by 0.2). As a result, it would appear that it is possible to increase both fairly equally if no attempt is made to radically increase either one.

Although these numbers must be read with a great deal of caution, they do suggest that perhaps the original proposition should be reformulated to read as follows: Despite the increased use of technology by a group fulfilling a need desired by the party, the political leadership will be able to interfere in the internal affairs of the group to produce a dual executive. Emphasis on one aspect of the dual executive will not necessarily result in a decrease in the other. Strong emphasis on one half, however, will decrease the degree to which the other increases.

As a consequence, the party leadership must make a basic decision: Does it want a strong increase in the technical half of the dual executive? If so, emphasis on the political half will increase at a lesser rate. The reverse is also true. At the same time, however, there is no reason why both halves of the military dual executive cannot moderately increase, as was the case in Periods IV and V.

From a methodological standpoint, placing equal weight on all the indicators employed in this study sometimes resulted in distortions. Some indicators were more important than others. This is particularly true insofar as political control is concerned. Two indicators, the role of the Politorgane and the role of the military party organization, were of particular importance and influenced other indicators strongly, especially beginning with Period IV. For example, regular officers were responsible for political indoctrination and work with the masses. But in reality their freedom of action was greatly limited by the activities of the military party organization and the presence of the Politorgane. The activity of these two structures meant, in the case of political reliability, that the regular officer's political behavior could be better watched and reported, thus increasing the importance of conformity to the party line. Insofar as disciplinary questions were concerned, the regular officer continued to have authority over the handling of these matters. Nevertheless, he could only hope to maintain this authority if he used it in accord with the party's wishes, because the activities of the Politorgane and military party organization meant that failure to do so would be promptly reported and could result in a reprimand if not dismissal.

Three indicators, although providing interesting information, were insignificant for this study: the level down to which the political officer is present, the level down to which secret police officers are present, and civilian work by the military. In fact, if the study had not included these indicators, the level of political control would have been recorded as even higher. This suggests that future studies would do well to avoid compartmentalization of indicators, and instead focus on the most significant ones, bringing others into play where relevant.

Before concluding this study, it would be appropriate to say something about the future of the military dual executive in the NVA. Will the high level of politicization continue to be necessary in a military force as technical as the NVA, or will the NVA officer corps begin to internalize the political ideology of the SED to the extent that these controls may be relaxed?

The NVA has concerned itself with this problem to the extent of making several studies on the degree of acceptance of party ideology by young officer candidates. A 1966 study revealed that, when asked whether a number of subjects were enjoyable, ideological studies did not fare as well as the party would have liked.[3] Responses (in percents) to the question, "Is the subject enjoyable (macht Freude)?" were as follows:

Subject	Yes	Partly	No
Tactics	39.4	47.4	10.5
Sport	55.3	31.8	5.3
Social science (ideology)	39.9	36.8	13.2
Military discipline	31.8	47.4	5.3
General training	26.3	55.3	2.6

The fact that ideology received the largest percentage of negative replies caused concern among the article's authors and led to a call for ways to overcome it.[4]

Another study completed in 1967 showed similar results. A questionnaire circulated at the air force officer training school asked young cadets to give the reasons why they chose the air force as a career. Much to the author's displeasure, the majority of future air force officers replied that they came to the air force in order to master modern technology. A sense of social responsibility or concern for protecting the accomplishments of the young socialist state was lacking.[5] Much would have to be done, they reported, to correct this onesided view during the time the officer cadets spent at the Franz Mehring Air Force Officer Training School.[6]

Although these studies were completed five or six years ago, continuing references to a tendency toward a specialist-only (nur Fachmann) attitude were cited many times in this study, suggesting that this continues to be a problem. In addition, the younger officers tend to be the best educated because, unlike the older officers whose education was interrupted by World War II and the postwar instability, they attended civilian and military schools that provide a good technical education and then supplemented that education by attending advanced schools in the NVA, such as the Friedrich Engels Military Academy. This exposure to technological education means that maintenance of a military dual executive will continue to be a problem for the SED leadership, to the degree that greater exposure to technology increases officers' tendency to view themselves primarily as technicians.

The NVA officer corps is young, averaging 29 years in 1966.[7] Most of the officers, particularly those in the middle and lower levels, have been exposed to a high degree to technology. Thus the real question is what they will do when they assume positions of leadership. Although it is impossible to say with certainty how they will react, if the past history of the NVA is any indication, the party will continue to emphasize the political half of the military dual executive as technology increases, thereby seeking to head off the possible development of an apolitical and technically oriented officer corps.

In the GDR, the party decided at the very outset that it would control the gun and not the other way around. As General Hoffmann stated:

> In the history of the Soviet armed forces the attempt was made twice to isolate the army from the party and to undermine the leading role of the party and its Central Committee—once by Trotsky and the other time by Zhukov. Both times the Central Committee uncovered these anti-party tendencies and put an end to these adventures. Our party has closely followed the experiences of the CPSU (Communist Party of the Soviet Union) and undertook in the still young history of the National People's Army to make any appearance of isolation of the army from the party impossible. Our Central Committee, under the perceptive (voraussehende) leadership of Walter Ulbricht, has consequently implemented the principle that the party is the main source of all military success and that the devotion of the army in things of the party of the working class is to be protected like the apple of the eye.[8]

That the SED has suceeded in preventing the rise of apolitical military technicians in the face of rising technology seems evident from this study. That it will continue its efforts to bind the military to the party in light of further increases in technology seems equally certain.

NOTES

1. Roman Kolkowicz, "Interest Groups in Soviet Politics: The Case of the Military," Comparative Politics, II, 3 (April 1970), 453.

2. Comparing the smaller GDR air force with the larger Polish one, one discovers that the Poles possess 500 interceptor aircraft mixed between MIG-17s, 19s and 21s, while the GDR possesses 256 jet fighters, all MIG-21s except for some trainers. International Institute for Strategic Studies, The Military Balance, 1972-1973 (London, 1972), pp. 12-13.

3. Oberstleutnant H. Lüttke and Oberstleutnant S. Mahn, "Erfahrungen bei der Verbesserung der Bildungs- und Erziehungsarbeit durch Klassenanalysen," Militärwesen, October 1966, p. 1426.

4. Ibid., p. 1424.
5. Major R. Wahnelt and Major E. Flau, "Die Notwendigkeit richtiger Vorstellungen über die gesellschaftliche Rolle des Offizierberufs," <u>Luftverteidigung</u>, February 1967, pp. 4-5. Unfortunately, no statistical breakdown of the figures was provided.
6. <u>Ibid</u>., 7.
7. Generalmajor W. Fleissner, "Die Revolution in Militärwesen und das militärtechnische Denken unserer Offiziere," <u>Militärwesen</u>, January 1966, p. 10.
8. Armeegeneral Heinz Hoffmann, <u>Das Militärprogram der sozialistischen Revolution. Lektion geb. an d. Parteihochschule "Karl Marx" beim ZK der SED</u> (Berlin-Ost: Deutscher Militärverlag, 1962), p. 31.

**APPENDIX:
SELECTED
STATISTICS**

	1949	1950	1955	1956	1957	1958	1959	1960	1961
Length of officer's training school	9 mos.	2 yrs.	3 yrs.	3 yrs.[a]					
Percentage of total officers having completed three years' officer training				10.7		23.5			26.8
Percentage of total officers with the mittlere Reife as highest educational level			0.1	10.0		12.0			
Percentage of total officers with the Abitur			8.8	11.0		13.0			
Percentage of total officers with Fachschulausbildung				31.0					
Percentage of total officers classified as engineers or technicians				1.7		5			
Percentage of total officers with an academic degree.				2.6					
Percentage of Army regimental commanders with an academic degree					2.0			8.0	
Horsepower, or PS level			15.0	20.0		25.4			
Percentage of officers who are party members			74.0	79.5	86.0				
Hours per year spent on civilian types of projects						1,050,000	1,361,979	3,278,623	

Note: Because of the variety of sources utilized and the fact that these sources are cited in the text of this study, they are not repeated here. Only those years for which specific citations are on hand are entered on this chart. The raw data provided for these indicators are far from complete. Rather than noting each case where data are not available, the space is left blank.

1962	1963	1964	1965	1966	1967	1968	1969	1970	1971	1972
	3 yrs.[a]		3 yrs.[a]			3 yrs.[a]				
				60.0			80.0		80.0	
36.0			41.0	47.0			52.0		53.9	
19.5			21.0	23.0			34.0		37.1	
				73.0					75.2	
	10		14	16.6			17.0			
	6.0			10.0		13.0	14.0		16.0	25[b]
	80.0	80.0	80.0	77.0						
		29.1				30.5	30.5		30.5	
	96.3	96.0	95.0	96.1	97.0			98.0	98.0	
				2,647,530						

[a]Schools with a predominately technical nature such as the air force and naval officer training schools are four years.
[b]By March 1973.

BIBLIOGRAPHY

WESTERN SOURCES

Public Documents

Bundesministerium für Gesamtdeutsche Fragen. A bis Z: Ein Taschen und Nachschlagbuch über den anderen Teil Deutschlands. 11th rev. ed. Bonn: Deutscher Bundesverlag, 1969.

_____. Die Kasernierte Volkspolizei in der Sowjetischen Besatzungszone Deutschlands. Bonn: Deutscher Bundesverlag, 1955.

_____. Der Staatssicherheitsdienst: Ein Instrument der Politischen Verfolgung in der Sowjetischen Besatzungszone Deutschlands. Bonn: Pohl, 1962.

Western Books

Biegler, Rolf. Der einsame Soldat. Frauenfeld: Verlag Huber, 1963.

Bohn, Helmut., ed. Die Aufrüstung in der Sowjetischen Besatzungszone Deutschlands. Bonn: Bonner Berichte aus Mittel u. Ostdeutschland, 1960.

Bromke, Adam, and Teresa Rakowska-Harmstone, eds. The Communist States in Disarray, 1965-1971. Minneapolis: University of Minnesota Press, 1972.

Childs, David. East Germany. New York: Praeger Publishers, 1969.

Clarkson, Jesse. A History of Russia. New York: Random House, 1963.

Dornberg, John. The Other Germany. New York: Doubleday, 1968.

Fainsod, Merle. How Russia is Ruled. Cambridge, Mass.: Harvard University Press, 1963.

Farrell, R. Barry, ed. Political Leadership in Eastern Europe and the Soviet Union. Chicago: Aldine, 1970.

Fischer, George. The Soviet System and Modern Society. New York: Atherton, 1968.

Forster, Thomas. NVA—Die Armee der Sowjetzone. Cologne: Markus Verlag, 1964.

———. NVA—Die Armee der Sowjetzone. Cologne: Markus Verlag, 1966-67.

Förtsch, Eckart. Die SED. Stuttgart: Kohlhammer, 1969.

Galtung, Johan. Theory and Methods of Social Research. London: Allen and Unwin, 1967.

Garthoff, Raymond. Soviet Military Doctrine. Glencoe, Ill.: The Free Press, 1953.

George, Alexander. The Chinese Communist Army in Action: The Korean War and Its Aftermath. New York: Columbia University Press, 1967.

Godau, Heinz. Verführter, Verführer, Ich war Politoffizier der NVA. Cologne: Markus Verlag, 1965.

Huntington, Samuel, ed. Changing Patterns of Military Politics. Glencoe, Ill,: The Free Press, 1962.

———. The Common Defense. New York: Columbia University Press, 1961.

———. The Soldier and the State. New York: Vintage, 1964.

Institute for Strategic Studies. The Communist Bloc and the Western Alliance. London: the Institute, 1962.

———. The Military Balance, 1966-1967. London: the Institute, 1966.

———. The Military Balance, 1972-73. London: the Institute, 1972.

Janowitz, Morris. The Military in the Political Development of New Nations. Chicago: Phoenix, 1964.

———., ed. The New Military. New York: Wiley, 1908.

———. The Professional Soldier. New York: The Free Press, 1964.

Joffe, Ellis. Party and Army: Professionalism and Political Control in the Chinese Officer Corps, 1949-1964. Cambridge, Mass.: Harvard University Press, 1967.

Kanet, Roger. The Behavorial Revolution and Communist Studies. New York: The Free Press, 1971.

Kolkowicz, Roman. The Soviet Military and the Communist Party. Princeton, N.J.: Princeton University Press, 1967.

Langenscheidt. Fachwörterbuch Wehrwesen: English-Deutsch, Deutsch-English. Berlin: Langenscheidt, 1957.

Lolland, Jörg. Zu Befehl, Genosse Unterleutnant. Stuttgart: Seewald Verlag, 1971.

Ludz, Peter C. The German Democratic Republic from the Sixties to the Seventies. Cambridge:, Mass.: Harvard University Press, 1970.

_____. Parteielite im Wandel. Cologne Opladen: Westdeutscher Verlag, 1968.

Moore, Barrington. Terror and Progress USSR. Cambridge , Mass.: Harvard University Press, 1954.

Mosen, Wido. Bundeswehr—Elite der Nation? Neuwied and Berlin: Luchterband, 1970.

_____. Eine Militärsoziologie. Neuwied: Luchterband, 1967.

Picht, G., ed. Studien zur Politischen und Gesellschaftlichen Situation der Bundeswehr. 3 vols. Witten and Berlin: Eckart, 1965-66.

Richert, Ernst. Die DDR-Elite. Hamburg: Rowolt, 1968.

_____. Sozialistische Universität. Berlin: Collogium Verlag, 1963.

_____. Das zweite Deutschland: Ein Staat, der nicht sein darf. Hamburg: Fischer, 1966.

Rühmland, Ulrich, ed. Nationale Volksarmee der SBZ in Stichworten. Bonn: Bonner Druck- und Verlagsgesellschaft, 1969.

Smith, Jean Edward. Germany Beyond the Wall; People, Politics
. . . and Prosperity. Boston: Little, Brown, 1969.

Vogt, Hartmut. Bildung und Erziehung in der DDR. Stuttgart: Kleh, 1969.

Waidhausen, Georg. Nationale Volksarmee als Parteischule. Pfaffenhofen-Ilm: Ilmgau Verlag, 1965.

Waldman, Eric. The Goose Step Is Verboten. Glencoe, Ill.: The Free Press, 1964.

Weber, Hermann. Von der SBZ zur DDR, 1945-1968. Hannover: Verlag für Literatur and Zeitgeschehen, 1968.

Zapf, Wolfgang, ed. Beiträge zur Analyse der Deutschen Oberschicht. 2nd rev. ed. Munich: R. Piper, 1965.

Articles and Periodicals

Baumann, Gerhard. "Die militärische Kapazität der SBZ," Wehrkunde, Vol. VI (June 1966), pp. 300-8.

Childs, David. "The Nationale Volksarmee of East Germany," German Life and Letters, Vol. XX (Winter 1967), pp. 195-204.

Deutsche Zeitung und Wirtschaftszeitung, 1950.

Fleron, Frederic, "Toward a Reconceptualization of Political Change in the Soviet Union: The Political Leadership System," Comparative Politics, I, 2 (January 1969), 228-44.

Holgert, Werner. "Die Ausbildung der Polit-Offiziere für die KVP," SBZ-Archiv, V, 22 (1954), pp. 341-42.

Kolkowicz, Roman. "Interest Groups in Soviet Politics: The Case of the Military," Comparative Politics, Vol. II (April 1970), pp. 445-72.

Ludz, Peter. "Continuity and Change Since Ulbricht," Problems of Communism, March-April 1972, pp. 56-67.

Mühlen v. zur, Heinrich. "10 Jahre Militärizierung," SBZ-Archiv, Vol. IX (August 1958), pp. 230-32.

Parole, 1955.

Pritzel, Konstantin. "SED und Nationale Volksarmee," Deutsche Fragen, XII, 3 (1966), pp. 144-45.

Der Spiegel, 1955.

Der Tagespiegel, 1971.

Die Zeit, 1971.

Dissertation

Baylis, Thomas. "The New Class in East German Politics," unpublished Ph.D. thesis, University of California, 1964.

Letter

Letter to author from Major Winfred Vogel of Leitungsstab 2 of the Bundeswehr, October 7, 1971.

EAST GERMAN SOURCES

Books*

Autorenkollektiv des Deutschen Instituts für Militärgeschichte. Zeittafel zur Militärgeschichte der Deutschen Demokratischen Republik 1949 bis 1968. Berlin-Ost: Deutscher Militarverlag, 1969.

Bendrat, Arno, and Alfred Nikolaus. Methodik der Politischen Schulung. Berlin-Ost: Deutscher Militärverlag, 1968.

Butter, Werner. Die Autorität des Offiziers. Berlin-Ost: Deutscher Militärverlag, 1966.

Doernberg, Stefan. Kurze Geschichte der DDR. Berlin-Ost: Dietz Verlag, 1969.

---

*Because of the difficulty in separating governmental publications from individual works in the GDR, they are listed together here.

Deutscher Motorkalendar 1971. Berlin-Ost: Deutscher Militarverlag, 1970.

Für den zuverlässigen Schutz der Deutschen Demokratischen Republik. Berlin-Ost: Deutscher Militärverlag, 1969.

Handbuch der Deutschen Demokratischen Republik. Berlin: Staatsverlag, 1963.

Handbuch Militärisches Grundwissen. 2nd. ed. Berlin-Ost: Deutscher Militärverlag, 1969.

Handbuch für Mot. -Schützen. Berlin-Ost: Deutscher Militarverlag, 1963.

Hartmann, Alfred. Die Abgabe von Straftaten an den Kommandeur zur Behandlung nach der Disziplinarvorschrift der Nationalen Volksarmee, DV-10/6. Berlin-Ost: Deutscher Militärverlag, 1968.

Hoffmann, Heinz. Das Militärprogram der sozialistischen Revolution. Berlin-Ost: Deutscher Militärverlag, 1962.

_____. Sozialistische Landes Verteidigung: Aus Reden und Aufsätzen: 1963-1970. 2 vols. Berlin-Ost: Deutscher Militärverlag, 1971.

_____. Zur Militärpolitik der SED. Halle-Wittenberg: Martin Luther Universität, 1966.

Honecker, Erich. Zuverlässiger Schutz des Sozialismus. Berlin-Ost: Deutscher Militärverlag, 1972.

Hundert Fragen, Hundert Antworten zur Wehrpflicht. Berlin-Ost: Deutscher Militärverlag, 1964.

Innendienstvorschrift (DV 10/3). Berlin-Ost: Deutscher Militärverlag, 1962.

Institut für Gesellschaftswissenschaften beim Zentralkomitee der Sozialistischen Einheitspartei Deutschlands. Wissenschaftliche Entscheidungen—historische Veränderungen-Fundamente der Zukunft: Studien zur Geschichte der DDR in den sechziger Jahren. Berlin-Ost: Staatsverlag der DDR, 1971.

Jahrbuch der Deutschen Demokratischen Republik, 1959. Berlin-Ost: Verlag der Wirtschaft, 1959.

Jahrbuch der Deutschen Demokratischen Republik, 1961. Berlin-Ost: Verlag der Wirtschaft, 1961.

Leitfaden für Militärschöffen. Berlin-Ost: Ministerium der Justiz, 1967.

Lenin, Vladimir. Ausgewählte Werke. 2 vols. Berlin-Ost: Dietz Verlag, 1959.

Leuschner, R. et al., eds. Taschenbuch Militärpolitik und Wehrpflicht. Berlin-Ost: Deutscher Militärverlag, 1967.

Militärakademie "Freidrich Engels" der Nationalen Volksarmee: 1959-1969. Dresden: Militärakademie Friedrich Engels, 1969.

Die Nationale Volksarmee der Deutschen Demokratischen Republik. Berlin-Ost: Deutscher Militärverlag, 1961.

Protokoll der Verhandlungen des V. Parteitages der Sozialistischen Einheitspartei Deutschlands. 2 vols. Berlin-Ost: Dietz Verlag, 1959.

Protokoll der Verhandlungen des VI. Parteitages der Sozialistischen Einheitspartei Deutschlands. 4 vols. Berlin-Ost: Dietz Verlag, 1963.

Protokoll der Verhandlungen des VII. Parteitages der Sozialistischen Einheitspartei Deutschlands. 4 vols. Berlin-Ost: Dietz Verlag, 1967.

Protokoll der Verhandlungen der VIII. Parteitages der Sozialistischen Einheitspartei Deutschlands. 2 vols. Berlin-Ost: Dietz Verlag, 1971.

Strafgesetzbuch der DDR -StGB- und angrenzende Gesetze. Berlin-Ost: Staatsverlag der DDR, 1969.

Taschenbuch für Wehrpflichtige. Berlin-Ost: Deutscher Militärverlag, 1965.

Taschenbuch Militärpolitik und Wehrpflicht. Berlin-Ost: Deutscher Militärverlag, 1968.

Uckel, Klaus-Dieter. Militärische Ausbildung. Für die militärpädagogische Aus u. Weiterbildung der Offiziere u. Unteroffiziere der Nationalen Volksarmee. 2nd. ed. Berlin-Ost: Deutscher Militärverlag, 1967.

Unsere Nationale Volksarmee. Berlin-Ost: Deutscher Militärverlag, 1964.

Articles and Periodicals

Autorenkollektiv. "Zu Fragen der militärpolitischen Propaganda," Militärwesen, June 1959, pp. 824-32.

_____. "Die Potenzen des geistig-kulturellen Lebens noch wirksamer für die Erhöhung der Kampfkraft und Gefechtsbereitschaft nutzen." Militärwesen, January 1971, pp. 46-59.

_____. "Gründliches Studium der Geschichte der deutschen Arbeiterbewegung—wichtiger Bestandteil unseres Kampfes um hohe ideologische Gefechtsbereitschaft," Militärwesen, October 1966, pp. 1363-72.

Beck, Major. "Offensiv mit den Lehroffizieren arbeiten," Parteiarbeiter, January 1966, pp. 41-42.

Benjamin, Hilde. "Zu den zweiten Militärschoffenwahlen," Militärwesen, March 1965, pp. 307-13.

Bergel, H. "Die politische Arbeit auf kleinen Kampfschiffen und -booten bei der Entwicklung und Festigung militärischer Kampfkollektiv," Marinewesen, September 1970, pp. 1037-45.

Bieler, F. "Die Geschichte der deutschen Arbeiterbewegung und einige Maritime Berühungspunkte," Marinewesen, March 1967, pp. 259-76.

Borning, W. "Die Nationale Volksarmee erfüllt ihre geschichtliche Aufgabe, weil sie von der Partei der Arbeiterklasse geführt wird," Militärwesen, December 1965, pp. 1635-46.

Braune, G. "Die Wachsamkeit—eine wichtige Bedingung für die Erhöhung der Einsatz—und Gefechtsbereitschaft der Volksmarine," Marinewesen, June 1963, pp. 643-55.

Butter, W. "Über den Einfluss der Parteiorganisation und des militärischen Kollektivs auf die Autorität des Offiziers," Militärwesen, April 1965, pp. 468-76.

Dethloff, K. "Probleme der Erziehungsarbeit bei den Maaten—und Matrossenausbildung," Marinewesen, February 1969, pp. 155-64.

Dickel, F. "Die Notwendigkeit einer allseitigen, wissenschaftlich-technischen Qualifizierung des Offizierskorps der Nationalen Volksarmee," Militärwesen, July 1961, pp. 867-76.

Eckardt, Oberstleutnant and Fritz, Oberstleutnant. "Einige Erfahrungen aus der Arbeit einer ZPL mit Arbeitsgruppen," Parteiarbeiter, March 1969, pp. 8-11.

Ehm, W. "Das Errichte ist die Grundlage für neue Erfolge im Ausbildungsjahr 1964/1965," Marinewesen, January 1965, pp. 3-20.

_____. "Wissenschaftliche Führung und klassenmässige Erziehung—Grundlage für die Erfüllung der Aufgaben des neuen Ausbildungsjahres," Marinewesen, January 1967, pp. 3-18.

_____. "Worauf kommt es in den letzten Wochen des Ausbildungsjahres an?" Marinewesen, June 1965, pp. 643-52.

Entschliessung der VIII. Delegiertenkonferenz der Parteiorganisationen der Sozialistischen Einheitspartei Deutschlands in der Nationalen Volksarmee am 22. und 23. Mai 1971, Parteiarbeiter, Special Issue, 1971, pp. 6-10.

Falke, S. "Einige notwendige Bemerkungen zum Artikel 'Organisationspolitische Aspekte zur Tätigkeit einer Arbeitsgruppe für politische Arbeit,'" Luftverteidigung, August 1970, pp. 9-11.

Fleissner, W. "Die Revolution in Militärwesen und das militärtechnische Denken unserer Offiziere," Militärwesen, January 1966, pp. 3-11.

Flohr, D. "Der Öffentlichkeitsarbeit der Volksmarine mehr Aufmerksamkeit," Marinewesen, September 1968, pp. 1027-39.

Franke, H. "Über einige Aufgaben der Truppenteile bei der sozialistischen Wehrerziehung in der Öffentlichkeit," Militärwesen, September 1964, pp. 1221-28.

Fritz, G. "Das aktuelle Gespräch wirksam gestahlten," Militärwesen, July 1972, pp. 28-36.

Gesetzblatt der Deutschen Demokratischen Republik. 1957, 1962, 1963, 1966, 1970.

Glapa, Fregattenkapitän. "Parteierziehung—nicht nur vor der PKK," Parteiarbeiter, June 1967, pp. 9-11.

Glaser, G. "Die Initiative der Zentralkomitee der SED im Mai und Juni 1957 zur Festigung der Einzelleitung in der NVA," Zeitschrift für Militärgeschichte No. 3 (1968), pp. 294-309.

Gleis, Hauptmann. "Die Verantwortung des Gruppenorganisators," Parteiarbeiter, December 1966, pp. 18-20.

Göbel, H. "Die politische Schulung ist Parteischulung," Parteiarbeiter, March 1967, pp. 13-19.

Grechko, A. "Reliably defend what has been created by the People," Sovestskiy Voin, No. 1 (January 1972), pp 2-5.*

Greese, Karl, and Alfred Voerster. "Probleme der Auswahl und Förderung der Offizierskader in der NVA (1958-1963)," Zeitschrift für Militärgeschichte, No. 1 (1966), pp. 32-47.

Grosse, H., and Neitsch, M. "Politisch-pädagosische und psychologische Probleme der Festigung der militärischen Disziplin in der NVA," Militärwesen, January 1972, pp. 29-35.

Hammer, W. "Einige Ergebnisse und Schlussfolgerungen aus den Parteiwahlen 1969 in der Nationalen Volksarmee," July 1969, Militärwesen, pp. 893-99.

Hasemann, E., and K. Morbitzer. "Erfahrungen und Gedanken zum wissenschaftlichproduktiven Studium des Marxismus-Leninismus," Militärwesen, November 1970, pp. 1584-94.

Hauser, H. "Die kulturelle Massenarbeit—wichtiger Bestandteil der soziaistichen Erziehungstätigkeit," Marinewesen, June 1969, pp. 643-58.

---

*This article is Soviet in origin.

Helbig, E. "Zur Arbeit der Parteiorganisationen bei der sozialistischen Erziehung in der Nationalen Volksarmee," Militärwesen, January 1959, pp. 22-33.

———. "Über die Aufgaben der neugewählten Parteileitungen der Grundorganisationen," Militärwesen, May 1962, pp. 651-58.

———. "Die Einheit von politischen und militärischen Führung verwirklichen," Militärwesen, March 1962, pp. 651-58.

———. "Sozialistische Offiziere erziehen," Militärwesen, November 1963, pp. 1603-10.

Hoffmann, Heinz. "Die Arbeit mit den Kadern—das Kernproblem der Führungstätigkeit," Militärwesen, July 1963, pp. 963-80.

———. "Wie erreichen wir in der Armee den wissenschaftlich-technischen Höchstand?", Militärwesen, February 1963, pp. 170-74.

———. "Worauf es im neuen Ausbildungsjahr ankommt," Militärwesen, January 1968, pp. 3-20.

———. "Das Ausbildungsjahr im Zeichen der fortgesetzten Offensive des Sozialismus," Militärwesen, January 1971, pp. 3-14.

———. "Die stolze Bilanz unserer Landesverteidigung und einige künftige Aufgaben," Militärwesen, September 1969, pp. 1180-91.

———. "Für die volle Durchsetzung der Einzelleitung in der Nationalen Volksarmee," Militärwesen, January 1961, pp. 7-21.

———. "Zu neuen Erfolg im Ausbildungsjahr 1963, dem des VI. Parteitages," Militärwesen, December 1962, pp. 1803-11.

———. "Mit neuen Erfolgen dem VII. Parteitag entgegen," Militärwesen, December 1966, pp. 1651-68.

———. "Friedenssicherung u. Sozialistisches Militärmacht," Militärwesen, January 1972, pp. 4-14.

———. "Zu den Grundfragen der Militärpolitik der Sozialistischen Einheitspartei Deutschlands," Militärwesen, June 1964, pp. 755-86.

_____. "Siebziger Jahre setzen hohe Massstäbe für die marxistisch-leninistische Bildung, für die Erziehung, Lehre und Forschung," Parteiarbeiter, Special Issue 1, 1970, pp. 2-14.

_____. "Kampfauftrag erfüllt—vor neuen Bewährungsproben," Militärwesen, February 1971, pp. 163-71.

Ilter, K. "Die sozialistische Offizierspersönlichkeit: Probleme und Gedanken zum Bild des sozialistischen Offiziers," Militärwesen, November 1967, pp. 1543-52.

Jäkel, H. "Die neuen Grundsatzvorschriften," Militärwesen, June 1963, pp. 842-48.

Junge Welt, 1965

Kalwert, G. "Als Mitglied der Partei erfüllt der Militärschoffe einen wichtigen Parteiauftrag, Parteiarbeiter, January 1972, pp. 22-25.

Kessler, H. "Die neuen Dienstvorschriften," Militärwesen, July 1972, pp. 3-9.

Kettner, K. "Die neue Technik in der Flotte erfordert höhere pädagogisch—psychologische Fähigkeiten der Offiziere," Marinewesen, September 1966, pp. 1079-92.

Knäfel, H. "Probleme der gesellschaftswissenschaftlichen Weiterbildung der Offiziere in den Ausbildungsjahren 1970/71 und 1971/72," Militärwesen, September 1970, pp. 1274-81.

König, H. "Mit dem Selbststudium steht und fällt die gesellschaftswissenschaftliche Weiterbildung der Offiziere," Militärwesen, December 1965, pp. 1714-24.

Koppe, E. "Einige Hinweise zur Einschätzung und Beurteilung der Kader," Militärwesen, May-June 1971, pp. 690-99.

Kubasch, H. "Zweite Kadertagung der Nationalen Volksarmee," Militärwesen, July 1966, pp. 1037-39.

Leiber, A., and G. Sarge. "Nationale Volksarmee und Rechtspflege," Neue Justiz, No. 20, (1966), pp. 129-31.

Leuschner, R. "Rundfunk und Fernsehen für die ideologische Erziehung der Soldaten nutzen," Militärwesen, January 1965, pp. 51-57.

Lolischkies, H., and W. Schmökel. "Die Kollektivität der Parteileitungen und die Funktionsverteilung," Luftverteidigung, February 1968, pp. 14-18.

Lüttke, H., and S. Mahn, "Erfahrungen bei der Vebesserung der Bildungsund Erziehungsarbeit durch Klassenanalysen," Militärwesen, November 1966, pp. 1420-32.

Lux, G., and T. Nelles. "Der Aufbau und die Entwicklung der NVA— schöpferische Anwendung des Leninschen Militärprograms durch die SED (II)," Zeitschrift für Militärgeschichte, No. 6 (1970), pp. 659-73.

Mähler, M., and H. Richter. "Methodische Hinweise für die Abschlussprüfung in der gesellschaftswissenschaftlichen Weiterbildung der Offiziere," Militärwesen, June 1966, pp. 861-66.

Matern, H. "Die Führung der Nationalen Volksarmee durch die SED— die Quelle ihrer Kraft und Stärke," Militärwesen, February 1958, pp. 197-204.

Mehner, H. "Eine Wende in der politisch-ideologischen Arbeit herbeiführen," Militärwesen, February 1965, pp. 147-55.

Müller, H. "Der sozialistische Wettbewerb—objektive Notwendigkeit auch an der Offiziersschule," Luftverteidigung, January 1966, pp. 31-37.

Müller, R. "Anwendungsmöglichkeiten von Lehrmaschinen im Ausbildungsprozess an der Offiziersschule 'Karl Liebknecht,'" Marinewesen, March 1967, pp. 298-306.

Münch, G. "Aus dem Protokoll der IV. Delegiertenkonferenz der FDJ-Organisationen in der Nationalen Volksarmee," Parteiarbeiter, Special Issue 2, 1965, pp. 2-28.

Munschke, E. "Sozialistische Klassenbeziehungen—Quelle der Kampfkraft der Nationalen Volksarmee," Militärwesen, April 1959, pp. 479-84.

Nelles, T. "Der Aufbau und die Entwicklung der NVA—schöpferische Anwendung des Leninischen Militärprogramm durch die SED (I)," Zeitschrift für Militärgeschichte, January 1970, pp. 19-33.

Neues Deutschland, 1959, 1972, 1973.

Neukirchen, H. "Aufbauend auf dem Erreichten zu neuen Erfolgen im Ausbildungsjahr 1962/63," Marinewesen, January 1963, pp. 3-16.

Nordin, W. "Einige Erfahrungen aus der Zusammenarbeit zwischen der Fakultät für Seestreitkräfte der Militärakademie 'Friedrich Engels' und dem Kommando sowie den Verbänden der Volksmarine," Marinewesen, April 1967, pp. 397-407.

Notroff, F. "Die Offiziersschule der Volksmarine 'Karl Liebknecht' ist die Kaderschmiede unserer Flotte," Marinewesen, March 1966, pp. 333-46.

Nowak, E. "Das Niveau der gesellschaftswissenschaftlichen Weiterbildung verbessern!" Militärwesen, March 1966, pp. 346-54.

Pahnke M. "Zur führende Rolle der SED in der NVA," Parteiarbeiter, Special Issue 2, 1968, pp. 10-13.

Pech, O. "Die richtige Arbeit mit den Kadern—Bestandteil sozialistischer militärischer Führungstätigkeit," Militärwesen, December 1964, pp. 1667-73.

_____. "Die Attestierung des Offiziersbestandes vorbereiten," Militärwesen, November 1970, pp. 1555-61.

_____. "Die Attestierung des Offiziersbestandes im Ausbildungsjahr 1967/8 gründlich vorbereiten," Militärwesen, May 1967, pp. 631-36.

_____. "Wachsende Aufgaben in der Nachwuchsgewinnung für militärische Berufe," Militärwesen, February 1971, pp. 198-205.

_____. "Über die Entwicklung und Perspektive des Offizierskorps der Nationalen Volksarmee," Militärwesen, February 1966, pp. 196-203.

_____. "Leninische Prinzipien sozialistischer Kaderpolitik und ihre Anwendung in der Nationalen Volksarmee," Militärwesen, April 1970, pp. 523-28.

_____. "Die ständige Sorge der Partei—und Staatsführung um die Entwicklung sozialistischer Militärkader," Militärwesen, September 1969, pp. 1236-42.

Pevestorf, D. "Patenschaftsarbeit—ein Mittel zur Unterstützung der sozialistischen Bewusstseinentwicklung," Militärwesen, November 1966, pp. 1546-51.

Pohle, G. "Wie wir den sozialistischen Wettbewerb zur Entwicklung unserer Kampfkollektive nutzen," Militärwesen, January 1970, pp. 115-18.

Politische Hauptverwaltung der Nationalen Volksarmee, Argumentation, December 1967.

Pretzsch, Oberst. "Der Einfluss der PKK auf die Erziehung leitender Kader," Parteiarbeiter, June 1965, pp. 10-12.

Raubach, R. "Einzelleitung, wissenschaftliche Führungstätigkeit und Parteiarbeit," Militärwesen, November 1964, pp. 1507-13.

Raulein, H. "Zur Verbesserung der militartechnischen Bildung in der Nationalen Volksarmee," Militarwesen, June 1960, pp. 1047-53.

Redaktion. "Fur unsere sozialistische DDR—unter Fuhrung der Partei—immer gefechtsbereit," Militärwesen, May 1967, pp. 611-20.

Riemer, W., G. Raschpichler, and H. Dittrich. "Das neue System der Heranbildung von Offizieren der Volksmarine—ein Erfordernis der wissenschaftlich—technischen Entwicklung," Marinewesen, August 1965, pp. 911-25.

Rothe, W. "In unserer Parteiarbeit den Massstäben der siebziger Jahren Rechunng tragen," Parteiarbeiter, March 1970, pp. 2-7.

_____. "Die Wirksamkeit der Parteiarbeit in der NVA allseitig erhohen!" Militärwesen, April 1971, pp. 517-26.

Sarge, G. "Die sozialistische Militärgerichtsbarkeit in der DDR," Neue Justiz, July, 1963, pp. 364-67.

Schierz, H. "Fordernde und hemmende Faktoren der Bewusstseinbildung," Luftverteidigung, January 1967, pp. 11-20

Schille, A. "Die Bedeutung der Strafrechtsnormen über die Verbrechen gegen die militarische Disziplin," Neue Justiz, July 1958, pp. 153-56.

Schirrmann, S. "Zum Problem der kollektiven Erziehung," Militärwesen, December 1966, pp. 1704-10.

Schneider, F. "Kulturwettstreit 1967," Luftverteidigung, January 1967, pp. 46-50.

Schmökel, W. and H. Jung. "Die Tätigkeit der Grundorganisationen bei der Erziehung ihrer Mitglieder und Kandidaten in der Gefechtsausbildung und im Gefechtsdienst," Luftverteidigung, June 1970, pp. 3-7.

Schottmann, W. "Mehr Aufmerksamkeit dem zweckmässigen Kadereinsatz," Militärwesen, July 1966, pp. 972-79.

Schreiber, R. "Der Einfluss der Kulturellen Massenarbeit auf die Gefechtsausbildung," Marinewesen, January 1966, pp. 387-95.

──────. "Sozialistische Kulturarbeit in der Volksmarine," Marinewesen, March 1964, pp. 285-94.

Schubert, P. "Der Erwerb der Klassifizierungsabzeichen—ein Mittel zur Erhöhung der Einsatzbereitschaft der Bewaffnung der Volksmarine," Marinewesen, July 1969, pp. 817-27.

Schulz, G. "Erziehungs—und Ausbildungsprobleme an den Offiziersschulen der Landstreitkräfte nach der Schaffung der NVA," Zeitschrift für Militärgeschichte, April 1970, pp. 438-47.

Schulze, G., and K. Kästner. "Die Aufgaben der militärischen Kollektive bei der Festigung der Disziplin und Ordnung," Marinewesen, March 1965, pp. 301-8.

Schunke, J. "Zur militärischen Bedeutung Lenins," Mitteilungsblatt der Arbeitsgemeinschaft Ehemaliger Offiziere, July 1970, pp. 11-15.

Seehaus, P., and A. Bendrat. "Der Platz des gesellschaftswissenschaftlichen Selbststudiums im Prozess der Ausbildung junger Offiziere," Militärwesen, September 1965, pp. 1243-52.

Spank, R., and B. Hillmann. "Einige Probleme der Verbrechen gegen die militärische Disziplin," Neue Justiz, June 1959, pp. 581-84.

Stöhr, D. "Jugendkommunique und unserer militärischer Auftrag," Militärwesen, September 1963, pp. 1763-69.

Teichmann, Oberstleutnant. "Die Schulung der Sekretäre der ZPL mit hoher Qualität vorbereiten und durchführen," Parteiarbeiter, May 1969, pp. 8-11.

Teller, G. "Einige Ergebnisse und Aufgaben der politischen Massenarbeit in der NVA," Militärwesen, August 1965, pp. 1050-60.

_____. "In der Führungstätigkeit der Politorgane und Parteiorganisationen wirksamer werden," Parteiarbeiter, December 1967, pp. 1-11.

_____. "Einige Grundfragen der Führung der politisch-ideologischen Arbeit im Ausbildungsjahr 1966/67," Militärwesen, January 1967, pp. 3-12.

_____. "Die Parteiwahlen in Vorbereitung des VII. Parteitages der SED festigen die Kampfkraft der Parteiorganisationen der NVA," Militärwesen, March 1967, pp. 291-300.

Teuber, D. "Das Offizierkorps der Volksmarine am 10. Jahrestag der Nationalen Volksarmee," Marinewesen, March 1966, pp. 361-71.

Tilgner, H. "Die Rolle des Kommandeurs in der Parteiorganisation," Militärwesen, April 1967, pp. 487-95.

Tribüne, 1962.

Trinks, H. "Auf die Abschlussprüfung in den gesellschaftswissenschaftlichen Weiterbildung gewisshaft vorbereiten," Luftverteidigung, February 1966, pp. 9-13.

Tülling, W., and E. Schmolinsky. "Kollektive Erziehungsmassnahmen— Voraussetzung für eine bewusste Disziplin," Marinewesen, May 1966, pp. 558-63.

Ulbricht, W. "Zur Eröffnung der ersten sozialistischen Militärakademie in der Geschichte Deutschlands," Militärwesen, Special Issue 1 (February, 1959), pp. 5-47.

Verner, W. "Die Ergebnisse und Aufgaben der 11. Tagung des Zentralkomitees der SED," Parteiarbeiter, January 1966, pp. 2-26.

_____. "Für die Erhohung der Kampfkraft der Partei und ständig hohe Gefechtsbereitschaft der Nationalen Volksarmee," Parteiarbeiter, Special Issue, 1971, pp. 10-57.

_____. "Wissenschaftlich fundierte Führungtätigkeit in allen Bereichen unserer politischen und militärischen Arbeit durchsetzen," Militärwesen, May 1964, pp. 611-19.

_____. "Die marxistisch-leninistischen Gesellschaftswissenschaften und die Aus—und Weiterbildung der Offiziere," Parteiarbeiter, January 1969, pp. 2-9.

_____. "Die Kampfkraft der Partei in der NVA stärken—unser Beitrag zum VIII. Parteitag der SED," Militärwesen, April 1971, pp. 467-75.

_____. "Den Marxismus-Leninismus wirksamer für die Erhöhung der militärischen Kampfkraft und Gefechtsbereitschaft nutzen," Militärwesen, August 1971, pp. 1011-20.

_____. "Die Parteiarbeit zur Entwicklung militärischer Kampfkollektive," Parteiarbeiter, January 1971, pp. 2-9.

_____. "Zur führenden Rolle der SED beim Aufbau und bei der Entwicklung der Nationalen Volksarmee," Zeitschrift für Militärgeschichte, No. 4 (1969), pp. 389-402.

_____. "Die führenden Rolle der SED in der Nationalen Volksarmee allseitig festigen und verwirklichen," Militärwesen, February 1968, pp. 171-78.

_____. "Für die weitere Stärkung der führenden Rolle der Partei in der Nationalen Volksarmee," Militärwesen, February 1964, pp. 163-70.

_____. "Ziel der Parteiarbeit—Sicherung einer hohen Kampfkraft und ständigen Gefechtsbereitschaft der Nationalen Volksarmee," Parteiarbeiter, September 1967, pp. 2-14.

Vogel, A. "Die Analyse der Entwicklung des Bewusstseins der Angehörigen der Nationalen Volksarmee—wichtiges Element der Führungstätigkeit," Militärwesen, June 1966, pp. 819-29.

Vogelsang, G., and P. Rath. "Kultur und Kunst erhöhen Gefechtsbereitschaft und Kampfkraft," Marinewesen, October 1970, pp. 1155-64.

Vogelsang, G. "Volksmarine volksverbunden," Marinewesen, May 1965, pp, 515-27.

Die Volksarmee, 1956-61.

Volksarmee, 1962-72.

Volkspolizei, 1950, 1951, 1952, 1955.

Wagner, K. "Anforderungen des Erzieungs—und Bildungsprozesses in der Nationalen Volksarmee an die Ausbilderpersönlichkeit, Militärwesen, February 1966, pp. 188-95.

Wahnelt, R., and E. Flau. "Die Notwendigkeit richtiger Vorstellungen über die gesellschaftliche Rolle des Offiziersberufs," Luftverteidigung, February 1967, pp. 3-12.

Wegner, R. "Die führende Rolle der Sozialistischen Einheitspartei Deutschlands ist die Quelle unserer Erfolge," Marinewesen, March 1966, pp. 297-307.

———. "Vor der Wende in der Parteiarbeit," Parteiarbeiter, March 1965, pp. 8-12.

Wiesner, H. "Zehn Jahre Militärakademie 'Friedrich Engels'—zehn Jahre erfolgreiche Heranbildung sozialistischer militärischer Hochschulkader," Militärwesen, January 1969, pp. 11-20.

Weiss, S. "Alle Vorasusetzungen für eine wirksame Qualifizierung schaffen," Militärwesen, January 1964, pp. 33-45.

Wettengel, R. "Vielfältig wie das Leben," Neuer Weg, No. 20 (1972), pp. 921-25.

Wolf, J. "Kontrolle—Bestandteil der Führungstätigkeit," Militärwesen, June 1968, pp. 800-9.

Zawichowski, M., and G. Fink. "Die Rolle des militärischen Kampfkollektivs bei der Erziehung sozialistischer Soldatenpersönlichkeiten in der Volksmarine," Marinewesen, December 1970, pp. 1418-27.

Zierold, F. "Sozialistische Soldatenkameradschaft zwischen Vorgesetzten und Unterstellten in den Einheiten der NVA," Militärwesen, May 1969, pp. 607-15.

Zöller, Oberstleutnant. "Vor den Schöffenwahlen," Parteiarbeiter, April 1965, pp. 13-17.

INDEX

Abgrenzung, 154, 165
Abitur, total officers with, 8, 46, 63, 96, 123, 155
Academic degrees, army regimental commanders with, 11, 64-65, 97, 124-25
Academic education, total officers with, 11-12, 64, 96-97, 124-25, 156
"Additional Education in the Social Sciences," program of, 108, 138-39, 168-69
Armeerundschau, 67
Der Ausbilder, 159

Bundeswehr, 156

Central party directory, 131, 133, 162
Charter city program, 132
Childs, David, 17
Civilian projects, hours per year spent on, 38-39, 80-82, 112, 141, 187
Civilian work by officers, 75
Collegium, 50
COMECON (see Council of Mutual Economic Assistance)
Council of Mutual Economic Assistance, 152
Criminal offenses, 38, 53-54, 79-80, 109-11, 140, 170-72

Detente, effect on the NVA, 153, 154
Discipline, handling of, 37-38, 53, 79, 109, 140, 169-70
Dölling, Rudolf, 70
Dornberg, John, 4

Education required for admission to officer training schools, 3-4, 44, 61, 95, 121-22, 154-55
Ehm, Willi, 157
Engineers and technicians, total percentage of officers who are listed as, 9-10, 63, 96-97, 125, 156

Fachschulausbildung, total officers with, 8-9, 62, 123-24, 156
Friedrich Engels Military Academy, 10, 64-65, 74, 97, 124-25, 161-62, 188

Gefechtsausbildung, 100
German Democratic Republic, 43-44, 93, 152-54
Gesellschaftswissenschaftliche Weiterbildung (see "Additional Education in the Social Sciences")
Godau, Heinz, 46, 48, 49, 52
Grünberg, Gottfried, 69

Hoffmann, Heinz, 9, 64, 98, 99, 107, 125, 136, 140, 156, 161, 189
Honecker, Erich, 83, 94, 153
Hungarian uprising, 59-60, 74, 186

Ideological commissions, 104-05

Janowitz, Morris, 11

Der Kämpfer, 47
Kasernierte Volkspolizei, 44, 46, 47, 49, 53
Kessler, Heinz, 170
Kolkowicz, Roman, 36, 183
Kollegium (see Collegium)

KVP (see Kasernierte Volkspolizei)

Length, officer training schools, 4-5, 45-46, 61-62, 95, 122, 154-55
Ludz, Peter Christian, 184
Luftverteidigung, 128, 158

Main Political Administration, 26-27, 50, 70, 105
Marinewesen, 100, 158
Massenarbeit, responsibility for, 34, 52, 77-78, 107-08, 137-38, 167
MBFR, (see Mutual and Balanced Force Reductions)
Militärtechnik, 16, 100
Militärwesen, 67, 158-59
Military court structure, 109-10, 171
Military dual executive, 24, 33, 34, 45, 52, 53, 56, 76, 84, 94, 99, 114, 121, 166, 174, 183, 186, 187, 188, 189
Military journals published, 16-17, 47, 67, 100, 128, 158-59
Military party organization, 29-31, 50-51, 71-73, 105-06, 133-35, 163-64, 187
Mittlere Reife, total officers with, 7, 46, 62-63, 95, 96, 123, 155
Mutual and Balanced Force Reductions, 152

New Economic System, 93, 120
NVA officer corps, average age, 188

Occupational categories, 15-16, 66-67, 100, 126-28, 158
Officer's education, value of, 6-7, 46, 62, 95-96, 123, 155
Officer's obligated length of service, 12-13, 46-47, 65, 97-98, 125, 156-57

Officer's technical qualifications, importance for promotion or retention in the service, 13-14, 65-66, 98-99, 125-26, 157-58

Paramilitary forces, 43 (see also Kasernierte Volkspolizei)
Parteiarbeiter, 128
Parteigruppen (see Party groups)
Parteikontrollkommission (see Party Control Commission)
Parteirevisionskommission (see Party Revision Commission)
Part-time ideological training, 34-35, 52, 108, 138-39, 168-69
Party Conference, SED: V Party Conference (1959), 59; VI Party Conference (1963), 31, 93, 105; VII Party Conference (1967), 120, 121
Party Control Commission, 26-28, 132
Party groups, 71-72, 133, 163
Party ideology, acceptance by officer cadets, 187
Party membership, total officers, -31-32, 51, 73, 106, 135, 165
Party Revision Commission, 26-28
Patentstandt program (see Charter city program)
PKK, (see Party Control Commission)
Polish Armed Forces, comparison with NVA, 184
Political Control: Discussion by period (Period I, 55; Period II, 83; Period III, 112-13; Period IV, 143; Period V, 173-74); Discussion of, 21; Levels (Period I, 54; Period II, 82; Period III, 112; Period IV, 141; Period V, 172); Soviet influence on, 44, 55, 152-53, 173
Political-Cultural Organs, 49-50, 52

Political indoctrination, responsibility for, 33-34, 51-52, 76-77, 106-07, 136-37, 166-67
Political officers, level down to which present, 21-22, 48, 68, 101, 129-30, 160, 187
Political officers, prior military service of, 24-25, 49, 69-70, 103, 130, 162
Political officers, length of training period, 23-24, 49, 68-69, 102-03, 130, 161-62
Political reliability, importance for promotion or retention in the service, 32-33, 51, 73-74, 106, 135-36, 165-66
Politische Hauptverwaltung (see Main Political Administration)
Polit-Kultur Organe (see Political-Cultural Organs)
Politorgane, 25-29, 38, 49-50, 70-71, 103-04, 130-33, 162, 187
PRK (see Party Revision Commission)
PS (horsepower) level, 18, 47, 67-68, 100-01, 128-29, 159

Relationship of technical level to political control, 55-56, 83-84, 114, 143, 174, 183, 186-87
Richert, Ernst, 44
Rückwärtige Dienst, 100

Schulz, Günther, 62
Secret police officers, level down to which present, 22-23, 49, 68, 101, 130, 160-61, 187
Self-criticism, effectiveness of, 35-37, 52-53, 78, 109, 139-40
Service by officers as enlisted men, 75
Single leadership principle (see Military dual executive)
Soviet armed forces, comparison with NVA, 152, 184

Soviet Union, influence on NVA, 43-44, 152, 185
Specialization, influence on political control, 11-12
Specialized military books published, 11-12, 67, 100, 128
Stalin, Joseph, 52
Stoph, Willi, 60
Sulzberger, C. L., 153

Technical awards, 66, 99-100, 126, 158
Technical level: Discussion by period (Period I, 55; Period II, 82-83; Period III, 113; Period IV, 141-43; Period V, 173-74); Levels (Period I, 47; Period II, 68; Period III, 101; Period IV, 129; Period V, 159); Soviet influence on, 44, 55, 152-54, 173
Three-year officer training schools, percentage of officers having completed, 5-6, 62, 95, 122-23, 155

Ulbricht, Walter, 35, 59, 64, 74, 75, 93, 120

Verner, Waldemar, 105, 136, 168
Volksarmee, 67, 76, 79
Die Volksarmee, 67
Volkspolizei, 47, 67
Volkskammer, 59

Wehrmacht, former officers in the NVA, 44, 52, 83, 186
Wilhelm Pieck Military-Political College, 162

Zeitschrift fur Militargeschichte, 100
Zentrale Partei Leitung (see Central party directory)

ABOUT THE AUTHOR

DALE R. HERSPRING is a Foreign Service Officer assigned to the U. S. Embassy in Warsaw. Until recently he was assigned to the Bureau of Politico-Military Affairs of the Department of State. Prior to that he spent two years in the Federal Republic of Germany as a Fulbright Research Fellow. In addition to numerous visits to East Germany, he has traveled extensively throughout Eastern Europe and the Soviet Union.

Dr. Herspring received his A. B. from Stanford, his M. A. from Georgetown, and his Ph. D. in political science from the University of Southern California.

**RELATED TITLES
PUBLISHED BY
PRAEGER SPECIAL
STUDIES**

ARMED FORCES OF THE WORLD: A Reference
Handbook
      edited by Robert C. Sellers

EAST AND WEST GERMANY: A Comparative
Economic Analysis
      Martin Schnitzer

EASTERN EUROPE IN THE 1970s
      Sylva Sinanian, Istvan Deak, and
      Peter C. Ludz

ECONOMIC REFORMS IN EASTERN EUROPE:
Political Background and Economic Significance
      Radoslav Selucky
      translated by Zdenek Elias

THE MILITARY AND POLITICAL POWER IN
CHINA IN THE 1970s: Organization, Leadership, Political Strategy
      edited by William W. Whitson

MODERNIZATION AND POLITICAL-TENSION
MANAGEMENT—A SOCIALIST SOCIETY IN
PERSPECTIVE: Case Study of Poland
      Dennis Clark Pirages